About the Authors

Simon and Rebecca live in Devon with their three teenage children. Simon is a civil servant and Rebecca a leadership development specialist. Since their epic global trip twenty-three years ago, family life has taken over—travelling is a distant memory—and recent adventures are of a gentler kind closer to home, in Devon, Dorset and Cornwall. At the time of writing, Brian, a recently purchased camper van, remains firmly planted on the drive, patiently waiting for Covid-19 social restricting rules to lift. Brian allows them to dream of further adventures. A four-mile round trip to the local supermarket is Brian's furthest journey so far.

South America for Starters

Simon and Rebecca Levi

South America for Starters

Olympia Publishers
London

www.olympiapublishers.com
OLYMPIA PAPERBACK EDITION

A CIP catalogue record for this title is
available from the British Library.

ISBN: 978-1-78830-839-7

First Published in 2021

Olympia Publishers
Tallis House
2 Tallis Street
London
EC4Y 0AB

Printed in Great Britain

Dedication

For Charlie, Jude and Yasmin. Devon is wonderful, however there is a whole world out there for you all to explore.

Acknowledgements

We would like to thank our family and friends for supporting our adventure—writing to us and thinking about us. Our adventures were the hopes and fears of our nearest and dearest. We would also like to acknowledge Matt and Hil. At times, we trod in their footsteps. We were not the first adventurers in the family. They dared to go ten years earlier; they were an inspiration to us and gave us the confidence to go forth.

"On the beach there is a hut with a bumfire. The perfect place for a fullmoon night"
Advert for hostel—Entel phone office, Coroico, Bolivia

How good is your memory? How is your general knowledge? Let's find out. Let's pick a time period covering twelve months. 1st May 1997 to 30th April 1998 is as good as any place to start. Did anything of any significance really happen then? I guess many of us will remember some events from this time. New Labour winning a landslide election and of course the tragic death of Princess Di. Who can forget where they were when they heard that news? Any more events that year?

Hong Kong was handed over to China—Chris Patten being its last British Governor. Amazingly, Britain won the Eurovision Song Contest (for the first time since 1981) with an effort by Katrina and the Waves. Can you remember the song? Lada stopped importing cars to the UK. Both Scotland and Wales were given limited powers of devolution after two close run votes. The last of the traditional old-style London cabs were produced, after a run of thirty-nine years. The Good Friday Agreement was signed, just over a year after the last British soldier was tragically killed by the Provisional IRA.

Until this time, Cornwall still had a working tin mine. South Crofty closed during this time, along with a long held and proud tradition of mining in this part of the world. Four proud northern football clubs opened brand new all seater stadiums—Derby, Sunderland, Stoke and Bolton. Can you remember the names of their old grounds? Could you guess who opened each one?

And there is more—shockingly, British nurse Lucille McLaughlan was sentenced to eight years imprisonment and five hundred lashes by a Saudi court for accessory to murder. Elton John's *Candle in the Wind* became the second biggest selling single worldwide, twenty-four years after it was first released. Rolls Royce was bought by German car maker

BMW. James Cameron's film *Titanic* was released and became the first film to gross US $1 billion dollars. Talking of large boats, the Queen's yacht, Brittania, was decommissioned and not replaced. It is now a tourist attraction in Edinburgh. At this time, we probably found out all news via the TV, radio or newspaper. However, some of us may have found out about some of these events via BBC online—this was launched on 4th November 1997. Anyone who could access BBC online probably used a desk-based computer at home to look up the details—most employers had very strict controls about internet access at the time.

Amazing events though these were, I will remember this time period in a slightly different way. I will remember this period as both an adventure and a love story. On 1st May 1997, my partner (now wife) and best friend and I took off from Heathrow for an eight-hour flight to Buenos Aires. The last thing we did before we left was to vote in the general election. It would be four days before we found out that New Labour had won by a landslide majority.

This trip had been four years in the planning. Rebecca and I had saved meticulously the £17,000 that we hoped would be enough to take us around the globe for a year, taking in twelve countries, three continents and a sub-continent. For four years of planning and saving, we did everything on the cheap. A treat might be just one pint (strictly limited to one) at the pub, very occasionally. For four years, we ate home-made sandwiches at lunchtimes, at home and at work, wherever we were. In these four years, we bought a house and decorated it ourselves—strictly on the cheap. Old thread bare swirly carpets were kept and not replaced. A 1950s bathroom and 1970s kitchen were merely repainted. Instead of buying a plant pot for the garden, we reused a butler's sink that we found at the property, long before this kind of look became vogue. Despite the frugal style of the house, we loved our home in St Albans, Hertfordshire.

So, where did we go? Argentina, Chile, Bolivia, Peru, New Zealand, South Korea, Hong Kong, Vietnam, Thailand, Sri Lanka, India and Nepal. We travelled by any form of transport that you can think of: plane, train, boat, taxi, bike, motor bike, horse and foot. We slept anywhere you can imagine—tents, the open, reasonably nice hotels (three times), very rough hostels (mainly) and one campervan. We ate like kings at times and like paupers at others.

We took two large backpacks. Rebecca's had a nifty large pocket that could unzip and become a small day pack. The contents of the packs were interesting. No mobile phones, tablets or kindles—we did, however, bring one book: —the South American Handbook. The other eight travel guides that we had already posted ahead to pick up from family in New Zealand. We had nothing else to read (I am an avid reader so, looking back, I don't know how I coped). I remember now, I coped because we brought four cassettes and a Sony Walkman. Four cassettes for a year! I seem to remember that one of them was a compilation of The Cure re-mixes. Many of our journeys were well over twelve hours and these cassettes were life savers.

We didn't bring sleeping bags. It may have saved space, but this proved to be a big mistake. My brother had undertaken a similar trip years before, but he spent most of his time in Australia and South East Asia where it was warm. We didn't experience anything like warmth until we got to Hong Kong— six months into our trip. In the first six months we had rain, cold, snow and ice. Rectifying such a mistake was impossible.

We finally managed to track down some incredibly heavy, but somehow not warm, sleeping bags in South America. Carrying these things on four-day treks through the dense jungles of Peru and Bolivia made tough journeys even tougher and nights in bed far colder. We also omitted to bring a tent. Another foolish mistake, but somehow, we managed to buy a half decent small tent in Bolivia.

We took one pair of trousers each, which zipped down to shorts—a brilliant invention. Our shoes were our walking boots. We took a list of twelve post offices and rough dates when we thought we might be in the general area. Our friends and family had copies of the same lists. I don't suppose "Poste Restante" exists now, but for us it was our lifeline. We had nine opportunities in the year to pick up letters from friends and family. They had no other way of communicating with us and could only wait for the expensive phone call or the regular long letters arriving on the mat.

I took my leaving present from my colleagues at work— an incredible Swiss Army knife. It did everything from having a tool to fix the stems on our glasses to a hook for creating somewhere for a clothes line to hang. The knife was pretty handy too. We also took a belt each that unzipped on the inside - all our money and travellers' cheques were rolled up within these belts. We also took a false wallet each that had some old ID in them and very little money. We thought they might come in handy if we were held up at gun point anywhere. More about that later in the book... We bought a couple of pens and a blank diary to record our experiences and then apart from a fleece, a water proof jacket, three pairs of undies and three T-shirts that was it. Oh no, there was one other thing. We brought a computerised chess game. Despite many long hours on this thing, away from home, I was still thrashed every time on level 0 out of 9!

We documented our trip meticulously and here it is for you to enjoy, maybe even be inspired to try something similar one day… it was certainly the best year of our lives!

SOUTH AMERICA

The poetry of motion! The real way to travel! The only way to travel! Here today—in next week tomorrow! Villages skipped, town and cities jumped—always somebody else's horizon!

(The Wind in the Willows—Kenneth Grahame)

Contents

Part One
Argentina
1 - 16 May 1997

Absolute Beginners
by David Bowie.

Not Sure About This

Simon

Buenos Aires
La Republica Argentina 1st May to 2nd May 1997

A long gruelling twenty-hour journey from London to Buenos Aires. We arrived at 8 a.m. local time. So far, we have been adjusting to the shock of our new life. Everything is just so different. Unpacking your bag every time you need something, planning the sightseeing for the next day, attempting to communicate in Spanish!

Buenos Aires is very much like an American city. Built on a grid and not very much of it is very old. We have been to the presidential palace (Casa de Gobierno), the Costanera Sur Wildlife Reserve and the Teatro Colon opera house. I have enjoyed all this very much. One thing that I have learnt so far is that I have a lot to learn—about "surviving" on a long trip, on getting the most out of it and about adapting to situations out of my comfort zone. I'm nowhere near to progressing any of these and I'm sure there are many other issues I'm not even aware of yet. But at least I now know I have a lot to learn.

Rebecca

5th May 1997 9.50 p.m.

It is only four days into the trip and its feels so much longer! So much has happened since this morning's arrival in Bariloche, amongst the dark and foggy cold air. Having spent a couple of days in a city, we thought it was time for some real fresh air amongst the hills and yesterday we began a twenty-one hour coach journey across Argentina's Pampas to a Swiss/Austrian chalet in the National Park of Nahuel Huapi. Bariloche has some very steep streets heading up mountain sides. It is at the bottom of the most beautiful lake and mountains all-round that I have ever seen! Spectacular, once the fog cleared by 3 p.m. this afternoon.

The coach journey here was not without mishaps. The place we stopped for dinner, ravenous for food and a stretch of the legs, turned out to be closed and our lack of handle on the Spanish language meant that we never really found out why! The only explanation we deduced was that it was too early for dinner in a country where a siesta in the afternoon spreads over the whole year (not just the summer) and therefore dinner does not begin until at least 8 p.m. We had arrived at the restaurant at 7.15 and they would not serve proper food. We made do with a portion of chips, a packet of Pepitos and a couple of yoghurts. We were beginning to realise that our normal healthy meal routine would not sustain very long!

The second mishap came in the middle of the night when most people had decided that as it had gone dark and the light in the coach for reading was terrible, they would get some sleep. It became apparent that there was something seriously wrong with the engine—it could not maintain power and we kept pulling off the main road for a budding engineer to tweak a few knobs. This lasted about one-and-a-half-hours (with no explanation, even in Spanish, of what was going on) whereupon many lorry drivers had stopped to offer assistance and eventually a spare part was brought which did the trick. Simon and I agreed that their contingency plan would always have to be "get the damn thing fixed" as sending another coach would be impossible, given we were hundreds of miles from any known town. The coach journey did, however, provide some lovely biscuits, sweet coffee and a chance to try my hand at the computer chess—"it" won!

Buenos Aires was a very interesting place which at first seemed cold and uneventful but after a couple of days we felt more at home. Teatro Colon was one of the most impressive buildings I have ever seen and what a treat to hear some live chamber music playing. The bus journeys were great fun, once we established how to get a ticket by telling the driver our destination and then putting the money in the machine. The underground was also very efficient, clean, uncrowded and to our amusement had televisions on every platform playing adverts! We have decided Argentinians love TV and football! It was a very safe, unintimidating city with an obvious lack of investment and money spent on it. Not altogether clean and coming out of the Retro Station yesterday we saw some incredible shanty like housing.

The YHA in Buenos Aires was basic but fine—our biggest issue being we were separated by single sex dorms causing a little havoc on our packs and what we were carrying for each other. I don't think either of us got used to not having anywhere for us both to sit and chat and be alone (as we have been used to at home). Neither of us liked having to share the living room with all and sundry! We met some interesting people—two Australian electrical engineers called Martin and Jason, some American girls, Maria the Mancunian who has flown from Auckland, Sylvie the Swiss girl who has stayed with her Monk uncle and the British guy who hadn't seen a British person for two weeks!

The South American handbook is proving invaluable—only when you are in the countries do you realise the use of such detailed information. A lot of our ideas are coming from this book. The next few days will be spent around this beautiful part of the world with snow-capped mountains and still pond-like lakes. We have organised a walk for tomorrow taking us up a mountain and to a Refugio owned by Club Andiho of Bariloche. Club Andiho has a lot of information about the surrounding hills, but it was only when we talked to a couple of old German men (whom Simon reckoned were war criminals!) that we realised as yet such a National Park does not have any such things as an Ordnance Survey map! The small scrappy diagrams they gave us are all we have to go by but sufficient.

My impressions of Argentina so far:
- Friendly and safe.
- Some English spoken e.g. bus station Bariloche, Club Andiho.
- No money to invest.
- Low expectations of service e.g. bus mishaps did not seem to cause much hassle from Argentinians.
- Lack of creative food dishes unless you pay a lot for it.
- Better sanitary systems than France.
- A huge country with great variety.

This is More Like it

Rebecca

7th May 1997 8.35 p.m.

Bariloche proved to be PERFECT! Yesterday and today, we have walked in the hills—both walks providing some spectacular scenery. Yesterday, we walked from our hotel up a hill called Cerro Otta that took us behind and high up above the town. It was mainly wooded.

Simon

San Carlos de Bariloche—The Lake District
3rd to 8th May 1997

Well, since I last wrote in this diary, we have left Buenos Aires and have spent four days in Bariloche in the Parque Nacional Nahuel Huapi. We took a twenty-one-hour bus ride to get here from Buneos Aires. We crossed the Pampas which are flat, unpopulated and vast. Hour after hour we travelled with absolutely no change of scenery. This was OK because we were well supplied with books, travel chess and a personal stereo. It did get very worrying when fifteen hours into the journey the bus broke down. I really did believe that we may have to wait for a second bus from Buenos Aires. Fortunately, the driver fixed the problem.

We arrived at 7.30 a.m. on Monday. It was freezing and a dense fog hung about the place. We couldn't see a thing. I think we both thought we had "boobed" by going to a place at the wrong time of year. However, as the day progressed the fog started to lift and gradually, we began to see, bit by bit, the scenery around us. Absolutely amazing, lakes and mountains! I couldn't wait to get into these hills on foot.

For the next couple of days, we did our second hike. Must rate among our best ever, probably the best. We hiked up Cerro Lopez to near the top. It was a 2,400 ft hike and we were 4,900 feet above sea level. The views were amazing. Mountains upon mountains as far as we could see. Mountains completely surrounded by lakes. Where we were, waterfalls crashed around us. The sun shone. We walked from 9.30 a.m. until 5.30 p.m. We were not tired. In truth, it was a perfect day and I don't use the phrase lightly.

The trip has been fabulous so far. I think the whole thing bewildered me at first. However, I'm getting used to it now and loving it. Before we left the UK, I worried that I would miss all our possessions. At the moment, I'm loving living out of a rucksack and seeing the world. I really hope the rest of the trip is as good as it has been so far. As I write these lines, I look out of the bedroom window and see a vast lake, calm as a mill pond. Beyond are forested mountains gliding out of the water. I see sunlight shimmering on the grassy hill sides and clouds mingling with the mountain peaks. Could life ever get any better?

Rebecca

10th May 1997 6.15 p.m.

Three days later, I shall aim to complete the diary up-to-date!

As I was saying, the first walk we did was mainly wooded and took us up to out of season ski pistes. It was strange walking along paths that during the winter would hold scores of skiers! The views were wonderful overlooking the Nahual Huapi Lake and Bariloche. The descent was over the other side again through woods and, at times, proved very steep and difficult due to the soil underfoot being quite soft and slippery. We weren't entirely sure we were going the right way, but signs on the piste indicated "Lago Gutierrez" which is where the walk was heading. At the bottom, the route meandered through forests where tree felling seemed popular and up to a river coming down from the hills. We saw a couple of locals dragging logs on a horse and cart and managed to ask if we were going the right way. They weren't particularly helpful, but he had grunted "yes" and we carried on. Within half an hour, it was obvious that heading into the flat/barren/desert like Argentinian land was not going in the right direction and Simon managed to work out on the map that we needed to get back over the other side of the river, needless to say we eventually found the right road that took us to the shores of Lake Gutierrez. It was so peaceful and beautiful and no one around. Unlike the Lake District in England, this is completely unspoilt and natural, devoid of tourism (certainly at this time of year!) and completely unassuming people living nearby. Our walk continued along a dusty, stony road to the corner of the lake where we had been informed, we would be able to catch a bus back. Local bus journeys are proving to be one of the highlights of our trip! They are old and battered with cracked/broken windows and used, torn and moving seats! Most of the roads they go along are just dusty, stony tracks causing a real rough and bumpy ride. Another theme to our walks so far has been dogs—this walk provided us with a walking companion from the lake to the bus. We named him "Poles" as, at the time, we were playing I-Spy and it was the one word that Simon could not guess! The bus arrived just on time and we got back to Bariloche as promised.

Bariloche proved a good base for us although on reflection it is quite touristy and can therefore give you a slightly distorted view of real-life Argentina. Food could have been very expensive if we hadn't really shopped around and for the first two nights, we ate in a place called Rock Chicken that did some good deals of meals, including a tumbler of wine! My stomach found the food with chips a little greasy and too much after two attempts so the third and fourth night we ate at Porkys. Again, they did a good deal of a big Mozzarella and Olive pizza with a bottle of beer for about £6 (for two). It was a real American type place with a TV showing football constantly! However, there were plenty of Argentinians there and we still had to speak Spanish!

Our second walk was even better! Arroyo Lopez (Lopez stream) was about twenty-five kilometres from Bariloche and was a walk highly recommended by Club Andinho. This was one, in as many days so far, that we saw the sun rise, as had to get a bus at about 8.15 a.m.—the sun is only rising at about 8.30 a.m. and setting at 6.30 p.m.! Another interesting journey with people going to work out to the sticks of Arroyo Lopez and a smiley friendly bus driver who showed us exactly where to go.

The Lopez stream was set in a wood on the Lopez Mountain and our ultimate aim was a Refugio at 5,000ft above sea level but we started the walk at 2,500ft! For the first half an hour, we took the wrong path and even though the information told us the first part of the walk was steep, the boulders and huge stones we were having to climb seemed ridiculous! We ended up turning around to find the right path marked with the infamous Club Andiho red blobs (small paint blobs on trees to show the way)! The walk was steep, but our legs got used to it. Unlike steep roads that can get tedious, this was a mixture of stone/sand surface through the woods, short undergrowth and forests before continuing on a winding makeshift road. It was the most glorious day—deep blue sky and warm sunshine and the views were absolutely unbelievable. We felt like we were on top of the world with mountains all around and the lake way down below. As with the walk the day before, a dog returned into it somewhere! "Lopez" became his name and he was extremely companionable, although we did wonder whether he was a wolf! He seemed too tame for that and was quite happy to come up all the way with us and venture all the way back down again. He loved the core of our apples and we thanked his company by giving him a slice of our "chorizo" (almost like salami) that we have been eating with bread for lunch. He loved it!

We eventually came to snow! An amazing feeling of being as high as the snow line of about five inches in depth, across the waterfall that went crashing down the mountain and descending to the Refugio that stood pink and very high up. We had climbed for over three hours and we decided that we should turn around if we were going to get the bus on time. It was sad coming down as the walk had been almost perfect solitude on the mountain with fantastic scenery all around and we knew we would never be there again. We followed the road all the way down which was at least six kilometres to the bottom. It turned out that we had some time to spare before the bus and decided to walk to the nearest village about one and a half miles away called Colonia Suiza.

A village built at the turn of the century in the format of a Swiss town. All the houses were hidden chalets with water coming from a tank on wooden stilts. The bus was, once again, on time and this time was very interesting. Just down the road was the local nursery/junior school. The bus stopped right outside and about three teachers watched about ten children get onto the bus and waved them off. The children's ages ranged from three/four to about ten. They were all gorgeous and so naive in their own clothes but each wearing a little cotton overcoat. We realised some schools did not have a uniform, only this 'science lab' type white coat over the top, to stop them getting their own clothes dirty. The nursery school children have to wear a coloured checked coat (girls pink and boys blue or green with their names on). The bus driver was obviously the same one they had every day. One of the boys stood next to the bus driver during the whole journey, an occurrence which did not seem to show much concern as the lack of traffic on the roads does not result in many accidents. That day was probably the longest day walking I have ever done, but it was exhilarating and a day I will never forget.

Our time at Bariloche was coming to a close and the following day was spent organising our next destination and seeing more nearby. We had decided to see one last National

Park in Argentina before heading for Chile and having read about El Bolson in our green book, we booked a bus journey for 8 a.m. the following morning, one hundred and twenty-five kilometres south of Bariloche. We also posted our first letters at the main post office with huge excitement that our parent's letters were now on their way, although the green book said they would take ten days. The rest of the day was a mish-mash! We got a bus to Llao Llao about twenty-four kilometres away from Bariloche and another lake away called Lago Escondido. Llao Llao was not how we expected it. It was a tiny street village at the corner of Lago Nahuel Huapi where it was obviously used as a port for boats to and from the lake. We found a small trail around the lake, through a wood to the shores of the lake and on the way back came through a bunch of Arrayan trees, thousands and thousands of years old and twisted, but still very much alive. It was a very windy day and on heading back to the port area where we could catch the bus, we decided to head back to Bariloche and stop at Cerro Campanario where we were informed by the green book that we could take a chairlift for only $5 per person and see some wonderful views. The chairlift was very much open, but with a 96% inflation rate since 1996, the price of this chairlift had doubled to $10. Of course, we were not prepared to pay £16 for a chairlift so we ended up getting the next bus to Bariloche and had a lovely cup of coffee (what a treat!) in a café.

For our stay in Bariloche, we had stayed in a hosteria on a road called Relando. The view from our room was right over the lake, but every night it was barred by the hanging of wet underwear from our super-duper washing line. The owners were very nice and I particularly liked the daily fresh towels, made bed and cleaned bathroom.

Friday morning, we rose early to get our bus to El Bolson and managed to get a taxi to the station in plenty of time. As usual, it was very dark still, but not as cold as they day we had arrived. The bus was a lot smaller than the previous "via Bariloche" bus and as the journey progressed it proved to be a local bus in places. We saw the sun rise and took a tremendous trip around three beautiful lakes and bottoms of mountains. A normal every day journey for some locals, this was amazing for us. The trip lasted about two and half hours and when we arrived at El Bolson, it looked at first glance like it could prove to be a more realistic picture of how Argentinians live. We headed straight for the tourist information centre that housed a delightful man whose English was actually very good. He answered all of our questions and provided us with information on the hosteria just down the road. This was the start of what turned out to be a very odd/funny/lucky day!

Rebecca

Monday 12th May 1997 3.30 p.m.

We headed for the hosteria in high spirits. It was relatively easy to find somewhere to stay and sure enough walking down this dusty stony track for a few yards, we found the hosteria we were looking for. An old man came out of a house, turned the corner to see us just as he was doing his flies up! What a shock he got. His wife then came tottering out and showed us to a room which was behind the house, through the garden and to an extension at the back. She opened the door straight into a room that felt very cold, damp and dark with two single beds and an open fire to heat the room. And that was it! It was awful and of course we did not have the language skills to say, "Sorry, it is not what we are looking for," and could only natter, "No gracias!" and shuffled out for her to get the message. She looked quite surprised we were not interested, but we headed back to the tourist office where the guy apologised profusely and promptly phoned up another hosteria to check for a double room with heating. This second hosteria was at the other side of the town and, with packs on our backs, we arrived at this house that looked better. It turned out that most of the house was taken by rooms for the hosteria, but they weren't all ready. The lady first of all showed us the room, again at the back of the house, through the garden and into what seemed a studio flat. The bed looked as if it had just been slept in and as her husband was all bleary eyed; we assumed that it had been him!

The kitchenette was dirty and we really weren't that impressed. She wasn't taking no for an answer and proceeded to show us every room available with hand signs that looked that she was shoving us away rather than beckoning us to come and see! I eventually chose a room myself that of course wasn't ready and the husband and wife team then spent about fifteen minutes changing the bed sheets and doing a spot of DIY in the bathroom. It turned out there was a pipe from the shower head to be fitted to the taps in the basin for us to be able to have a shower. The place was really not that clean, but we realised we would probably have to put up with a lot less in other countries and we would have to make the most of it. I had got used to the nice little hosteria in Bariloche where the room was cleaned every day, gave us fresh towels and made the bed. I realised that this had been luxury and we were going to have to settle for less.

As with any first day in a new place it is quite important

to get your bearings, finding out where things are and do a little exploring. El Bolson is a town set in a valley with its unique microclimate. As I found out, it had its own weather each day. Not far from the National Park, Lago Puelo and surrounded by various mountains and hills, El Bolson is a true Argentinian town, quite like a Western film looking and no money. It isn't an attractive town in itself, but the surroundings are amazing and the people are genuine and friendly.

With our tourist info map, we headed along a road that took us over a one-way bridge over the Rio Azul. We were trying to find a small walk they recommended near the river, but ended up getting a little lost. However, the views that we did see were new to us and all part of the experience. We had discovered the true shanty town area. Usually set beside rivers/water, these areas are a mass of small houses, almost little huts/sheds in England. They all had smoke coming out from makeshift chimneys, dogs running around and clothes hanging outside wherever they could find a gap on the fences for them. Children were wandering around, sitting on the ground and were just as fascinated by us as we were by them. One of the interesting aspects of these places is that, of course, we felt bewildered and slightly afraid. There was no need. We were quite safe and, unlike other countries we will visit, these people are not interested in our money nor our possessions. They are keen to get on with their lives the best they know with no violence or crime involved.

With no success on this walk, we decided upon another one at the other side of the town that was to take us up a hill called Cervo Amigo. It forced us to walk through the centre of the town and just have a scan around at the restaurants for that evening. We also found a place called Grado 42 that supposedly arranged rafting and horse-riding trips. This place was closed for the siesta, so Cervo Amigo came first. Near the start of the upward climb, we came across some wooden built chalets in a field advertised as cabanas and looked like holiday homes. Being nosey, I said to Simon we should just have a peek through the window of one and, on looking through the glass, we saw some beautiful furnished Swiss/Austrian looking chalets made entirely of wood, fitted with kitchen, bathroom etc.... None of them seemed open and we left wondering how much they would cost to rent etc. As we ventured up the road to Cervo Amigo, we came across a sign for other cabanas on the left which stated that it could be rented for a number of nights or a period of time. Our eyes lit up and we ventured a little way down the drive to ask what it all meant and what was on offer. We both assumed that this was the house of the owners of cabanas down the road, but we were mistaken. There did not seem to be anyone around and we, therefore, decided to leave. As we were about to pass back through the gates, a lady's voice shouted "hello" from behind us and we turned to see a lady about forty-five to fifty wearing a pair of black jeans, black jumper and a red neck scarf. She reminded me of Auntie Ros with a lovely smile, dark hair and natural country ruggedness about her. We quickly deduced that her cabanas were different to those down the road and on asking the price which turned out to be about $3 more per night than we have been paying, she took us to have a look at it. It had been built on the right-hand side of their garage and on entering the door we both melted. This was absolutely perfect! Another chalet made entirely of wood with a fitted kitchen to the left, a dining area to the right raised by a step and housing a great sturdy wooden table and six chairs. A bathroom on the left and some double doors ahead leading into an open plan living room with windows all around with little wooden furniture and cushions on the settee, which was obviously also a bed. To the left was a small bedroom with single beds at right angles to each other almost like bunk beds and to the right a double bedroom with a lovely cream throw over the bed and windows all around overlooking the magnificent mountains. We were gobsmacked! This place was idyllic for a few days stay and it became apparent that it was also available. We knew we would never have this opportunity again and although we both felt inclined just to move in there, we decided to stay at the hosteria one night and move to the chalet the following day. There was one problem—there was a man who was interested in the chalet for a long period of time and he would be phoning that evening to let them know for sure. We would have to phone later to find out. Our hopes were not entirely dashed, but we left so excited about the prospect of staying in such a beautiful place, where we could cook our own meals and come and go as we please. We walked up the hill in a daze and no sooner had we walked a few yards, the lady shouted "Rebecca!" from below and she was heading our way. This was it! Yes or no? Her husband had just told her this gentleman would not be coming that soon and we, therefore, could have the chalet. OH JUBILATION! We were ecstatic!

That evening, we ate at a restaurant called Colobaza and talked constantly about our temporary home and the experience we had just had in Grado 42. (What a day it was turning out to be.) At about 7.45 p.m., we walked into Grado 42 to enquire about rafting and horse riding. It was not as simple as we had thought and proceeded to be there for about half an hour—a small basic office where people could also come and buy tickets for a bus operator. This was a company that wasn't used to tourists at this time of year. Having understood what we wanted, they kept us waiting and eventually beckoned to the telephone. We finally had a conversation with one of their friends (Paul) in English about having a two-hour horse-riding lesson! We arranged a horse ride on the Monday and when we came to the phone, the guy in the shop then ummed and arred about rafting and proposed a three-hour trip on Sunday for $35 each including a sandwich. It seemed a lot of money, but in comparison with what you can pay in England, and the fact that they were being so nice, we accepted. A visit to Grado 42 had proved to be expensive, but such laughter when we don't speak Spanish and they don't speak English! We all ended up laughing at each other! We expected some fun ahead.

The following morning, we were away by 8.20 a.m., both desperate to get to our new home. It was still dark and there had been no sound in the hosteria and obviously breakfast was not included! We left a broken Spanish note and the money on the table and left. The landlady caught us sneaking away. She was hanging out of her bedroom window all bleary eyed and asking about money. We explained where we had put it and left!

The chalet was still as perfect as we remembered and after unpacking our things and having a shower, we headed for the supermarket to shop for our forthcoming meals. Certain foods are cheaper or more expensive. For example, tinned food is very expensive (tinned tomatoes about 75p each) and fresh mushrooms did not exist! Baguette bread is lovely when fresh and there were also croissants and other delicious cakes and biscuits. We were so thrilled to be able to buy fresh vegetables and, for the next few days, we would be eating home cooking.

On the way back from the supermarket, we stopped at Grado 42 for a "talk" that they had asked us to attend. We had wondered what on earth this would entail and whether we would be able to understand a word of it and who would be there. After a lot of experiences in Argentina, nothing is as it seems and the "talk" consisted of when we needed to meet them there the next day and to bring some spare clothes! We did explain as best we could that we didn't have any spare clothes and we did become a little concerned ourselves that we hadn't brought enough clothes. On reflection, we should probably have brought a pair of tracksuit bottoms with us, certainly for the cooler countries.

The rest of that day was spent at the beautiful Lago Puelo, where supposedly there is a trail to the Chilean border but at this time of year this is impossible due to the rivers being too big to cross. It was a very peaceful lake, still and natural with mountains all around. We walked around the side of the lake, where beaches are used in the summer and had our picnic lunch on the rock by the water. We had noticed a guy walking endlessly around on this own and having bitten into our sandwich, he reappeared and started speaking to us in English. He turned out to be Spanish. We never found out his name and we had an interesting conversation about each other's experiences so far. He had been down south in Patagonia with knee deep snow—camping! He was a student about to start university in Barcelona and had worked in the 7–11 supermarket in London to save up for his trip to South America. One of his stories was about the day he fell into a lake, was rescued by the Park Ranger and taken back to his house for food and to dry himself and all his belongings. On our way back to the bus, we stopped to chat with some Argentinians and we never saw him again.

By evening, Simon made a delicious pizza with meat empanadas to start and Roquefort cheese and bread afterwards—delicious! Our evening is spent writing diaries, letters, playing chess, scrabble and talking about the day's events and planning ahead. Reading is also a great past time that you never get around to at home and of course at the moment, cooking! Tonight, we are having roast chicken, roast potatoes, cabbage and super-duper gravy—a mixture of last night's sauce, wine and beer.

Sunday morning brought the proposed rafting activity and we packed nearly all our clothes in case—we are anticipating falling in!

Rebecca

El Bolson
Wednesday 14th May 1997

The guy from the shop picked us up as promised in this BMW! Not a new one, mind you, but an eye opener in an area where old cars are the norm. We set off for his home first, about ten kilometres away, and we found his name was Christian. Really nice guy, he tried so hard with his English as we did with our Spanish. He lives in a beautiful house with a big open fire in the lounge that was already burning—out in the countryside. He introduced us to his wife, Marianne, his brother Martin and his girlfriend who I think was called Lorraine or something. Christian had two daughters, one about four and the other, one. They were very sweet. It turned out Martin spoke very good English and it almost looked as if Christian had invited Martin down, especially for our trip. By the way, we were the only people they were taking. This was the first time I was offered tea that was dried chopped up tea leaves in a mug with some hot water and a silver straw with a filter on the bottom of it—an extreme Argentinian habit that we have been aware of ever since. The funny thing is it gets passed around to everyone and anyone, with no thought for the mixed saliva. It tasted bitter and grassy, but quite refreshing, although Simon wasn't keen! Martin had brought the gear for the day, including wetsuits, which we promptly had to put on in their bathroom! We were also able to borrow some old trainers/shoes of theirs that fit us.

It was arranged that the two men were coming with us and the two women and children would make a picnic and meet us somewhere in a few hours. We piled into Martin's red 4 x 4 Jeep and set off amongst the jackets, the boats, the oars and a bag of our dry clothes.

The journey to the river was an experience in itself, down bumpy stony tracks with trees which had fallen and Christian had to jump out and remove branch by branch, as well as a few boulders. No other car would have made it but we got to the river bank and proceeded to unload the jeep. Within half an hour we were on the water, proceeding a demonstration from Martin on how to manage the boat, what you do if you fall in the water etc. These conversations lasted for ages with guffaws of laughter at various stages when understanding became impossible or when the two brothers cracked brotherly jokes. The sun started to shine as we forward paddled downstream, one foot under the piece of rope and each of us sitting at all corners of the dinghy. It was obvious that both brothers knew the river very well and it turned out that Martin runs the Youth Hostel in Bariloche and runs the same excursions there. If we had known, we may have stayed with him. The river was not as rough as expected with about ten rapids altogether. At one point, we witnessed a kingfisher bird fly past us, mainly grey and black with a bit of white on its feathers. We also stopped to view some forty-five-million-year-old fossils on the river bank from when the whole place was covered by the sea— amazing! After each rapid we went through, it was imperative that all four oars went up in the air like a tepee and yelps and whoopees start to signify success and that rush of adrenalin.

We must have been on the river for about two hours, witnessing some magnificent scenery and hardly a soul in sight, except a farmer getting a bucket of water from the river. The end of the trip was a small picnic on the beach eating ham and cheese sandwiches with salad which included egg, beetroot, carrot and lettuce—an odd combination, but really delicious. We couldn't believe that it was 4pm and we were only just eating some lunch. It had all been such great fun and we were led up the hill to where the girls had left the cars in the campsite. The infamous tea was even drunk there with hot water from a flask. Martin very kindly brought us back to El Bolson and Christian went home with his family. Unfortunately, I didn't have the right change to give him the exact $70 and neither of us had any change from $100. To our amazement, he was happy to leave it until Monday when we could pop into the shop and pay then. No deposit—no problem! He was so laid back and so trusting. He was fortunate he could trust us and it was nice to feel he could when really we were just strangers.

In the evening, we reminisced on the fabulous day with some really nice people. Such fun and easy to get on with. We ate rice with a tomato and ham sauce and went to bed looking forward to our horse-riding expedition.

Simon had arranged with Paul that he and his brother,

Alan, would pick us up from our cabin at 9 a.m. and although it felt like a work morning being awake at that time, we didn't mind that. It was at the heart of Argentina. We were still on holiday! Paul did not actually turn up, but his brother, Alan, was bang on time in his white van, which we later discovered was about to collapse! It was a good twenty miles back to his farm called El Monje—named after a big stone on the mountain above his land. We never actually saw Paul, but we met Alan's wife Patti and we discovered that they had four children (ten, eight, seven and six). As well as running horse riding expeditions (Calbalgatas), when demanded, usually in the summer, he has a jam producing factory and therefore a lot of fruit growing all around. Alan didn't waste any time saddling up the horses ready for a ride with a mixture of very old-fashioned looking saddles and sheepskin rugs, and no helmets/hats or whips. Simon's horse was dark brown coloured named Tornero (Tornado in English). Slightly worrying name for a beginner rider! My horse was the same colour as my hair and a name I couldn't begin to write. It was apparently the same word as his colouring. Once saddled, Alan invited us into his house for a cup of tea. We stepped into the lounge from the front door with a roaring big open fire and to our surprise, a fairly loud Supertramp CD was playing—the first familiar music in an Argentinian home. Patti not only made us a cup of tea but decided to set out a light breakfast: toasted small baguette pieces of bread, butter and a small amount of each variety of jam that they produce. Alan's English was superb and it turned out that not only was his mother English but he had attended an English school in Argentina. We were, therefore, able to hold a relatively good conversation with him and learn about the Argentine way of life as the day progressed.

Before leaving for our ride, Alan told us of an uncle from England who used to sail across to South America quite regularly and write books about his trips and the people he met. Frank Mulville was his name and on flicking through what looked a really interesting book of travelling experiences; Frank quoted a visit to see Alan and Patti in Argentina. "Alan has a very laid-back attitude to life," was one quote, partly due to a tap that used to come out of the wall in the bathroom when used and Alan's idea of fixing it was banging it back in with a hammer each time. Alan was laid back, certainly by English standards, but he assured us that this had changed since having four children and running a business! Both Simon and myself seemed quite capable of getting on and off a horse and the use of the reins to control the horse seemed a lot easier than I remembered way back in Austria, when we rode as a family. There did not seem to be very much legwork involved, just pulling the reins from side to side to steer and pulling straight on to stop. My horse however did lag behind a little at first, content only to eat the juicy grass beneath its hooves. However, Alan knew the horse well and provided me a leafy cane to tap the horse's backside a little, like a whip, if the pace was too slow. It seemed to work and a couple of times I even went into a canter and didn't fall off! Simon also enjoyed his ride but I discovered later that his small bottom became quite bruised from the whole experience whereas my fat arse was not in the slightest bit affected— padding sometimes comes in handy!

The trail took us around the edges of his farmland and at one point we stopped and walked up to a small waterfall where his water comes through from the visible black pipe down the hill. The scenery once again was marvellous and this time we could appreciate even more as we didn't have to keep watching our feet. Unlike walking, you are not actually using many muscles and there was a tendency to get a little chilly but this didn't divert away from the enjoyment. Through bracken, along a track, up a hill and even through a river was the route we took until we came back to his farm and factory that he promised to show us.

A very simple operation making jam in a building that used to be the main farmhouse. Although quite clean, I was sure it was not EC (now European Union) standards of a food producing environment but nevertheless very interesting. At high season, they would employ fifty to seventy neighbours to pick fruit, usually surrounding locals in need of the work. The jam is sold locally and as far away as Buenos Aires at the moment, although they are considering exporting again. Again, because it was low season, we were unable to see them making anything but there were plenty packaged up to look at. In England, this farm would be considered small. Here in El Bolson they consider it to be big! To us, its existence is quite laid back with no rush hour traffic to contend with at school run time or taking jam to local markets. The pressures are obviously very different, but we felt that there was a lot that we could learn from a seemingly simple existence. Alan informed us there is a lot of unemployment around here, no money and nobody really needs it. Everybody seems relatively self-sufficient. His brother runs the business with him and also has a house on the same land by the river. Unlike a lot of Argentinians, Alan was relatively well-travelled. He had visited London in 1976 and some of the European countries, but his heart was still in El Bolson.

He very kindly brought us back to El Bolson at lunchtime; whereupon, we did a few errands in the centre of town and proceeded back to the cabin. The day had come to wash our trousers and with no others to wear instead, we hauled on our shorts and left the trousers to dry on the line whilst we walked up the hill above our cabin, Cerro Amiga. The sun was out by now and we managed to explore some of the paths winding up and down the wooded hillsides. An hour or so later we came back to discover our super-duper traveling trousers were almost dry, so his sales patter hadn't just been sales crap! A strange material that obviously doesn't hold water.

Washing today has been a bit of a chore. Washing underwear by hand isn't too bad, but when it comes to T-shirts, you know that your hands can never really clean clothes as well as a machine. However, since Simon's first load was swamped by an overpowering smell of sweaty feet, it hadn't been too bad. The log cabin has a special big washing sink and clothes lines outside. We have also used the walls around the gas heater to dry the larger clothes, using the backs of chairs. Improvisation is the name of the game and this trip is certainly teaching us how little we can manage with in terms of possessions and money.

Rebecca

Thursday 15th May 1997 5.25 p.m.

We deliberated for a couple of days whether we should leave El Bolson before Simon's birthday and Tuesday was the decider. We found out what other walks there were in the area. Cascada Escondida was about two hours walk away from the town centre and we decided that it was ideal for that day. It took us along the river the other side from where we had walked on our first day and found a path at the end of the road that took us through wooded areas to where two rivers met.

Here, the path went over the first of a few wooden footpath bridges. What dodgy bridges they turned out to be. Built on wooden slats with metal ropes. The trick was to go over one at a time so the bridge wouldn't bounce too much and make you even more sick than normal. Once on the other side, the walk followed a river/stream up a small valley, but the path was lethal. It was narrow with such huge drops beside you and the ground was wet and slippery. It was probably the most dangerous walk we had ever done, but the trick was to watch every step you made and help each other along. It was a miracle we made it. I had visions of one of us breaking a leg and putting an end to the whole trip, but we didn't. The thought of the walk back wasn't something I was looking forward to. Cascada Escondida is one of many beautiful waterfalls in Argentina and this was no exception. It was beautiful with three main paths of water hurtling down. It was probably a forty-foot drop and at one point in the path you could feel the spray off the fall. It was nestled away in this valley far away from civilisation. Having taken photos and eaten sandwiches of chorizo and baguette, we braved the way back. It was actually a lot easier than we had anticipated, although by the end of our walk our pristine clean trousers were no more!

Simon

El Bolson—The Lake District
9th to 15th May 1997

Case of "déjà vu" at the moment. The last time I wrote in the diary was at a hosteria table in Bariloche. I talked about the scenery of mountains etc. I am now sitting at the dining table of a log cabana that we have been renting. As I look out the window, the scenery is of a deep valley in which sits the town of El Bolson with mountains all around.

Anyway, a lot has happened over the past week. I will try not to duplicate what Rebecca has already written. Our time here in El Bolson has been packed with excitement. We looked at numerous places to stay ranging from downright disgusting to pretty awful. In the end, we settled for a room in a hosteria, but it has to be said that we were not all that happy with it deep down. On our first day here, we went walking on the back roads out of town and found this amazing place, a log cabana. Cerro Amigo made a proper little home for us: luxury for two people with bathroom, kitchen, dining room, lounge plus two bedrooms. We couldn't really leave our existing accommodation that day as we had already accepted it, but we set our alarm for early the next day so we could move in as soon as possible. We also booked a white-water rafting trip and horse-riding excursion at the local agency. On making a routine enquiry on what was available, we seemed to cause havoc at the agency. It felt like the stock exchange as numerous calls were made, faxes sent off, return calls came back, none of which we could understand. By a mixture of mime and us speaking to the owner's friend on the telephone (someone who could speak English), we believed we had booked a rafting and horse-riding excursion.

The rafting was excellent with some good rapids and beautiful scenery, but we both didn't know what to expect. We didn't even know if our guide would pick us up as arranged. The journey there was an experience which involved the use of a 4x4 Jeep and the guide, Christian, jumping out at regular intervals to clear away anything that blocked the road. The M25 it wasn't—well, there's a relief!

The next day, the horse riding went as planned. I have to say that both excursions were money well spent. We ended up trekking around the man's farm for a couple of hours, taking the horses across rivers and seeing the views via horseback. The horses, thankfully, were well behaved, apart from one time when mine decided to enter a gallop. I think Rebecca almost fell off hers with laughter!

Every day of our trip has shown us something new. Up to now, there has always been one part of the day that has amazed us. In El Bolson, we have seen our first taste of real poverty, many people live in little more than garden sheds. Many have no windows, all their washing hanging everywhere and a guard dog. You may think that these slum areas would be unsafe. Perhaps they are, but I would be surprised. Kids playing with stones on the ground, dogs barking, the odd passing horse, babies cried as babies do, but everywhere there seemed to be smiling faces and we felt very welcome and very safe. People here have so very little, but it doesn't seem to make them bitter.

In El Bolson, we have been given a small taste of Argentinian life. By taking the two excursions, both times we were shown to the guides' houses and shown great hospitality. Before horse riding, we had breakfast. Before rafting, we were given tea. I hope that this is a very typical Argentinian trait. It may be that this is typical only in the more remote rural areas. Wherever it may be, I will have pleasant memories of the people of El Bolson.

El Bolson translated into English means 'the big bag'. It is surrounded on all sides by huge steep mountains, therefore the name. Beauty surrounds the place from all angles. The rafting excursion was on the Rio Azure, the blue river. The water was blue in colour, but so clear as well. We have seen a kingfisher. We have seen parrots in the valleys. A sure sign that snow is due allegedly. Today, we saw the Cabeza de Indio which is a rock formation that looks like the face of an Indian. Beyond the face, there was a steep drop below the river and forests. In the far distance were three peaks, glaciated mountains. Yet, in the middle of all this, kids go to school, some people go to work, and others don't. Life goes on all around in a very real sense. I wonder if the people here appreciate it. Whenever I say, "Muy bonita," as knowing a little Spanish I am accustomed to do quite often, nearly always receive a very sincere "Si," anyway. I also learnt that nothing is what it seems in Argentina. Can we have a map? There are no maps. Can we change some money? Maybe tomorrow… maybe. Do you know any walks? You get to the route and the river is too wide to cross, thereby cutting a walk short by eight miles. Planning is easy. Having the confidence in achieving the expected results becomes impossible. People here are very laid back, but it doesn't really matter. I wonder if this will be a theme throughout Latin America or even the whole trip.

Today is my birthday. When I awoke, Rebecca gave me a card and a bundle of presents. Socks were never so gratefully received. For some reason, I had packed thick walking socks, light cotton ones for my birthday are a real treat. Today, we wandered down into town and looked around the market. They hold the market here twice a week. The traders are selling produce and goods that they made and grown. None of it was tacky. I spent my birthday hiking to Cabeza de Indio, the "Indian head" mentioned earlier. We had lunch on top of the rock overlooking the valley. It was wonderful. Rebecca has prepared a tasty looking meal and the vino is not in short supply. The only disappointment today has been that I have been unable to get through to Mum and Dad on the phone. It was engaged three times. So, we pack our bags tonight and head for Chile tomorrow. I didn't expect to be able to self-cater in style on the trip at all and it has been great. If the trip carries on like it has so far, it will indeed be the trip of a lifetime.

Rebecca

Chile—Puerto Montt
Saturday 17th May 1997

When I last wrote, we had been on a walk to Cascada Escondida. Wednesday was the day we had planned to head to Cajon del Azul, another mountainous/valley with a refugio (a mountain hut). The tourist information recommended we go up and then stay there, but without access to some luggage and lockers or something we felt it would be impracticable. We, therefore, decided to go as far as we could in a day and then back again. The bus left El Bolson at 7.45 a.m. We thought we were mad, never mind anyone else. It was really cold and all we could think of was crawling back to bed, but we knew it would be worth it.

We arrived at the start of the walk just as it was light at 8.30 and headed down to where two rivers meet which are crossed by cross two bridges. It was actually a very clear day and the views over the rivers as the dawn broke over the bridges were magnificent. I don't think we had ever seen such clear rivers as we have in Argentina. The walk then basically followed one of the rivers up along the valley bank, a mixture of ups and downs, clear paths, woodland, forest etc. It was extremely peaceful, but at times very cold and after two-and-a-half-hours walking, we decided to turn back. This was partly because there were only two buses back that day, one at 1.30 and the other at 6.45. This later bus would have meant a three-hour wait and we decided that a five-hour walk would suffice and therefore turned around. The bus journey back was fun, it was jam packed full of school children coming home from school, although looking as if they could do with dumping in a bath and giving them a jolly good scrub, and their clothes!

Later that afternoon, I was able to pop to a couple of shops for Simon's birthday. When travelling, we decided it was pointless buying each other anything major, partly because of money and partly because we would have to carry it, whatever it was. Simon had already mentioned the socks. I thought it was a chance to buy him what he wanted and found a lovely little shop with a lady who was very patient. She even wrapped them in paper like a real birthday present. Buying a card was, however, more difficult than I had anticipated. Any cards that I did find were really tacky, old, lots of words that I didn't understand and very expensive. My next route was a postcard, but for some reason, it did not exist. I eventually found a small shop that sold just what I was looking for.

I love surprising people and on Thursday morning, Simon's birthday, I surprised him with a bag of goodies including a card from his mum and dad that I had hidden for two weeks. He was chuffed to bits. It certainly was a little strange celebrating his birthday in a different country and not having any phone calls or cards from people. We both really enjoyed the day, having a wander around the market and all the handicraft stalls and food stalls. None of the walks we have done so far have been made out to be a big deal, probably due to the lack of commercialism/tourism in Argentina. I have been amazed that they are not talked about a lot more and are not marketed more. The walks we did that day were no exception. Cabeza del Indio was great. Who has ever heard of or seen a rock on top of a hill in the shape of an Indian head! It took about one-and-a-half-hours from the bottom of the hill, with views on the way overlooking the Mirador del Azul. This was the valley with the Rio Azure, the river we had rafted down last Sunday. Superb view!

We have certainly eaten well whilst staying in the log cabin and, for Simon's birthday, I made chicken and veg soup, a veg and ham sauce with rice and sweetcorn cob on the side, and some Roquefort cheese for dessert. It is incredible what you can cook with so little. We didn't have any herbs or spices or even salt and pepper, but it all tasted really good.

The family who owned the cabin were really nice to us all week. We only had to ask and they would give us what we needed or help in any way they could. They brought us candles, gave us fresh towels, a pen, a Spanish/English dictionary and mended the toilet on numerous occasions. Even the dog treated us like one of the family and was always delighted to see us when we got back. One evening, their cats came into the cabin and made themselves at home in the kitchen.

When you have been on holiday, packing always seems a lengthy process, but packing our belongings at the moment takes about ten minutes! Another advantage to hauling nothing with us.

Part Two
Chile
16 May – 17 June 1997

Learning to Fly
by Tom Petty and the Heartbreakers

Here comes the Rain Again

Simon

Puerto Montt—The Lake District
Chile 16th to 18th May 1997

It has been a funny few days. We are now in Chile in the southern most largish town, Puerto Montt. There are no real signs of civilisation south of this town and that is an area that must cover some 25% of the country. All there is south of here is mile on mile of fjords and the rough Pacific Ocean culminating in the famous Cape Horn at the foot of Latin America. Yes, we are in the gateway to the end of the earth.

Yesterday (Saturday 17th May) and the day before when we arrived it sure felt like it! Chile has had no rain fall for two years now apparently. So true to form to form, we arrived at Puerto Montt bus terminal in torrential rain—thirty seconds in that weather would be enough to soak you to the bone. We were out in it for ten minutes looking for a bed for the night. Our traveling gear really has been used in anger now.

The place that we are staying in is basic but clean. There is a lounge with a fire which is good seeing as there is no heating anywhere else in the house. We could really hear the rain crashing down on the roof, but thankfully none got into our room. It did elsewhere in the house.

We had a good day on Saturday, despite the torrential rain. We ended up buying raincoats in the morning. We had our best meal yet at lunchtime. Cazuela is a very Chilean dish. Meat in a soup with lemon, rice and other vegetables. It was very warming. We needed it! In the afternoon, we went to the local museum. As we wandered around the museum, where the rain dripped into strategically placed buckets, I started to wonder what on earth we should do. I even started to think of other countries in Latin America that we could visit. At this stage, we didn't know the rain was the exception not the rule. Later on, we saw reports on the news thereby indicating that the rain was not expected.

When we woke up today (Sunday 18th May), the sun was shining and the rain had apparently stopped. We decided to stay and despite initial reservations, I am very pleased we did. We got the bus to Chinquihue. Chinquihue is a small fishing village about thirteen kilometres outside Puerto Montt. We walked along the coast for about an hour or so. We realised what we missed yesterday because of the weather. Today, we could see all across the bay that Puerto Montt nestles in. The sea was blue and the wind fresh. We had lunch at a seafood restaurant. I had congrio. This is fried conga eel, another national dish. Rebecca had a huge piece of salmon. It was cooked beautifully and there was heaps of it. After that, we paid someone to row us to Isla Tengla which is a small island in the bay. The view from the top of the island across Puerto Montt and the bay was impressive.

All in all, I have enjoyed our stay here. There have been low points because of the weather largely. However, I am pleased we stuck it out because we saw Puerot Montt today, a large vibrant fishing town in an amazing geographical position. It was tempting to leave as soon as we arrived, but we didn't. Our experiences here also made us aware that at times we may get a bit low. Before we came, Bob Hope, someone at work who went travelling, told us that there invariably would be some low points. However, whenever this happened, he advised we look back to the truly great days I had had ten years ago and then to look back at the great days experienced whilst travelling. Sound advice!

Simon

Ancud—Chiloe
19th to 20th May 1997

We have taken a slight detour on the advice of someone we met at the hostel at Puerto Montt. We have taken a ferry south to the island of Chiloe. We have read that the culture of the island of Chiloe has been heavily influenced by isolation from Spanish colonial currents, the mixture of early Spanish settlers and Mapuche Indians, and a dependence of the sea. To be honest, we don't think we were sure what we should do. We were really conscious of the rain which could severely limit our activities and to head further south might not be such a good idea in that respect. On the early morning ferry, the weather turned very wet and I had a sinking feeling in my stomach. We arrived at the bus terminal at our chosen destination, the small fishing port of Ancud. This was on the outskirts of town and from the geographical position; Ancud looked like a "dredges of the world" kind of place. That sinking feeling had left my stomach and was creeping towards my toes. The weather was grey. I had no clean clothes and was concerned my underpants and socks were on for the second day in succession. Then everything changed. We found a laundrette. We then found a great place to stay. We have been staying with a wonderful family. Once again, we are the only people in the hostel, but the owners have taken us into their home. We share their food and we eat with them, use their lounge, and warm ourselves by their fire. The view from the living room is unbelievable. Ten yards from the sea, a deep blue blanket of ocean is a feast for the eyes as we sit at the dining table.

Upon arrival yesterday, they gave us breakfast (my second of the day—one being from the hosteria in Puerto Monnt). Before we left to explore Ancud, we were asked for lunch. It was 'free—no money'. Sounded good. We explored the town and we were really impressed. There is much to remember, but mainly the small harbour with lots of small fishing boats, the sea air and also the wildlife. Yesterday, we saw pelicans. Lunch turned out to be a feast, Cazuela (a typical Chilean casserole) with bread and a desert. We spent the evening in front of the fire, playing chess, writing etc., but mainly attempting to communicate with the family and the countless friends that come and go on an hourly basis. We have managed to get by with the help of a phrase book and Spanish/English dictionary. The lady of the house, I believe, is a direct descendant of Don Quixote—if I understood correctly (I now realise that this is not possible as Don Quixote is a fictional character). We have even discussed Lord Byron and Charles Darwin's *Origin of Species*. Today has been great as well. After a huge breakfast, we took a walk along the beach around the peninsula. It was great to walk along the coast with the Pacific crashing onto the beach. The sun was out and the views were beautiful. Again, we were asked to come to lunch: salmon with all the trimmings, side dishes and desert. If they carry on like this, they will go bankrupt within two weeks! We are only paying £18 a night for both of us and they have given us feasts at every meal. This afternoon, one of the sons (Hector—an artist who normally lives in Santiago) gave us a tour of Chiloe in a car he had fixed especially for us. This type of friendliness has given a magical feeling to Chiloe. It is the type of stuff I had dreamt of when planning the trip, but didn't seriously believe it would materialise. Today, we even saw a sea lion dipping its head in and out of the water as it swam past—how can anyone be so lucky.

Rebecca

Castro Chiloe
Thursday 22nd May 1997—7.15 p.m.

Again, I've got a lot to catch up on so I will go back to where I left off. Last Friday, we got up really early and finished off tidying the cabin before, torch in hand, we headed down into the town to catch the "via Bariloche" bus back to Bariloche. It was the first time we hadn't got a complete ticket for the whole journey. We hoped to be able to get this at the bus station. Having got up so early, we both spent most of the bus trip asleep and before we knew it, dawn had arisen and Bariloche was in view again. Cruz del Sur are a bus company who have monopolised the bus system in Chile to the extent that they also run a cheaper service around Chiloe called Trans Chiloe so that they do not miss out on any market. We were able to get a ticket to Bariloche very easily and we settled ourselves in the bus station for a couple of hours wait. This was also the first of such hanging around at bus terminals and I quite enjoyed it! Being so nosey, I find such places fascinating. The comings and goings of travellers; locals and foreigners. People arriving from destinations you know nothing of but try and guess by looking at their clothes or luggage. The little shop / kiosk where people come and buy last minute bits for journeys—mainly biscuits in Argentina—and the porters who are hanging around waiting for something new to happen The bus station also houses the train station, a lonely track that has one or two trains a week going to so few destinations. I do like trains and I am looking forward to some future train journeys, but for now the bus system is working admirably.

The Cruz del Sur bus was fine, quite basic and old, but clean and functional for the six to seven-hour trip. It did, however, smell of cheap room spray that was a little off putting, but there were so few of us on the bus that we were able to spread out our belongings. The first part of the journey was around a few local lakes providing yet more excellent scenery and soon the Andes were coming more into force and the bus was winding its way up very steep tracks with huge drops each side and tall trees, bearing down. As we got nearer to the Chilean border, the rain began in earnest. I think we both thought it would just be showers. How wrong we were, but for now we were warm and dry in a coach and it didn't matter.

An odd situation arose at customs in that the two borders were about thirty kilometres apart! We arrived at Argentina and we all had to troop out and go across to the custom officers who wanted to check out our documents. The driver's assistant, someone all buses seem to have, had taken our details as well as all the other passengers and transposed it onto other sheets of paper which he typed on a new typewriter at the back of the bus. At customs, one guy read out our names from a list and one by one we had our passports checked and a "Salida" stamp in a different colour put onto them. Why are those moments always the scariest? Almost as if we were guilty of something we haven't done or haven't got! Anyway, at the Chilean border we didn't have to queue up again as they seemed to accept the assistant checking our passports and adding stamps. They did decide to X-ray our luggage though. Quite wisely, Simon remembered our camera was in his rucksack and having read that these machines were not quite camera friendly, we realised it might ruin the film. So that was instantly removed. They also pounced on our bag of bits of food where we had two lovely oranges that we were looking forward to eating. These were taken from us as harmless as they are, but apparently Chile disallows any other produce but their own for fear of bugs and infection. Paranoid or what!

The funniest thing was an older woman on the coach who was Argentinian and would have obviously known this hiccup. She had wrapped up some huge butter fruit in newspaper in a tightly taped box in a bag. They found out and confiscated them. She was obviously embarrassed, but it was hilarious for us to watch as these evil big vegetables got taken away, probably to be eaten by the Chilean officers.

The rest of the journey to Puerto Montt was relatively uneventful and comfortable with a bottled drink in with the bargain. There was a decided lack of scenery because of the rain and this never eased. We briefly stopped at Osorno where my concern for lack of Chilean cash overcame me and I went in search of a supposed money exchange café. Sounds dodgy, but their rates can be cheaper and I didn't do that badly. The exchange 'cash in hand' happened in seconds and I was on the bus again. We had quickly worked out that 500 pesos was about £1, but at least we were not going to be dealing with thousands of pesos and such valueless change.

Puerto Montt bus station was very busy and quite daunting in the rain. We felt like a really easy target when hosteria owners kept trying to persuade us to stay at their place—just around the corner! One of the problems you find at a new town is not finding accommodation. We managed to get a local bus and went a few hundred yards before being told to get off. It was pouring with rain and we made our way as quickly as possible to a recommended cheap hosteria that was about fifteen to twenty minutes away. We were wet through when we found it and to be honest, we took it purely because we couldn't face going out in the rain with our heavy packs and trying to find somewhere else. It was also dark by now and we were just glad of a bed. The hosteria was very big and old, but very cold and our room at the back was cold and damp with not even a double bed to keep each other warm at night. There was however a communal lounge with fire, settees and a TV with about seventy channels! That evening we went back into town to find something to eat and plumped on a café that had been recommended by the green book. We both chose spicy sausage and chips and regretted it as it was very greasy and disappointing. We still haven't seen anything of the town and our experiences so far haven't been very favourable. It was cold and wet; the hosteria was basic and the food yucky. We both missed our cabin. We agreed that if the weather was still very bad in the morning, we would move on, but the morning was beautiful and our spirits were lifted a little.

We deduced that the hosteria was owned by an older

couple whose daughter ran the hostel side of things. The father spoke very good English and always dressed in a three-piece suit. He recommended somewhere for us to go along the harbour and then divulging the fax information. He had a fax machine and for about £3, we could send a fax to England if we wanted to. What a great idea, except we didn't have any family with fax numbers—what fools! We did find Sacha and Jez's new fax number that they had handed to us before we left Heathrow and we promptly wrote a one-page fax to them purely for contact and any news. We also asked them to phone our parents in an attempt to let them know we were OK and had been trying to phone them.

Simon

Castro—Chiloe and Chonchi-Chiloe
21st May to 24th May 1997

I really feel the trip has taken off in a big way. Basically, every day holds something new. On Wednesday 21st, it was a Chilean National Holiday—'Navy Day' and from what I could gather, it celebrated a sea battle about one hundred years ago. Today, Hector, who is the artist at the place we are staying, took us on another tour of the island. From this tour, the highlight was visiting a place called the Wild Sea. You couldn't see it unless you have a car; this was a major bonus for us. The scenery is what I imagine Cornwall to be like. The rocks were pentagonal cylinders perhaps similar to the Giants Causeway in Ireland. Upon our return to base, we went to town to get a present for the senorita of the house as it was her birthday. The place was alive with people; bands were playing and traditional dress being worn. It was great. For lunch, the family served us curanto. This is a Chilean dish of potatoes, different meats and shellfish, the mussels were stacked so high in huge bowls that we couldn't possibly eat them all. It was amazing. I dread to think how much this meal would have cost to make back home. Anyway, when we left, the family would take no extra money from us. We had eaten a total of eight, mainly superb, meals there and all we paid was £36 for our accommodation. They treated us like part of the family and after Hector dropped us off at the bus terminal, I think we were very moved and won't forget it.

Castro was the next stop—friendly and worth a visit, but one day was enough for us. However, we decided to head further south. Chiloe had not been on our original plans at all, but we just couldn't get enough of it. It is a beautiful island, but not spectacular. I suppose it is my romantic guess at what Britain may have been like fifty years ago. The people here have a hard life, live from the land and the fish caught from the sea. In the bigger towns at night, the shops are still open at 8.30 with people buying groceries. The place feels alive with life, but never threatening.

So, we are now in Chonchi, staying at a hostel on the beach. As I write this, the sea is lapping against the front not two metres from me. I have just come back from a trip around the harbour in the owner's rowing boat. We had a great day yesterday after we arrived at Chonchi. We got a ferry to the remote island of Lemuy. Lemuy has a total population of 4,200 and as Rebecca said yesterday, "Now I feel like we are at the ends of the earth." We both hitched across the island to the end of the peninsula, about twenty miles across the island. We walked along the beach looking out across the sea towards the distant snow-covered volcanic mountains of Southern Chile. It was then that we saw dolphins, loads of them swimming in groups, dipping in and out between the sea and the air. We saw a dolphin about 9 a.m. from the beach leaping out of the water. All I can say is unbelievable!

I wanted to walk for hours along the beach, but it was getting late. We started walking along the road back to the ferry terminal, some twenty miles away. To say traffic is sparse is an understatement and in some ways, we took a risk going that far across the island. I must admit that I was getting a bit worried that we may have to walk all twenty miles in the dark night, but after some thirty minutes of walking, we hitched a lift with the first car that came along. Phew!

Rebecca

I have decided to leave out what I haven't covered today as Simon seems to have covered most things. I would reiterate Simon's words about Ancud in that the family were immensely generous and so friendly. Hector, the son, was the same age as us and a really nice guy. It was such a shame we couldn't communicate a little more freely, although Simon managed to have quite deep conversations about music and various other topics. Jo and Nelvida, the parents, were so good to us and the food was out of this world, not to mention the raspberry torte we had for breakfast and the homemade bread with chilli. Hector and one of their friends, Miguel (who exports shells to the USA) were brilliant chess players. They beat level 9 (the top level of our computerised chess game) within half an hour. We can't beat level 0 yet! Seeing sea lions by the harbour was amazing along with the wild sea. The house was very cold away from the main fire, but their warmth made up for it and was an experience we will never forget. I even learnt to dance the bolero!

Chonchi has proved almost as fascinating. We arrived yesterday morning. We caught the 9 a.m. bus from Castro to Chonchi which is about thirty miles. Chonchi is another fishing harbour town with a population of about 4,000; a beautiful location with a B&B right by the water called Esmeralda owned by a Canadian guy called Charlie, who claims to have lived nearly everywhere in the world, including Wales. His heart is in the right place, but his mouth never stops moving. He just doesn't stop talking! He gave us maps, details, opinions and we decided to go to Lemuy for the day, a small island off Chiloe. The ferry turned out to be three to four miles from Chonchi. Nice walk, but further than we expected. A small ferry holding only a few vehicles, we managed to persuade a lorry driver to take us to the main town, Pugueldon, on the island. Charlie recommended that we stopped there for lunch and then head down south, which is exactly what we did do. On the ferry, we managed to see another sea lion and the drive on the lorry was rutted and stony, but good. Our first ever hitchhike and in Chile it is extremely safe.

Once in Pugueldon, we found a Super Mercado where we got a couple of rolls and cheese and ham. We headed down to the harbour and sat and ate it down by the water with a puppy dog jumping around our legs and licking our bags, and pigs that were roaming around the street munching at any grass that came in sight. Probably the smallest town we have seen in South America. It has a school, a church, library, tourist info etc. We started walking along the road to the south of the island and after about thirty minutes a car came nearer that seemed to be happy to stop and give us a lift. It was such a rally car ride for about eighteen kilometres up and down the hills on Lemuy. The scenery was fantastic and, at various points, we saw water either side as the island was so narrow. The town at the south was called Detif and we then realised we would have to walk another three to four kilometres to get to the coast and be able to see the views of the Andes. It was a lovely sunny day and the walk was great. We did, however, bump into a local who introduced himself as Jo. He seemed very friendly and spoke nice and slowly for us to understand. He had been standing amongst a pile of wood by the side of the road when we found him and, after a few minutes of chat, he invited us to his house/hut across the field. Open to new experiences, we agreed and promptly followed him into a house entirely made of wood. It was one biggish room and, on the left, was a raised platform and a pulpit with what looked like prayers written on poster sized paper on the walls. We both realised what we had found, but not wanting to appear rude, we stayed a little while listening to him preaching the word and trying to convince us of the need to follow Christ! We were sitting on a bench with his stove to the right and a few odds and ends around. No apparent bed and no luxuries—all basic. He offered us milk to drink, apples to eat and told us he used to be a drug addict in Santiago who had seen the light and was now free to live his simple live. We made our excuses about wanting to see the mountains and left, although we were a bit concerned, he may not let us go! We quickened the pace to get away and got to the coast within half an hour.

The beach was beautiful, so peaceful, quiet and deserted. The views were magnificent of the Argentinian Andes; all snow-capped and majestic, I would have loved to be amongst them, but the view in itself was breath taking. Looking out to sea, we were suddenly aware of some animals and realised we were witnessing a few schools of dolphins swimming around and jumping out of the sea. It was a wonderful sight to see and I managed to take a few photos before the camera decided to pack up on us! Can you believe it! Fortunately, the camera has a rewind button to the film so we were able to save the twenty-five photos, but would have to buy a new camera. Anyway, the beach experience was magical and as time was pressing, we knew we still had to find a lift back up the island, all twenty miles.

We were both secretly unsure we would make it, but we walked swiftly back to Detif and it wasn't too long before we heard engines and a couple of Chevrolet vans pulled up and let us in. Fortunately, they were going all the way to Chonchi too, so our luck was in. The pickup had two women and one man who had obviously been doing some work somewhere and it became apparent it was based on fish and in particular salmon. We had only gone a few hundred yards when they stopped the car and got out, the man, donning a life jacket and some welly boots. No explanations made, but the women told us to go with them so we did. Down some steep steps built into a cliff onto a deserted beach. The man and his mate were already out in the boat heading for some platforms which, when we asked, turned out to be a salmon farm. It was only the following day that I found out from Charlie that salmon farming is all about rearing salmon from eggs. I had no idea. Anyway, the man on the boat obviously owned them and he made his way to all five platforms and spent at least fifteen minutes on each talking to the men and obviously sussing out how they were getting on. Having a lift from them, we had to wait a further one-and-a-half-hours before we set off again in the car. We couldn't exactly complain when they were giving us a lift. They did take ages. In the meantime, the two women had given us some ideas to where to go in Northern Chile and whether some of the places we were contemplating to visit were any good. We arrived back to Chonchi in the dark, tired and hungry. Charlie was his normal talkative self, wanting to know what we had done and telling us his life story. He recommended a restaurant in town where they did curantos (a fabulous meal of fish and meat with potatoes), the best on the island, but we would have to order it for the following evening, Saturday. We decided to try a different restaurant on Friday too and by 8.30 we were there. This restaurant was just above a house—just one room, much red furniture and a TV (of course!). Having been in that morning to order curantos, they recognised us and we sat down to eat congrio (conger eel). It was delicious, served with boiled potatoes and tomatoes. To drink, we had the recommended 'grande' glass of crystal Cristel Schopp beer. The meal did just the trick and by the time we got back to the hostel, the sea air had already got the better of us and we went to bed exhausted. The room we had was basic, overlooking the sea with a Chilean sized double bed that was more like a big single, but it was comfortable and we awoke to the smell of a cooked breakfast. This wasn't included in the price of £12 per night, but it was a treat for one of the mornings and meant we wouldn't need much lunch. Charlie provided half a banana, a glass of fresh orange juice (up until then what we had has not been fresh), warm fresh rolls, a plate of spicy sausage, sauté potatoes, scrambled eggs and coffee. Delicious!

After breakfast, we decided to do a beach walk along to the next town and set off stomachs full and raring to go. It was quite a long way and Charlie had also recommended we go and see a secret waterfall about half-way along. It was great walking by the sea again, although more difficult on stones than sand. The waterfall wasn't easy to find and at first, we took the wrong track, but we found it. Not as big and spectacular as others we have seen, but good. We didn't manage to reach the town as the sea had come in too far to get all the way up. We found a path in some fields and made our way to the road and headed back to Chonchi.

Back in Chonchi, I once again tried to phone home, but was told I couldn't get a line. So frustrating! I was told to go somewhere else in town, but time was ticking by. So, I decided to get up early the next day and do it then. Whilst in town, I also found out about bus times and prices for Frutillar, our next destination and then headed back.

Charlie had been quite generous in allowing us the chance to use his little wooden rowing boat and we decided the time was right to do it then. The deal was that Simon would row and I would read some sections of the South American Handbook to him. So we set off. We only stayed within the harbour and pushing the boat out, my boots and feet got soaked. Simon found it quite difficult against the tide and after about half an hour, we went back. The boat also leaked so it was essential to keep bailing out every now and then. It brought back memories of us in Auntie Doris when bailing water out that kept coming back in. Auntie Doris was the tiny tub boat that my family owned and used on Lake Windermere as a child. Back at the house, we had a quiet hour reading and writing. Whilst staying at Esmeralda, there had also been another two people, an Australian girl and a French bloke. Both of them were extremely quiet to a point of being almost rude. Neither seemed to want to say anything and when asked where they had been, they said "Around," and what they thought of Chile was replied, "It's nice."

Rebecca

Frutillar, Chile
Monday 26th May 1997—5 p.m.

Having tried some conversation, we went out with them as Charlie had promised us all a trip to the museum, even though it was closed. Being a member of the committee, he could gain entrance. We all set off and were provided with a quick guided tour around Chonchi, not just the museum. As a fireman too, he was able to show us around the fire station with engines which were housed there. To our amazement, there was a Brockway 1921 old fire engine that they still used as their main support for putting out fires. It was really spectacular. The hoses were not original as being made of material meant them needing hours of drying from the tower and rubber hoses were therefore now much more practical. Upstairs from the main engine room they were building a big function room, all in wood, which they would use for dances and events of some description. The firemen themselves were slowly building the whole place and hoping it would be complete by next summer. Once Charlie had obtained the museum key from the owner, we spent an hour looking around an 'old house' that had been done up to look like the original. Simon and I did not feel that much has changed in sixty to seventy years as they still use old Aga's as main cookers, fires for heating, and old furniture. It was all really interesting and we managed to see the only Cocina Fogon (I think was called!) This was a room that had been transferred back in time to early last century where a room was a house for a family, all made of wood.

Apparently, it was the only real example of it in the whole of Chile and next year they are hoping to use it for real and offer visitors food cooked there. It was really interesting, especially as the local oldies had all had some say as to what was correct from what they remembered. In general, the museum was well kitted out. They had a spent a lot of effort making it look fascinating. Locals had donated all the furniture and knick-knacks, and the opening ceremony seemed to have been quite a big thing. We left the museum and walked up to buy our tickets for the following day's trip to Frutillar, and walking down the other side of the road were a travelling couple with backpacks who looked decidedly English. We all waved. On arriving back to Esmeralda, we found them sitting talking to Charlie. The South American Handbook had obviously taken them there as well. Kate was from Highbury, London and although Scott was from Sydney, he had been living in London for a while. They had been traveling for seven weeks in Ecuador, Peru and Bolivia. This was their first trip to Chile and their first impressions were based on it being a bit like England. They were a little disappointed with this as I think that had hoped to go back to England next week and with a feeling of having been somewhere really different. Anyway, they had lots of tips and ideas of places to go to in Peru and Bolivia. We ended up having dinner with them as we were going to eat our curantos and they needed a restaurant for dinner, so they came along. It was actually a really nice evening and we gained more confidence about Peru and Bolivia, having had Charlie tell us everything bad about it, including cholera!

Both of them work for Price Waterhouse in London and were going back to their jobs, although Kate was hoping for a transfer to Sydney by October this year. They both loved Peru and Bolivia including Machu Picchu, Salt Lake, Lake Titicaca and tried to persuade us to go to the Galapagos Islands, even though the flight cost £800. They said that both countries were a lot cheaper than Chile and warmer. It was great to be meeting some people who had done what we were about to do and it was also nice to talk to some likeminded travellers and learn a thing or two as well as being able to give recommendations to them. The curantos were good. The shellfish were huge. It had a nice soy sauce with it and some of the ribs were a little salty, not as good as the family one in Ancud, but good for £5.

The following morning, Sunday, it was my plan to get up at a decent time to phone Mum and Dad before we got the bus at 9.50. Whilst having my shower, I suddenly had a horrible thought that I had made a slight mistake. I knew that we had to change buses at Castro, but I suddenly wondered whether the 9.50 was from Castro and not Chonchi. When I got back to the room, Simon was still in bed and on checking the ticket; sure enough, 9.50 was from Castro—mild panic! It was a good job I got up early, but once again I couldn't phone home—was I ever going to speak to my parents ever again?!

We got to the bus stop at about 8.55, hoping there would be a bus to catch to Castro. Of course there wasn't one until 9.45, so we managed to get a "collectivos" taxi and got there in plenty of time. These taxis charge a fixed rate per person to go to the next town and usually like to have a full car before setting off, but our driver was generous. Castro was very quiet on a Sunday morning to the extent there was only one shop open for any food and drink. Thankfully, they had rolls and ham and things, so we managed to eat some breakfast. On the bus, I recognised a couple of lads I had seen in the café in Castro a few days previously. They both looked British, but we heard one of them speak American. It was only on the ferry that we chatted to them. One of them, an Englishman, was over in Chile studying Spanish in La Serena. He was showing his American friend the south and they were loath to go back to university. He was due back at Hull University for his final year in September. Nice guy!

Puerto Montt looked disturbingly different in the dry weather. It actually looked quite nice. We arrived in Frutillar at about 2.30 and decided to walk the four kilometres to the lake side down the road instead of getting a taxi. It was a long way. I wish we hadn't.

Bajo Frutillar is beautiful, situated on the third largest lake in South America, Lago Llanquihue. It seems like the sea, even with small waves lapping at the shore, and is surrounded by snow-capped mountains and volcanoes. It looked beautiful. The town is situated along the lake shore and we eventually found the hosteria recommended in the book. Kaiserseehaus is owned by an old lady whose descendants were German (as are many around here). She and her daughter, and a helper, run the place. Looking nothing from the outside, inside it smelt a little damp and cold, but old and wooden panelled and huge. Our room is the only bedroom overlooking the lake and you can hear the sound of the waves quite clearly. A very soothing noise.

Rebecca

Frutillar, Chile
Tuesday 27 May 1997—6.05 p.m.

The daughter showed us the room and gave us a price which

seemed expensive in comparison with what we have recently been paying in Chile She told her mother we were not happy and managed to knock off £4 per night. This would include breakfast and they also told us about their three course dinners which they do charging £5 per person. Not being used to paying less than this, we decided to accept it and try it out. The book had recommended it for budget travellers and we have been warned of big portions. The portions were not huge, but they were happy to give us second helpings and three courses which were quite a lot.

That first evening, we had vegetable soup with egg (very tasty) and the first taste of their homemade white bread, very similar to my mothers and very nice. They then served a pork chop and potato and lovely garlicky sauce and salad. Unfortunately, my chop was a little pink and for the fear of food poisoning, I decided not to eat it, only the cooked bits. However, I then decided to ask them to cook it a little longer and she was extremely obliging to the point of bringing me another fully cooked chop. The dessert was a thick set mousse made of some ingredients which I still can't put my finger on! Overall, the meal was very good and then she offered a bottle of wine. We accepted and it was delicious. We still don't know whether we will be charged for it. We have been the only people staying here since we came and have had all their attention to the extent that the mother wouldn't stop talking to us! In two days, we have found out:

• She has poison in her blood and her legs are so bad she has open wounds to let it out rather than go to her head or heart!

• Her daughter has probably had some kind of breakdown

where she needed a lot of drugs and cannot now think straight, often talking nonsense so we must ignore her (the daughter looks about thirty-five to forty and constantly looks worried, overworked and old fashioned in her dress sense). She used to be married, but the husband was very bad.

- In 1974, the mother told her husband she would leave him at the end of the year and she did. He only allowed her to have two children, but she really wanted four.

- He sold the farm and hostel and kept all the money saying she wasn't able to have any because she had slept with her daughter's husband! Apparently, the whole family believed him because she was the only one who liked him. So much so, her son's children are not allowed to visit her here.

- The mother is having a house built for her daughter and helper (who is extremely sweet) and family.

- Mother will be homeless soon (but is used to it and it doesn't bother her) as the other owner of the house has decided to sell the house and land to a company who will be building lots of houses.

- Her father had dinner with Rudolph Hess!

The gossip goes on and no doubt we will find out more this evening.

Yesterday, we decided to do a walk along one of the lakes and having taken some washing down to the laundrette, we set off. It turned out to be a very humid day and for most of the walk, we were just in short sleeves. Our jumpers were having their first wash in four weeks! A lot of the scenery was very British with green fields and rolling hills, but every now and then we would meet up with the lakeside again where I trimmed Simon's beard with his penknife scissors. This time, it was a proper hack that isn't too patchy. The client approved!

This ritual has so far taken place in very beautiful surroundings, the last time looking out to the Pacific in Ancud. Where would be next?

The whole walk took just over four hours. We were quite tired at the end of it, but I had decided to try and phone mum and dad again so I was anxious to get on and do it, hoping that I could at last speak to them. It coincided with picking up the washing and buying a bit of fruit and as it was a small taxi ride away, I went on my own to save money. The answer machine was on! I, therefore, phoned them direct and left a quick message. I could have said so much more, but I really wanted to speak to them properly so I kept it brief. Hopefully, they will have got that by now. I may try again tomorrow morning.

I bought our bus tickets to Valdivia, bought some fruit, picked up the washing and came back to the hostel for a cup of tea. Quite homely. The meal last night was also good. Fish soup with a piece of Corvena (don't know what that is) a tasty rice soup liquid. She also let us taste raw shellfish which to be honest neither of us particularly enjoyed. It was very fishy, slightly slimy, although Simon let it slide down his throat like an oyster and I chewed it like a true northerner! The main course was a piece of chicken, tagliatelle (which could have been cooked in stock for flavour), lovely carrot and onion and cold tomatoes, and a bit of onion on top. It was really nice and for dessert we had a bowl of preserved home grown plum that was delicious. Another bottle of wine was polished off and, again, we were ready for more tales of family gossip.

Today, we woke up to the sound of rain which fortunately subsided quite quickly. For the second day, we had a huge breakfast. Breakfasts are great. Fresh bread, cheese, ham, jams, and today three types of cake. Simon had them all! Two of them were apple strudel type (German) cakes and the third a plain sponge coffee cake. They were really nice and a couple of rolled oat date and nut like balls. Yum!

It is extremely relaxing around there and very quiet so we are recharging our batteries ready for tomorrow's jaunt to Valdivia. We did the walk around the other side of the lake for another four-and-a-half-hours and it was better than yesterday for views of the volcanoes and interesting ups and downs. Again, housing here is all wood, but quite colourfully decorated and Germanic in style. No traffic on the roads and only the sound is of animals or the water. We also bought some photo postcards as our camera is out of function. We planned to buy a new camera in Valdivia as ours can't be fixed. We also tried to get money out of a local bank with a credit card (Visa), but were told they would only accept national visa, not international. You just have to accept these things and we are hoping they won't charge us for the wine as we may not have enough to pay for it!

Back at the house we had tea and this time they also gave us honey bread which was really good. We are not sure what is for dinner. It may be soup made from the shellfish we tried raw yesterday. They are much better cooked. We have both really enjoyed Frutillar, a much more western looking town than others we have experienced, but small quiet and beautifully situated. We were fortunate to have clear views of the volcanoes when we arrived as they have been amongst cloud ever since. It is great to experience more off the beaten track places, away from the city and big towns. Who knows what Valdivia will bring? It is all an exciting risk.

Simon

Frutillar—The Lake District
25th to 27th May 1997

As usual, Rebecca has done an outstanding detailed account of our time at Frutillar. Therefore, I will merely attempt to briefly summarise my thoughts of the time we have spent here.

Bajo Frutillar is beautifully situated on the Lago Llanquihue. Lago Llanquihue is immense—the biggest in the Chilean Lake District. The town is very organised, neat and tidy, very different to the fishing villages on Chiloe. Here, there is no sign of poverty. Supposedly, in summer, it is probably the most tourist-y place we have been to. However, at this time of year it is empty giving the place a strange ghost town type of atmosphere. I have really enjoyed it here and will not forget the tranquillity of the place. We are staying on the seafront in a huge old house run by a mad old lady (Vida) and her middle-aged daughter. Vida has spent many moments telling us about her problems and the fact that her daughter is mad. I don't think either of them have all their marbles, but I don't think (I hope) they are dangerous. The biggest danger probably being that a guest will strangle the old dear one day to get her to shut up! That said, the food has been great and the breakfasts superb. According to Vida, the best in Latin America.

I won't forget the constant crash of the waves on the beach outside our window. I can hear them as I write this at 10.45 on our last night here. It's great to hear the water if you wake up in the night. The volcanoes on the other side of the lake are simply incredible. Calbuco, in particular, is really impressive—a perfect cone; the combination of its stature and the size of the lake make it look like it ascends straight from the water. According to my map, this isn't the case as it is quite some distance away from the lake. Whatever, impressive it is. We have done a couple of lakeside walks over two days and have spent much time relaxing here. Money is starting to give some cause for concern so the eating out every night might have to stop. Ham sandwiches here we come!

Rebecca

Corral (Valdivia), Chile
Wednesday 28th May 1997—6.15 p.m.

I can't believe I am up-to-date with this diary. We had rather a shock last night when we paid our bill. The wine was not inclusive of the meal price and we were charged £3 per bottle! It taught us both a huge lesson about asking all prices, however petty it may seem, as we are on a tight budget and we can't afford to overspend or that will mean going home early. We were both really annoyed with ourselves for not asking and the woman for selling it to us so willingly with no mention of the cost. Anyway, last night's meal was good, shellfish and veg soup to start, homemade burgers, mashed potato and salad and fruit salad. We then played scrabble which caused some amusement amongst the household. I won of course—the highest score ever of three hundred!

Today, we were up and away by 9 a.m. to get our bus for Valdivia. The breakfast was a little disappointing. There were no fresh cakes made so she asked if we would like eggs (however we wanted them). Agreeing to scrambled eggs and ham, we both got half-cooked scrambled eggs with a minute amount of ham. I could hardly eat it. Anyway, we filled ourselves up on bread. I tried the avocadoes she had mashed up with garlic for breakfast!

At the bus station, we had about half an hour to spare so decided to tot up our expenditure over the last four weeks. We had already spent £300 over budget which we are hoping to get back by being very careful and spending more time in cheaper countries like Peru, Bolivia, and India etc. The bus journey went very smoothly. I managed to read some more of the other areas in Chile that we could visit and managed to see some great countryside views on the way. Once in Valdivia, we decided to attach the small backpack back onto my bag to leave my hands free. It was really heavy, but I managed to plod along for a little while feeling like I was walking on the moon. Valdivia seemed like any other big town but had some interesting areas around the riversides. We walked into the centre and found a bank as well as a few camera shops to suss out prices. We saw some disposables for about £5, crap cameras for £20–£30, zooms started at about £90 and good cameras go up and up in price. We decided to buy disposable until we get to Iquique in Chile where they have a tax-free zone shopping area. We are hoping to pick up a decent one from there; however, we had passed by the disposals and the shop had shut! We will have to buy it in a couple of days when we get back into Valdivia. On asking a passer-by, we managed to find the bus stop for buses to Niebla, a coast resort outside Valdivia where there is a boat crossing to Corral. We chose this place because it is a good central stop for all the major forts and it says there are some very good coastal walks. The little boat trip was rather wavy, but fun. When we got to a damp and miserable Corral, we found the recommended hostel that looked huge and clean and well suited to travellers. However, they are asking for £16 a night for the room and weren't prepared to budge so we had to leave. It didn't look that good! We had been told by the British guy, Andy, that we shouldn't pay any more than £10. They recommended another hostel which we eventually found. Not as big, but clean and they seemed friendly. One of the women could speak English! They too were asking £16, but when haggling, we got it down to £12 including breakfast so we are here.

At the moment, there are some very odd band noises coming from outside. Trumpets, drums and whistles, all out of tune and sounding as if children are practicing. Very weird customs in Chile probably means something really significant. We had a look around the town earlier and found one of the forts with all its guns and high walls. Quite an impressive view across the big harbour, but not so clear to be able to see the Llaima volcano as the book promises. We sussed out where the coastal walk should start and then we decided to have a look at a few restaurants. The recommended one had no menu so we asked to see it and the man took ages finding it. A very basic fish menu all starting at £5. We decided to give the meal a miss today and just get some bread and cheese. By then, most places had sold out of bread and it took a while to find somewhere with any left. Anyway, we did so this evening; we are looking forward to rolls, cheese, crisps, fruit, yoghurt, biscuits and beer! What a feast! Lunchtime had been stale rolls and a packet of chocolate and vanilla filled biscuits. This is what living on a budget is all about. If we can get hot water, we may have soup tomorrow. What a treat!

Corral is not particularly attractive, especially in the rain, but hopefully we will see some great coastal scenery and who knows, the sun may even shine.

Simon

Corral—The Lake District
28th to 29th May 1997

Today, I saw a cow waiting by the bus stop near our hostel. Our hostel is in the high street and it is not as if we are on a farm or anything. Cows, sheep, pigs, dogs, chickens, turkeys, you name it; they roam around Chile (and Argentina for that matter) as if they own the place. These are the type of details that have become the norm when you spend some time in a place, but I don't want to forget them.

We are staying in the tiny port of Corral near Valdivia in the Lake District. It took ages to get here from Frutillar because after getting to Valdivia we had to get a bus and then a boat across the massive estuary that Corral sits alongside. It has been worth the effort for many reasons. Firstly, the weather has felt decidedly uneasy. You feel like it will rain any minute. In bed last night we could hear the rain against the tin roof that protects us from the weather. This morning I wondered what on earth we were going to do. We went out anyway. It wasn't raining, but it was very cloudy. We followed some information set out in the South American Handbook and walked for forty minutes to Castillo San Luis de Alba. This is one of three local Spanish forts built to defend the entry to Valdivia. We got there, looked around and then carried on walking. We ended up doing a five-hour coastal walk. The views were spectacular with huge seas and waves crashing against the wild and craggy coast. It was fabulous. Secondly, we have decided to budget even more than we have done. Whilst waiting for our bus at Frutillar, we worked out that we were £300 over budget. Our camera was broken and needed replacing. It was time to pull the horns in. I was dreading this because I feared that morale could take a dive. For the past two nights, we have locked ourselves away in our room. Once again, we are the only people here. We have eaten bread and cheese, and I for one have really enjoyed it. We even went to bed late last night after previous night of little sleep for me. In short, I believe we have proved to ourselves that we can have fun even if the weather is poor and funds are low. By the way, Corral is in a fabulous location in a huge estuary that is like a lake but has huge waves. Around the neck of the estuary is some of the best coastline I have ever seen. Well worth seeing.

Rebecca

Pucon, Chile
31st May 1997—5 p.m.

How would you feel staying near a volcano, all snow-capped and smoking at the top amongst fantastic hills, autumn, colours, rushing rivers and blue sky and sunshine? Believe me, it is beautiful. Volcano Villarica is just outside our bedroom window in a lakeside town Pucon. Yesterday, we left Corral at about 8.30 a.m. having had basic breakfast. The rain was torrential and we hoped that we would leave such weather behind us. No such luck! A boat, a bus and another bus later, we arrived in Pucon at about 2 p.m. and it was still raining. When buying our bus tickets, we were given a little card advertising a hosteria and we decided go and check it out. On the way up, a man started chatting to us and asked us where we were going and could he help. Having had such annoying people before we were a little wary of him and said, "No, there is nothing he could do." He then said we may be heading towards his place which was why he was asking. He was Patricia and he spoke very good English. He seemed knowledgeable of the area and happy to help us look around. It also turned out he organised excursions all around, supposedly cheaper than other agencies—an entrepreneur businessman, conman, whatever you want to call him, he is making all this his business as he is constantly trying to sell people something. We took the room that was more than we wanted to pay but included a big breakfast (which it was), cooking and laundry facilities. There are another couple staying here, Jonathan and Sarah Newman who married on 12 April (same day as Jenny), went to Ireland for a week's honeymoon and are now completing an around the world ticket. A little complex, but Jonathan is Australian, Sarah originally from Cornwall and both used to live in New Zealand. They are physiotherapists and have travelled a lot as well as working a bit as they have gone around. They went to England last summer for Sarah's sister's wedding. They stayed for about seven months whilst Jonathan could work for about six months, got married in April, lived near Crystal Palace and are now unsure where to settle. The choices are New Zealand or Ireland but they are visiting Australia in August, when their flights run out. A really nice couple. Sarah reminds me a little of Susie (David and Susie). Jonathan is really into surfing and even brought along his surfboard which got sent to Rio by mistake, but came back to Santiago, amazingly enough. They have chosen to do the five-day Spanish course here (that Patricia does) which includes two, one and a half hour lessons a day, one morning and one evening. They are planning to go further south, but eventually see something of Peru. Maybe we will meet again in Macchu Picchu.

The place here is very good in that Patricia lives in a house next door and this one is just for the use of all residents. There is therefore a lounge, dining area, big kitchen and roaring fire that goes on all day. He has a cleaner who comes in, makes breakfast, cleans the place and keeps it ship shape. The only downer is that most of the people smoke. It can taint the air somewhat, including our bedroom. Having chatted to Jonathan and Sarah a little yesterday, we headed out and ended up absolutely soaked. Patricia recommended that we have a look at the monastery. We set off and got incredibly lost in the woods, ending up behind some people's shed houses amongst their rubbish tip! We eventually found the right road up to the monastery and did have some great views across the town and Vallarica which is supposedly the most beautiful lake in the district, partly because it is surrounded by woods. As yet, we haven't explored the lake shore, but we may do that tomorrow. We headed for the supermarket and spent about an hour choosing some food for the next three days. It was great picking out some fresh veg again. Last night, we cooked a tomato, veg and salami sauce and rice and bread. It was delicious. Then we had a great evening chatting, drinking beer, playing Boggle and having a good laugh. There is also an American bloke staying here. He comes from Pittsburgh, Pennsylvania and is called David. He has a very slow drawling voice and has been in South America about two months. He has been having Spanish lessons here and in Santiago; having said that, he has no Spanish accent—all said with an American twang and so slow. It is so funny to listen to. There is also a Brazilian girl here called Anna and there are some suspicions that things are happening between them as they tend to spend a lot of time together. Anyway, as part of his eight-month trip that he started back in January, he stopped over in England for two weeks and drove all over the place, including the very north of Scotland. Typical American and mad to drive so far, but he did actually admit that he regretted it.

Rebecca

Pucon, Chile
1st June 1997—4.45 p.m.

June already! A month has been and gone, so much has happened and yet I can still visibly remember the day we left and almost each day since. Last night was really good fun. We didn't get to bed until 2 a.m. We cooked our own meal of lentil curry sauce and rice. All the others started organising a barbeque. I thought we hadn't been asked and was a bit offended, but Simon told me later that Patricia had actually mentioned it yesterday. Anyway, we played Boggle a couple of times, drank wine and chatted. Patricia started by providing some brain teasers which caused great fun for a while. Simon had a good one with three bottles, knives and a box of matches. Most of them went to the disco—again! But us, Sarah and Jonathan stayed behind and just talked for ages. The evening ended off a good day which has been glorious weather.

We had decided to go for a walk, which can be done by mountain bike too. It is a twenty kilometre stretch to another lake called Carbuga. We knew we wouldn't be able to walk so far, but we got a taxi to the bridge, over the river and walked for about five hours in total. What a fantastic walk—the blue sky, the snow-capped volcano Villarica and the colours. It was a well-used track which winded itself along the river bank, Rio Pucon. The route was peaceful and so well situated. We also had great views of two volcanoes nearby. We had our lunch of bread, salami and fruit at La Puntilla, the point at which two rivers join up. It was a beautiful spot with a small platform jutting out into the river which we decided could be used for diving off in the summer. The rivers were so deep and so clear. It was so quiet—no sounds apart from nature. Heading back to the bridge and the taxi we had booked, we heard voices the other side of the river and noticed two boats about to set off water rafting. It brought back memories of our experience in Argentina in El Bolson, but the difference was there were only four of us in one boat and yesterday there must have been at least ten!

The river did have quite a few good rapids for them and we ran ahead at one stage and got around the riverside just in time to catch them coming past. They all waved and made certain signs that they were having a great time. I felt a bit of a fool standing there in my shorts that we had to wear because all of our clothes were drying on the line from Simon's washing load in the cold-water machine. It was such a superb walk and we got back tired, but well exercised. The taxi driver was there as promised and when we turned up in the town centre, I tried phoning home again to no avail. The answer machine was on!

Last night, we were able to see the glow from the volcano in the distance, such an awesome sight. I never thought I would witness an active volcano. Sarah told us yesterday she had read that Pucon would be wiped out if it ever erupted. Great—I don't think it has spat out for about ten years. Maybe it's due, but we hope not!

This morning, we got up for a good breakfast—crispy bread, eggy bread and a bowl of apple, kiwi and yoghurt. Delicious with a cup of coffee and everyone having breakfast together. Anna left today for Puerto Varas. David may feel a little lost now she has gone, but he is still around. Patricia has mentioned a local Mapuche horse racing session somewhere today and we decided it would be a good laugh to see what the locals get up to on a Sunday afternoon. We would be going about 2.30 so until then we decided to go and explore this beautiful area that we had now been staying in for a couple of days and have not actually seen. The book recommended "La Peninsula" walk that supposedly took you onto private land owned by a hotel. We were supposed to get permission from them, but eventually finding the peninsula we couldn't be bothered to find the right hotel. The walk was OK; firstly, through an upmarket condominium of flats and houses via the lake and eventually through some wooded areas along a path. It really did take us to the edge of the water, past the golf course, tennis courts, rocks, little miradors and such wonderful views of the calm lake and the awesome volcano in the distance. It took about three hours and we even managed to get another great spot for lunch overlooking the lake and volcano with the warm sun on our backs. At times today, we have walked around in short sleeves as the sun was so warm.

On arriving back in Pucon, we saw Patricia who told us the racing was taking place about fifty kilometres away—too far really for us all to get to so it was all off! We walked around the local handicraft market which was disappointing in relation to the ones at Castro and Angelmo in Puerto Montt.

With time on our side, we decided to phone home again and this time, for the first time in four weeks, I got through! Oh, joy and rapture it was—a delight to speak to my mummy! It felt normal, but weird to speak to her so far away and having done so much. I was so glad that everyone was OK and it was great to hear that my letters had got through telling her all about where we are and what we have been doing. It sounded strange and made me realise what wonderful things we really are doing and seeing. Such a shame we are missing out on Jonathan's (my brother the actor) play that they saw on Friday. It would be great to experience the Globe Theatre now on its first opening. Sounds like the weather has been really good the last week, especially for Charlotte's (my sister) week away in the Lake District. I bet Chris (Charlotte's boyfriend) is glad to finish his work; really good he got a distinction for his presentation. Really feel for Oliver (my brother) at the moment doing his finals, but I am convinced he will be OK, bless him. He will be so pleased to finish them but gutted to end his university days. I do miss them all so much and it was sweet when mummy said she could just do with giving me a squeeze. I certainly could have done with one too, but I was satisfied with hearing her voice and at the end of the phone call I felt so pleased to have phoned and put the phone down with a lump in my throat! I am so looking forward to reading the letters she has sent. Simon was thrilled to hear that I got through and we headed for a quick walk by the lake and a sit down whilst I told him all the news.

Simon

Pucon—The Lake District
30th May to 3rd June 1997

The town of Pucon is situated on the south eastern slope of Lago Villarrica. For me personally, this town is a little bit non-descript. A rich tourist-town, miles removed from the life of your average working-class Chilean. Still the surrounding area is fabulous. For Rebecca and I, there is so much to do here. The hiking potential around the town is first class. Indeed, we have completed two great walks, one through the mountain valleys. We had lunch at the confluence of two rivers. Must sound like I am repeating myself, but the water was so crystal clear. We have also walked around the peninsula which Pucon is situated on. We only meant to go out for an hour or so, but we ended up staying for about four hours. This particular day was on Sunday. As we had our lunch perched on a rock looking at the smouldering volcano Villarrica, we told each other not to take all this for granted. Can you imagine? A Sunday stroll in the sunshine in a place where we are staying around a beautiful lake with a back drop of mountains and volcanoes as added extras. On Sunday, we were wearing T-shirts and then the rain set in. Rain here really means rain. For the first time on the trip, the rain has driven us out of an area. It started on Sunday evening and has not stopped since. It is relentless. We rescued the day yesterday by going to some thermal baths with another couple who are staying in the same hosteria, Sarah and Jonathan. It was excellent sitting in natural steaming hot pools in a deserted valley drinking cerveza in the rain. It got so hot at times I had to climb out of the pools to cool down. It's a tough life!

Today, we take things slow. Our bus does not leave for Santiago until 19:45. It is still raining so we have the unusual situation of pure slobbery forced upon us. So far, I have been presently surprised at how much I have enjoyed it. Now that takes me onto another aspect of our stay here. I feel like a student again. It is a good hosteria. We arrived to a full house with Sarah and Johnathan (she is Brit, him an Aussie) Anna (madly energetic Brazilian) and David (dry American at the age of thirty-five handed in his notice on the oil rigs to travel). He speaks Spanish in the most incredible way, in a slow drawing Pennsylvanian accent. At first, I thought he was taking the piss—I now realise he doesn't realise! Music plays constantly. People drink beer, make food, cook, someone even stole my beer from the fridge the other night. That's how much of a student feel the place has to it. It has been a different experience for us, but one that I have really enjoyed. I will be sad to leave our house. Now writing this has taken forty-five minutes out of the day, now for the other seven until our bus leaves. Just how long can I spend brushing my teeth?

A City, a Desert and a Beach

Simon

Santiago, Chile
3rd June to 8th June 1997

Please excuse the handwriting on this entry. I am currently on the bus travelling across the Chilean heartland. OK, where were we? We left the house in darkness at Pucon. The whole town had a power cut so we were forced to cook, eat and pack up in the dark. As a result, we boarded the bus without this diary, but luckily for us we were able to retrieve it at Santiago. The overnight bus was uncomfortable but saved us the cost of a night's accommodation. The bus company did their best to keep us amused. We even played bingo! I was never really confident that the numbers I crossed out were those that were being called out so I spent of most of the time hoping I wouldn't have to call Bingo! Anyway, we found Jock's place in Santiago. This was a hosteria that had been recommended by two other hostel owners, Charlie of Chonchi and Patricio of Pucon, so now it is Jock of Santiago. More on Jock of Santiago later.

On our first day, the first thing we did was go to the Post Office to pick up any mail. Miracle of miracles, despite us being three weeks late, we had some post. We caught up on some of the news back home, namely the following.

1. Dad had been pretty depressed that Labour had won the election.
2. The rest of the country hadn't been.
3. Berni was off travelling as well.
4. Rebecca's parents had eaten lots of meals out.

It was great to hear from friends and family. We gorged ourselves on McDonalds and hamburger fries and news from home. Next item on the "to do" list was to get some US dollars and some more travellers' cheques. This proved impossible to do in the towns and villages we had stayed at in other parts of Latin America. Surely, it shouldn't prove a problem in Santiago?

Four hours, ten banks, three cambios de change and countless clerks later, we realised we had been a little naive in our assumption. It was infuriating. A simple transaction had taken so long. We went from bank to bank and person to person. After that ordeal, we walked to the foot of Cerro san Cristobel. San Cristobel is a sharp conical hill to the north east of the city. It is the biggest of the parques within the city and a most unusual one. It houses a zoo which we went to. I really enjoyed it, but I am not sure that Rebecca did. We got the railway to the summit. From the top (three hundred metres), we had a fabulous view of the city as it got dark. There were very few people at the top, so all we could hear was the sound of the city below. It felt great to be in the city again after a month of comparative wilderness. I was really looking forward to exploring the city the next day.

Explore we did, with the help of a free guide booklet from the tourist information office. We saw museums, churches, plazas and cathedrals. We spent half the time wondering why most of the travellers we had met had told us Santiago was boring and Buenos Aires was better—answers on a postcard please! For me, this was the best day we spent in the city. The next two days we explored some of the city's museums, galleries and parques. In my mind, some of the architecture in Casa Colorada, the neo-classical Bibliocteca Nacional, the Universidad de Chile and the Plaza de Armas, rival many buildings in some of the cities of Europe, more famous for their history. The city was largely free from litter and well-kept. The Cerro Santa Lucia parque is also worth a special mention. This is a park laid out on a hill with a myriad of paths, buildings and walkways covering its slopes. Very unusual.

As I mentioned earlier, I did enjoy Santiago and would recommend a four-day visit to anyone who valued my opinion. Having said that, as I watch the sea, sky and surrounding countryside go by, it feels good to have left the big city. Our experiences there have, for me, confirmed me a country boy at heart, if not by recent past experience and practice.

The hostel was OK. People were friendly enough and they included;

1. Bjorn (German) and Sammi (Indian) who have spent six months biking across Argentina and Chile until their tandem had packed up. She was now pregnant and the cost of the bike repairs would include shipping expenses.

2. Simon, the Australian, who was very enthusiastic. He tried but failed to capture a Piranha in the Peruvian jungle.

3. Jock. I have written a song for Jock and it goes something like this;

"There was Jock, Jock playing with his cock. There was Jock doing what he should not in this room, in his room".

Yes, Jock did enjoy playing with himself in his bedroom.

Fair enough, but his bedroom was in full view of the kitchen area and it had glass doors. Strange person! It was only near the end that it struck me what he was doing. Each to their own, I suppose, but there is a limit!

Rebecca

Chile—San Pedro de Atacama
Monday 9th June 1997

Another week has gone by without writing in the diary, partly because we left it in Pucon and had it bused down to Santiago! I was so worried it had gone forever, but we picked it up safe and sound and I can continue tracking our trip.

Last Monday in Pucon was torrential rain again and we were on the verge of leaving that night for Santiago. However, Patricio assured us the weather was supposed to be getting better so we held off for a day and decided that going to one of the thermal springs might be a good idea in the rain. We persuaded Sarah and Jonathan to come and Patricio organised a taxi to come and pick us up, take us, wait for us and bring us back. Seemed quite a good idea and we set off with a couple of bottles of beer. The trip was a lot longer than any of us had thought, but we arrived by 4 p.m. and walked down the cliff side of the pools below—steaming! There was a small shed to get changed in. It was a fair distance from the pools and without shoes to wear, it was quite painful walking from pool to pool—very odd but pleasant experience sitting in outdoor natural pools with the rain pouring down around us. I couldn't quite get to grips with the pool being natural. I was convinced that they must have been heated from somewhere, but the only non-natural thing about it was the small pipe protruding cold water into the pools so that they weren't too hot. We sat and chatted in the pools for a couple of hours until it started to go dark and we had to get dried and dressed in candlelight. As promised, the taxi driver was at the top waiting for us and we got back to Pucon safe and sound.

Patricio's words of wisdom on the weather did not come true. Tuesday rain was worse! The puddles extended the breadth of the street and going out for two minutes was a soaking experience. We agreed there is no point in trying to do anything outside in that weather and, therefore, resigned ourselves to stay in and have a slob day before getting our Santiago bus at 7.45 p.m. It was amazing how time goes so quickly. We read, wrote diaries, letters, ate, drank, and chatted. Sarah and Jonathan had decided to leave that day too and David had gone the day before. By 4 p.m., we were the only ones left and it felt weird. I felt quite choked saying goodbye to Sarah and Jonathan. We spent quite a bit of time with both of them and seemed to get on very well. Unfortunately, when travelling, you always know that everything is short term and making friends can only really be short term. This was the case with Sarah and Jonathan. To avoid feeling disappointed and upset when it is all over, you hold back your feelings and don't really allow the friendships to evolve as naturally as they might in other circumstances. This was quite weird. I gave them our address and hopefully they will write to us with their eventual home address wherever they may be in the world.

Our hosteria in Pucon was a great place for us to be on a rainy day. We had a warm fire, tables and chairs and lounge area. We were able to be on our own and not have to sit in our pokey bedroom for hours. However, by 5 p.m., the electricity had really gone off. There had been one or two power cuts throughout the day, but this was the big one. Just when we wanted to cook a big meal and play a game of scrabble. Our torch came in really handy. Patricio meddled with the wiring a little and managed to get the dining area and the kitchen lights working. We had already packed earlier in the day, thank goodness, but at 7.15 we checked to make sure we had everything and set off to get the bus in the rain. We got soaked but managed to dry off in the bus in the twelve hours we had to Santiago.

Tur Bus was the name of the company, and although it was the basic bus, it seemed quite plush. The leg room wasn't brilliant, but the seats were comfy and they provided a pillow and blanket each. As Simon explained earlier, we even played bingo. What a joke that was when we don't speak the language! Thank goodness neither of us won. There were no refreshments all evening, but we did sort of get breakfast in the morning. A packet of small biscuits and a milkshake. They showed a film which, unfortunately, we had seen before called *12 Monkeys*. We just listened to our stereo and tried to sleep. This proved more difficult than we expected, partly because it was so hot on the bus. There wasn't much leg room and we just couldn't really sleep much.

We arrived in Santiago at about 8 a.m. We had brought the rain with us! We thought we were getting away from it, but the roads were like rivers. So many cars were getting stuck, but thankfully we were in a bus. Patricio has already recommended a hosteria owned by an American guy called Jock. Charlie had also given us his card and Patricio allowed me to use his phone. I telephoned Jock the evening before. I asked all the details on how to get there, how much it costs etc.

The taxi driver found the place OK and did not overcharge us as they seemed to have done with so many others. The place had a metal fence all around and the gate could only be opened from the inside. Jock had been in bed and in fact Simon glanced and noticed his bum as he came to the window to see who was at the gate. He opened the gate and door to us in a grubby yellow sweatshirt and very short yellow shorts. An odd greeting from the landlord. We tried not to look too shocked. He showed us to our room which was clean and airy. A double bed with six bunk beds, all single. He told us this was our room and I didn't think he would think about letting anyone else in it. There were no curtains or shutters or anything in any of the rooms, not just ours, but the house was big, the breakfasts sounded big and the whole deal seemed good for Santiago. We chatted to Jock for a little while over a cup of coffee. The information we gleaned about him.

1. He doesn't like Santiago and wants to go south and have a hostel there as well so that he can live there.

2. He decided to run this place because another business venture fell through (we never found out what).

3. He was ill in the army for four years doing a dead easy job working on nuclear missiles.

4. He doesn't really drink.

5. He loves to butt in on conversations, is highly opinionated to the point of knowing exactly how to run a country!

6. He is very messy and untidy (as shown by the obvious state of his room and the kitchen).

7. He is a stickler for water, not allowed to wash up as we use too much water.

8. Comes from Alabama.

9. His mother was paralysed by the time Jock was eleven and his father didn't really help him with his schooling much.

Anyway, enough of Jock for now.

Although we hadn't slept much, we were determined to go out and see some of Santiago. Jock was good at explaining the bus system and where to get off etc. We also had a few essential things to do, including getting some dollars.

The yellow buses are a fast breed in Santiago, but most of the roads were paved, so not so bumpy. We were vigilant the whole time we were there, hearing all sorts of stories about people getting money stolen etc. The time we were in Santiago, we had no problems and saw no troubles. At first sniff, Santiago seemed bubbly, bright and quite cosmopolitan in parts. Much better than Buenos Aires in that it appeared to have a soul and a centre to go to, whereas Buenos Aires was very bitty. We found the Post Office and promptly found the poste restante section. There were two lists on the board, one for men and one for women, and our names were on both. Oh joy! It was so exciting getting some mail. We had to write down the numbers and hand them over to be picked up. I got two letters from Mum and one from Christine. Simon got one from his mum and dad and cards from Berni, Matt and Nick. We read our own standing in the Post Office hall to much ohh's and ahh's and isn't this great! I definitely had a big lump in my throat when I started to read the letters from mum. Such a strange experience reading a letter your mother has written on the other side of the world. We were starving by this stage and headed for McDonalds, mainly because they had a good deal on. Not because we loved their food! It always seems criminal eating food like that in another country, but sometimes on a budget you don't have much choice. It tasted great and we swapped letters to read. We are now really looking forward to Arequipa to pick up some more. It was actually quite unfortunate. Mummy told me she had sent four letters, but I only got two. I went back twice in the week and never got them, although they did search for me.

Rebecca

San Pedro, Chile
Tuesday 10th June 1997

After catching up on the post, as Simon has already described, we spent forever getting some dollars and travellers cheques, mainly for Peru and Bolivia, both countries needing them. It was a nightmare, but we stayed as calm as we could and having obtained them, we explored a little of Santiago. It was showery for most of the day, but we managed to see Santiago from the top of San Cristobel Hill and we picked up a guide booklet from the tourist information which we thought we would do ourselves the next day instead of spending two-and-a-half-hours with a guide. We have experienced that before at Edinburgh and decided that it was too much! One thing that really struck us about Santiago was of course the smog. Never seen anything like it. A permanent dark haze hangs over the city and just gets thicker by the hour. From many high points in the city, it is very obvious. We couldn't believe how dirty our trousers were when we left. We were also aware of the incredible Andes all around the city, but on a smoggy and wet day, they are impossible to see. In fact, we were told it was very rare to see them at all. We were exhausted that day and the last thing we needed was to get lost. This is was exactly what we did when we took the bus back to Jock's place. A sudden realisation hit me that we should have got off and we were now heading towards the airport! We asked in the shop just near where we got off and all we could understand was that we needed to get the bus back from the other side of the road. This we did and half an hour out of our way later we were back.

One of the problems we had at this hostel was the lack of space. The kitchen was not very big for any amount of people wanting to cook. Bjorn and Sammi decided to cook incredible meals every night and unfortunately, they always managed to get into the kitchen before we did and use up all the pans. We managed to eat there for two nights but gave up for the other two as more and more people arrived. Thursday was glorious and we headed back into the centre to do our guided tour of the centre of Santiago. It was brilliant. Just what we needed: a simple way of getting to know the city and finding out its history. We took it at our own pace and having seen museums (from the outside), churches, cathedrals, plazas etc. we felt we knew Santiago quite well and felt more confident about finding our way around. Santiago was very busy when compared with some of the small towns and villages. I suppose this is expected from a city!

Simon

San Pedro de Atacama
9th to 11th June 1997

It's amazing how you develop skills on a trip such as this. Today I beat the computer at chess on level four, only another five levels to go. I will be bored by the end of the month.

San Pedro de Atacama has been a complete change to the rest of our trip. Gone are the green fields of Chiloe. Au revoir to the coast of Corrall. Ciao to the lakes of the Lake District. San Pedro de Atacama has a population of 1,600. Like many Chilean villages, it is small, peaceful and the people here don't have much. However, here you have to consider your actions very seriously before committing yourself to actually doing them. Go for a number two at 10.25 p.m. and by the time you have finished, you could be left with either a dirty hand or a dirty bum! Take a walk to the nearest main town, you may be found as a skeleton. San Pedro de Atacama is in the middle of the Chilean desert, one-and-a-half-hours by road to the next town. It has electricity from 6 p.m. to 10.30 p.m. only, but I love it here.

Yesterday, we did our first desert walk. We walked to Pukara de Quitor, a pre-Inca fortress restored in 1981. The fortress was huge and not expecting very much, I have to say that it was really great. We were free to wander around the rooms at will. It cost nothing. It just stood there on the side of the hill resisting the march of time. At the top the view was incredible with the most spectacular overall landscapes I have ever seen. Sand dunes, endless desert and a backdrop of mountains and volcanoes, some snow-capped. We decided to continue our walk to some Inca ruins at Catarpe. The ruins were exactly that, ruins and were not spectacular. However, I will never forget walking through the deserted desert valley to get there. The valleys were a rich red and heavy wind would occasionally whip up the sand and sting our legs. It was great. We even saw the odd shack or two. Why and how does anyone live out there?

Today, we went to the Valle da la Luna. It is three hours walk from San Pedro de Atacama across a relentless desert, heat and sunshine. We left at 8.30 this morning to avoid some of the heat. Two hours along the road we saw a van and it stopped. Only two hours before the first vehicle. The Valle de la Luna was beautiful; a combination of sand dunes, rocky outcrops and the backdrop for volcanoes made it a memorable experience. I had never walked on a sand dune before. Now I have. That is why we decided to go travelling. We could hear the rocks cracking as they bathed in the sun. All too soon it was time for the walk back. I like walking, but I wasn't looking forward to grilling ourselves as we journeyed and, grill we did, but judging by our arms and legs I think we got off lightly. I daren't look at myself in the mirror. However, after two hours, another car stopped and gave us a lift so that probably saved us from becoming complete lobsters. Hasta Luego!

Rebecca

Calama Bus Station
Thursday 12th June 1997—10.30 p.m.

I am sitting in Calama Bus Station waiting for another overnight bus, this time to Iquique. I am really keen to catch up on my thoughts from the last week, so I shall continue with Santiago. Our own tour of the city took most of the day, but we thoroughly enjoyed it and again gave us an idea of what to focus on the following day by way of museums etc. We were determined not to get lost on the way home and we didn't.

Another evening of fighting for the limited number of kitchen utensils! But good to eat home cooked food with a few fresh vegetables. They eat veg here to a point in soups and cold salads, but we haven't really experienced crunchy vegetable in stir fry or something. Can't beat a lump of crunchy carrot, broccoli and cauliflower!

By Friday, we felt pretty used to the bus system, but unfortunately have another job to do. We had to collect what we had left in Pucon. Both of us were so worried it wouldn't be at the bus office, but it was there—another person who laughed at my passport! Is it the photo by any chance or the stylish passport itself—who knows. Patricio put it in an envelope and had put a wad of his hosteria notepaper as a souvenir. Thankful for Patricio's help, he could quite easily have read everything we wrote about him. We headed for the Plaza de Armas, a square that exists in every Chilean town and one of the museums next door to the Post office. Simon had been attracted to it because it would tell us all about Chile's history. I was a little sceptical that it may be written in Spanish and therefore impossible to understand, but sure there would be plenty to see. It was all in Spanish! There were some interesting artefacts, pictures, costumes, figures, furniture etc. but it was a lot smaller than we had expected but only about 80p for both of us. We then decided to find out a little more about Santiago and visit the highly recommended museum dedicated to the capital's history. This was much better as we had an English written guide that took us through each room. The detailed small figurines and housing displayed were excellent and we learnt how the city had expanded over time and used a grid system that a lot of modern Americanised towns use today (Milton Keynes!). It wasn't as big a museum as we expected and certainly not commercial as a lot of London museums are, thank goodness!

It was another lovely day and we managed to go and find a museum that again had come highly recommended by Jock and other travellers. The museum was actually the house in Santiago of Pablo Neruda—a supposed famous poet and writer—we had never heard of him. We eventually found the house that looked nothing from the outside and found ourselves in luck. There would be an English tour in half an hour. The house was in the popular Bellavista area of Santiago, housing lots of restaurants, cafes and bars. Quite similar to Camden or Covent Garden, but not as developed. It was near to San Cristobel where we had been two days previously. The tour group consisted of Simon, me and the American. It was the highlight of our day wandering around the house of an eccentric, exactly as it was in the 70s. All the furniture and bits and piece were just as he had left them. The house had been built for his mistress, Mathilde and was designed to ensure that nobody could see in; therefore, keeping her a secret from his wife! The house and windows etc. were, therefore, all in the back, hence the reason why it looked nothing special when we turned up. Pablo loved food and drink, had bars in nearly every room and loved basing his house designs around boats and the sea. The dining room had portholes and used to have a river outside it with blue paint on the wall, creating the feeling of being on a ship. There was a lot of his furniture and big wacky lamps and a huge library with different sections separating different books in all different languages.

Rebecca

Harbour Iquique, Chile
Saturday 14th June 1997—2.10 p.m.

We loved the house. The only downer was that the zoo was behind it and caused quite a smell to pervade around Pablo's garden. The American guide was quite chatty and seemed interested in giving us a very thorough tour. He covered most points, but certainly needed prompting as to what everything was. We both felt quite inspired to read some of Pablo's works eventually.

Parque Forestal was a long thin park with highways on one side and the city on the other. At the end of it was the beautiful building of the Belles Artes Museum. From Pablo Neruda's house, we walked along the park and back through the centre of Santiago to get to the bus station to find out about moving on to San Pedro de Atacama. We eventually found the right bus terminal and were horrified to find the bus journey would take us twenty-four hours! A mere 2,000km! Having taken the bus times and prices, we were left to think about it and decided that going back to the hostel and starting to cook would be too much. Very often in Chile the South American Handbook has recommended cheap but good meals in bus terminals and we, therefore, decided to try this place. Most restaurants here have boards outside showing the offers of the day and good deals. We noticed 'Lomo a la pobre', poor man's steak in the book that we had wanted to try for a while. We went in with eager anticipation of our meal and were completely gutted when the waiter brought a rubbish hot roast beef sandwich and a few chips each. Our Spanish isn't up to scratch. As our Spanish isn't up to scratch we thought we had asked for something else and we thought we had been quite clear but by the time we had shoved it down our necks we were convinced the waiter had made the mistake and regretted not saying anything. We were so disappointed. Our first meal in Santiago and it was crap! We had a laugh about it and that evening Sammi and Bjorn took pity on us and gave us a piece of their delicious homemade pizza. We also found out on arriving back at the hostel, that Jock had put a French girl in our room. He said an Australian had also turned up and I was sure that Jock would have made Sammi and Bjorn share the room with him. That was not the case. I can't believe that "Laure" (strange name) would be comfortable sleeping in a room with a couple. Anyway, we wouldn't be there much longer so we bit our tongues and said nothing.

By the following day, another girl had arrived in our room and by now I really felt sorry for Simon. It felt that he should be in another dorm with the lads. By this point, we knew Jock was very weird.

1. On Saturday morning, I was eating my breakfast and I was sitting in direct view of Jock's room. Unfortunately, he had glass doors and he chose to sleep in a bed (being about six in the room) that was in direct view of people sitting at the table in the kitchen. My eyes diverted to his room at one point and I was horrified to find him touching himself in full view of everyone! I felt decidedly ill all day and could hardly look at him for the rest of the time I was there.

2. He had no curtains or shutters on any windows.

3. He goes around the house in dirty clothes and a very small pair of shorts.

4. He puts double beds in with single and bunk beds and puts single girls in a room with a couple without asking if we minded!

Our last evening, however, he did revive his image a little. We saw quite a different side to him, chatty, funny and very nice. He was quite a moody chap and you never really know what mood he would be in that day. We weren't altogether sorry to be leaving him. Our last day in Santiago was spent going up Santa Lucia, going to see the Belles Artes Museum and going up San Cristobel again for the view. It was a beautiful day and first thing in the morning we walked up Santa Lucia, a park built into the hill.

Rebecca

Same in hostel
7.15 p.m.

It was a mixture of steps, paths, trees, greens and incredible views of the city, the smog was just beginning, but the snow-capped Andes around were amazing. Then we descended and headed for the Belles Artes Museum which houses some fine art. The entrance was incredible, all white, glass roof and pillars everywhere, some carved into men and women. The collection wasn't very big, but it was a recent collection from a guy called Martinez which looked interesting. The paintings were a mixture of modern and Chilean, 1800 to the present day. Some of the landscapes and seascapes were fantastic as was the still life. I must admit that some of the scrawly modern stuff left a lot to be desired. We spent a good one-and-a-half-hours looking around.

Lunches in Santiago were nothing grand for us. This is partly because of money and partly because I struggle to eat a lot at lunchtime rather than in the evening, even though I know it is supposed to be better for you. We will probably not eat anything until about 3pm as Jock's breakfasts were huge. Bread, cheese, ham, jam, muffins, bananas, yoghurts, juice, coffee and our favourite, kiwi fruits. We became addicted to these, partly because they were so moreish and partly because they cost about 10p per kilo! Deliciously refreshing. Anyway, lunches might be a bit of bread and fruit, or one day we ate our first 'completos', a hotdog with tomato, onions, avocado sauce, mayonnaise and chilli sauce. Yummy!

After the museum, we decided to see the view of Santiago one last time from San Cristobel, but this time go up on the chair lift and not the train. Little did we know that the chair lift was going to be such a walk away. Three quarters of an hour later, I found it amidst some beautiful gardens that we never managed to explore. The chairlift is a longer trip up the hillside and quite spectacular when you look back over the Andes. It was a four-seater car so quite small and very precarious so high up. The summit was far busier than the other day. The views were worth it and the smog was by now disgusting! We came down by the train as it was a much quicker walk back to our bus. We then had to go and buy our bus tickets for the following day. By then we were exhausted, but managed to get there and book up with a really cheap company. Again, we were starving and tired with a supermarket shop ahead of us ready for the next day's trip, so we popped into a "Schop Dog" and had a Completos and Chips... not very good food I know, but it filled a hole and gave us the strength to carry on!

We were up with the larks the following morning, packing and preparing ourselves for a journey. We never anticipated a journey any longer than Buenos Aires to Bariloche, but this was it. We walked to the terminal which, upon reflection, was not a good idea. It was such a long way. Anyway, we bought some fresh bread for our trip and arrived in time for the bus, Flotas Barrios. The bus was very basic, but so much more leg room than any other. We had also been informed that we wouldn't get food, but they gave us a cheese roll for supper and breakfast. The trip wasn't too bad. We stopped at a good picnic location for lunch, but didn't really stop properly again, except at other bus terminals. There were toilets on these buses, but my experience of them has been smelly and dirty, so I avoided them at all costs. It is so much easier being a man when you want a wee.

They showed a French film, but dubbed over in Spanish so not particularly good. I did get the gist of some of it. We also slept pretty well thanks to our blow-up neck pillows. We arrived in Calama, one-and-a-half-hours from San Pedro at about 10.30, and were told that there was a bus leaving San Pedro in half an hour. Perfect! This is when we realised what a desert looks like. Sand dunes, flat hard sand for miles, blue sky and sunshine. No greenery and no water for miles. Amazing!

San Pedro was fantastic. A small oasis town so unique. Never seen anything like it. Roofs made out of mud and streets watered every day to stop sand blowing everywhere. Just like the frontier of the wild west. We found the hostel that had been recommended by Jock, popular with western tourists and students, but it got quieter. The place catered for travellers with showers and big sinks for washing clothes (had to get used to washing by hand again, but in cold water!). San Pedro has electricity for a few hours in the evening which meant no hot water until then, but you just work around this and it was great. The rooms were purpose built, basic and clean, but no breakfast included. Our first afternoon, we had a search around the town, visited a museum which had really good mummies in it, but the rest was all in Spanish and we got our bearings for the next couple of days. We had a lovely lunch at such a basic restaurant, a cazuela and a beer. We also bumped into a Canadian couple who had actually been on our bus from Santiago. They had spent the last five weeks working and studying in Lima and were now travelling around for a few weeks until going back to Canada. They tried to recommend Lima to us, but she said it took her a week before she felt comfortable so I don't think we will bother unless we have to.

We managed to find one or two grocery shops, but they seemed a bit few and far between and I started to wonder how people survived around there. The church was also worth a visit. Seventeenth-century, very basic inside and another mud roof. Bread and cheese were our staple diet that evening. We stayed in our room catching up on the diary, letters and reading. One downside of the hostel was that there were no lounge facilities to congregate in, except outside and that would have been fine, but it was freezing in the evening, but warm during the day (I never mentioned Santiago's underground system that we used a couple of times. Very much like the Paris system, on tracks and wheels, creating a very similar dusty rubber smell. A small two-line underground, crowded, clean and lots of room inside the trains. Buses in Santiago were fast, yellow and furious, and loads of them!)

The other thing was most of the other guests were students and quite cliché in their groups, totally disinterested in talking to us. Anyway, it was quite a nice change just keeping ourselves to ourselves.

The next day we decided to go on one of the few walks from San Pedro to Pre Luca, past Pukara, along the river. The river was a channelled manmade stream, but easy to find and it was a beautiful day. We had found warm weather at last.

Rebecca

On Beach, Iquique
Sunday 15th June 1997—12.40 p.m.

The walk itself was our first experience of walking amongst sand, cactus, small rivers and sand dunes around us and snow-capped Andes beyond. The pre-Inca fortress was breath-taking. Imagine a small hillside of sand and top to bottom the remains of mud and stone-built walls from the Inca's houses. So clear and really not as much in ruins as you would expect for somewhere over 7,000 years old. There were not many people there and hardly any tourist signs. In England it would be heaving and would probably cost a fortune to see. Here it was as if we had discovered it ourselves. We walked to the top of it amongst the walls and saw San Pedro from above and the huge view around. Spectacular!

Next to the ruin was another hill with a manmade path winding its way up. We climbed this too out of curiosity and found a cross at the top and almost a platform and some grills for barbeques. Bizarre, but higher up than the ruins and an even better view. This was definitely one of the highlights of the trip. The South American handbook also pointed out another ruin about four kilometres more along the road and we set off hoping to once again be surprised by another spectacle. How disappointed we were. There was hardly anything there except for a small wall in the hillside jutting out. The walk to it and back had however been good, amongst sand dune hills either side of us and some plants and vegetation. It was so dusty underfoot. That evening was once again bread, cheese, Yoghurt, fruit and biscuits. The things you do to save money and avoid having to cut the whole trip short and go home early.

The next day, by now Wednesday, was another beautiful hot sunny day and we set off at about 8.30 a.m. for the Valle de la Luna. The book said it was twelve kilometres away and we should therefore allow three hours there and back, and not to expect any lifts. The walk took us along the old road to Calama, unpaved, stony and bumpy, and was so set out into the distance it was a little disheartening at times when it seemed we were getting nowhere. We had to be careful of the sun and covered up sensibly. Although the sun was obviously here, there was a constant cool breeze meaning that at times short sleeves were not enough. We had another dog join us along the route. Goodness knows where it came from. We were miles from anywhere. It was about 10.15 a.m. and we were hoping to reach it quite soon when a four-wheel drive came along. Oh joy, a lift! Again, hitchhiking was not a problem and there was room. We hopped in and were only gone two minutes when the sign for Valle de la Luna appeared. It was absolutely magnificent. A valley, flat, sandy bottom with sand dunes either side, and salt made crags sticking up in the sky. We climbed up to one of the sand dunes. It was actually very difficult in soft sand, but well worth what was waiting for us at the top. The view went for miles, salt/sand, rocks, crags and hills, thousands of years old. Standing on top of a sand dune was bizarre, but fantastic. We had really made it to the other side of the world and it was so far removed from anything I had seen before, but I realised then that I was traveling! Again, not a soul about and absolutely quiet, except the sound of the wind whistling around the hills. We sat in silence for a while, just taking it all in and then stood up and hugged each other. We had made it!

We came from there feeling quiet and sad knowing that we would never see it again and we were both a little anxious about the three-hour walk in the sun ahead of us. Doing that walk in the summer must be suicide. We were doing it in their winter. At the edge of the area, we found a small path which took us right amongst the slated crags. The sound of them cracking in the sun was weird. Another strange feeling was walking down the sand dune. We felt that we were walking on the moon, going right down into the sand, step by step. We also wondered if the moon would look like the view we had just seen. Amongst the slated crags we ate our lunch in the shade with the haunting silence surrounding us. We set off back at about 12.30 and felt it would be nice to walk for about one and a half hour and then get a lift. Just as we were feeling as if we were frying, sure enough another four-wheel drive came along in the right direction and we got another lift saving us about three quarters of an hour walk. Someone had heard us! We were glad to be back in the shade, even if it was quite early in the afternoon. We decided to try and find out about getting to Iquique which was a town even further north where we were hoping to buy a new camera at the tax-free shopping centre. Unfortunately, the buses from Calama only went overnight and we would have to spend another whole day at San Pedro. We weren't concerned as we loved the place, but our hostel had signs everywhere saying they wanted people to be out by 11 a.m. and no one could leave bags in other people's rooms etc. We would be on the streets! One of the bus companies, Tur-Bus, agreed to look after our bags for the day so we decided to go to a place called Tulor, a supposed Stone Age village. That evening we enjoyed a meal out and it was delicious. In the restaurant called Banana Chavez, we had a three-course meal for £5 each—quite a popular place for travellers, but supposedly the cheapest.

Rebecca

Restaurant in town! Iquique Beach
Monday 16th June 97—10.55 a.m.

Now that we have a new diary, I am determined to catch up so I can tell you all about Iquique!

Back to this restaurant in San Pedro called "Banana Chavez" that almost looked like a restaurant out of the Flintstones! Each table was basic thick wood and surrounded by mud small walls as bench seats with a plank of wood on top to sit on. The waiter was German and quite cool looking, wearing a similar pair of trousers to ourselves i.e. same make but no zip off shorts! As with most restaurants in Chile, there was a "Menu a la Casa", standard two or three course meal costing about £3–£5 dependent on where you go. This restaurant only served this menu; no other food, which was obviously easy for them. There was, however, a choice of 2 starters and two main courses. I had a crunchy vegetable salad, beetroot, carrots, peas, sweetcorn, tomato, green beans, absolutely delicious and then a steak with sauté potatoes, again delicious. Simon had a homemade soup to start, tomato and croutons which was really good and then a Tortilla which is a thick omelette with very fine shredded sweet carrot with the same potatoes, another superb dish. Desert was a choice of fruit salad or pancake and we both had pancake with the infamous caramel/chocolate sauce in the middle so yummy! We polished it all off with some red wine and the whole meal probably cost about £10! It was great to eat proper food again and not bread and cheese.

The following day was our last day which we took quite easy as we knew we had to hang around all day somewhere! We took our bags to the "Tur Bus" office where they were happy to look after them. Chile has been so safe and trusting, we put them in the corner of the office where anybody could have taken them but she was adamant they would be okay and I knew they would. We vowed that there was no way we would be able to do the same thing in Peru! We then headed off towards Tulor which had caused some confusion as we had asked several people the way and how far away it was and we had had different responses. The most consistent was about four and a half km. It was another lovely day, cloudier than the rest which we didn't mind, for a rest from the sun. We took the old road out of San Pedro which was to take us to a village called Sequitor and then beyond to Coyo and Tulor. On route we passed an old woman in a small field pulling out her dead sweetcorn crops and laying them on her cart pulled by a donkey! She was wearing a simple blue smock and straw hat and I think some kind of wellies on her feet. It was an amazing sight and we asked her whether we were going the right way. With our minimal understanding of the language, we deduced we were going the right way, but it might be easier to go round the other road out of San Pedro back through the centre of town as this way we had to cross a river! We had come too far to turn back so we carried on with the knowledge that we would probably have to cross the water. She also said it was one kilometre away, Tulor that is. We then came to the town of Sequitor and again asked some men if we were going the right way, we were but it was five kilometres away! Confused, we continued and the track led out into the desert, not far from where we had walked the day before. I recognised Coyo in the distance and decided to head for it as we knew Tulor wasn't far from it. We soon came to the river which was almost dry and, therefore, no problem at all to cross. As we trudged along, a little deflated that our six-mile walk was going to turn into more like ten miles, the wind was gradually picking up and quite gusty every now and then causing sand to blow up everywhere. This got worse and it was only when we were nearing Coyo that we realised it was a real sand storm! Coyo was amazing, absolutely nothing there except a few farms that contained mud walls for cattle to graze in and a falling down community centre! It was like a ghost town and I was convinced we hadn't gone far enough into the centre, but by now we were tired and we realised we hadn't got a clue about the way to Tulor. There was no one around to ask, the wind was really strong and we didn't have much water left to see us through walking further and all the way back. We decided to turn back and neither of us were looking forward to the return walk.

The wind was really strong and we both experienced our first true sand storm! It was very frightening and quite painful as the sand whipped around our heads. Now I realised why you need to wear clothes all around your body, covering head, ears and just making a peep hole for eyes! The views around us had just disappeared through the sand forming hazy clouds. There was just nobody around and we carried on as best we could. We eventually found the river and the track back to Sequitor which was also blowy, even with trees, shrubs and buildings to protect us. We were so glad to get back to San Pedro. I had washed my trousers the day before, but by now they were so incredibly dusty. We didn't recognise our boots; Simon's were now brown having been blue and mine were just a dust colour!

We collected our bags and sat in the Plaza for a few hours with a bottle of sprite, books, Walkman etc. We had decided to eat at 'Banana Chavez' again with our bus at 11.10, but we found in good time that our bus was leaving Calama at that time and not San Pedro. We, therefore, had a one-and-a-half-hour bus journey to Calama first and we would eat there. Why does this keep happening to us when I am convinced, we have made sure we know where the bus is going from?

We got to Calama in one piece having seen a beautiful red sky sunset in San Pedro and over the desert. *Tur Bus* office had a custodia for our bags so we left them and went in search of food. We found a place that was recommended in the South American handbook and had a really good meal for £5! Again, they brought it; we didn't have a clue what we would be eating. It was a warm cheese empanada to start with chilli salsa sauce then a pork chop in sauce with rice and cold potato and veg salad. Dessert was a pear pie (no cream or ice cream or both!) and a bottle of coke, which we thought was included but wasn't! It was a very basic cafe/restaurant, but ideal to set us on our way for ten hours on a bus.

During the meal, Simon had been telling me about going to see a really good Genesis concert at the age of seventeen. He really wasn't into them at the time, but had really enjoyed it. As we came out of the restaurant, we decided to go and find a bar for a drink to while away a little more time.

Same day 6.45 p.m.
Hostel

On searching around the busy streets of Calama we came across a seedy/normal looking bar with a huge screen at the end showing a video of something. The bar wasn't very busy and anyway, only men were in there. I reckon there must be more men to women in this country! Anyway, we almost didn't go in until we realised, they were showing a video of the same Genesis concert we had been talking about not ½ an hour earlier! It was really freaky and seeing it as fate we went in. The video turned out to be a whole host of songs and videos from the '80's and even '70's including ABBA, Tears for

Fears, John Lennon and the Bee Gees! They seem to love that era of music here, play it all the time in bars. It turned out really well and we left with about half an hour to spare at the bus station, hence the entrance in the diary at that point.

The bus journey was fine. We had had no choice in which seats we sat in (for some reason!) and ended up with the first two seats behind the driver which I felt a little dubious about, but had no choice as the buses do get very busy. They showed a film which we missed the title of but we knew, Glenn Close playing a Colonel who realises her homosexuality. It was okay as it was subtitled and therefore in English, but a little cheesy! Didn't sleep brilliantly and we were woken at 6 a.m. by the driver's assistant handing round biscuits and orange juice for breakfast.

We arrived at Iquique a lot sooner than we expected and felt that 7 a.m. was a little too early to go knocking on hostel doors! We chose a couple of places from the book and headed that way on foot. It was about twenty minutes from the bus station and the first place was actually open.

Simon

San Pedro de Atacama & Iquique—Northern Chile
12th to 16th June 1997

Well, we start on diary number two. The first one didn't last long (Rebecca); let's see if we can make this one last slightly longer. When will you learn? We are on a budget and paper costs money.

Anyway, I thought I'd start this day by summing up a few things on our trip so far. Let's cast our minds back to Argentina and let's see what springs to mind.

1) Very bumpy roads.

2) Incredible big journeys doing the school run in the middle of nowhere.

3) Not eating beef because we couldn't afford it

4) The blue in the Rio Azul.

5) Buenos Aires—for better or worse.

6) White water rafting with Christian & Martin.

7) The views from Arrap Lopez.

8) Our cabana.

9) Bewilderment—trying to get into the swing of travelling.

10) The Teatro Colon in Buenos Aires—superb.

Whilst I'm in the swing of things I may as well do a similar list for Chile. Tonight, is our last night in Chile (if all goes to plan) so it is as good a time as any.

11) Being greeted by rain.

12) The turning point in our trip—meeting the Garcia family at Ancud.

13) The wildlife on Chiloe.

14) Falling in love with Chiloe.

15) Staying at Chonchi & Corral—real Chilean towns

16) The Valle de la Luna.

17) The quiet at San Pedro de Atacama.

18) Jock's antics!

19) Thinking that Santiago was miles better than fellow travellers had described.

20) Beaching it at Iquique.

So anyway, back to 12th to 16th June 1997. Well, the bus times from San Pedro de Atacama were not helpful and neither were the hospedaje owners. Earliest bus to Iquique 23.10.

Check out time from hospedaje 11.00. Brilliant! Over eleven hours to kill time with nowhere as a base. This is the sort of thing that makes planning in too much detail completely nonsensical. I like San Pedro de Atacama, but in a town of 1,600 inhabitants, there is only so much you can see in one day (complete with your world on your back). Besides from 6.00 p.m., it gets freezing in the desert.

We managed to store our bags "safely" on the dirt floor of the bus sales office and we went for a walk. We wanted to go to a Stone Age village called Tulor. Our book informed us it was twelve km away across the desert. The local tourist info said it was 4.3km. In confirmation, the man at the post office said it was an easy walk. Great. It wasn't to be a wasted day after all. Three hours across the desert later and no water left we had reached the village of Coyo, but we still hadn't got to Tulor. Coyo consisted of an old lady, two children who were amazed at the sight of us, lots of sand and two cows, plus a few walls. And I thought this was Stone Age enough for me. I didn't need to see Tulor.

So, in view of the lack of water, we decided to turn back. The great thing about travelling is that you get to do a lot of things that you see in films and would like to do e.g., walk along a sand dune, get stared at by small children etc. However, on the way back from Coyo, we got caught in a sand storm. Lawrence of Arabia or not, I wouldn't choose to do it again. Once was enough. The view was completely obscured by sand and we were battling against the burning heat of the sun and the painful lashings of the sand.

We were grateful to get back to San Pedro de Atacama. We sat in the Plaza de Armas and read, played chess etc., just passing the time. About three dogs kept following us as we moved from bench to bench to keep in the sun. One of them was a randy sod and kept trying to get his leg over one of the other ones. Please, there were ladies present.

In a not untypical scenario of our trip so far, we suddenly discovered the 23.10 to Iquique bus left Calama and not San Pedro de Atacama. Calama is almost two hours away by bus. This meant the usual clammer to get to Calama on time, which we did with something to spare. Another overnight journey awaited us.

Iquique was supposed to be a one-night stop. The plan was to replace our camera at the tax-free zone shopping centre there, send the other one home and move on.

The shopping centre was amazingly cheap and after much deliberation, we ended up buying a semi-professional camera. It is not just an 'aim & shoot'. The instruction manual is bigger than a Rebecca entry into the diary, but what the hell; we do have ten months and two weeks to read it.

We also bought a couple of sleeping bags as we had heard from many fellow travellers that they would be essential for the Peruvian Andes. Unfortunately, they are Latin American sleeping bags and like most products here they are brand new but fifteen years out of date. They fold up to the size of a football pitch but at least we should stay warm.

The overnight stop turned into four nights as we discovered a beautiful beach and thundering pacific waves. The waves were massive. They are probably the first waves that I have ever been scared of. The sea was warm, the beach clean and very empty and the sun scorching. All this in the middle of their winter. What on earth are the summers like? The plan was to re-charge our batteries for Peru, of which we had heard so much about. More of that to follow.

Part Three
Peru
17 June – 19 July 1997

The Magical Mystery Tour
by The Beatles

What Goes Up Must Come Down

Simon

Arequipa—Southern Peru
17th June to 19th June 1997

The day had arrived. We had read the warnings and heard the stories. When the guide book describes beautiful coastal walks with sea lions, pelicans and flamingos, with the added extra of "Don't attempt alone as kidnappings have been known", dreams of tropical rainforests, strange hidden tribal villages are somewhat marred. Guidebook requests to check the political situation in Lima before going into a potential guerrilla warfare area, further dampened spirits. "I was OK, but my mate had his bag snatched," said one fellow traveller. Caroline (Rebecca's cousin) wrote to us saying that her boyfriend had his watch stolen from his wrist. Alan Bancroft (a friend of my brother) ran after the thief who mugged him in Lima to get his wallet back. "Look on taxis as an insurance policy against attack," said the guide book. "Police are generally friendly as long as the particular officer is not corrupt," was another warning. "Beware of corrupt policemen planting drugs on you," was another helpful piece of advice. What on earth was going on in Peru, and more importantly, why are we determined to go there?

Notions of seeing the world's deepest canyon. Visiting a tropical jungle. Walking to the infamous Inca city of Machu Picchu. The guide book talked of discovering (literally) still unchartered Inca ruins. It also talked of, "A good set four course meal for $1.25."

We were prepared for Peru. We had listened to other people's advice, read the handbook; we knew where we wanted to go.

It took one minute from arriving at Tacna (the first town in Peru across the border) before we were ripped off. So called guides hassled us, changed money for us, bought our bus tickets (at a price of four times the face value we soon discovered) and we gave them a tip at the end for some reason. Not a good start!

The bus to Arequipa was a rickety one at first, until we changed to a nicer bus that showed films that were a curious mix of tits and martial arts. No toilet for seven hours. A taste of things to come. We changed buses at a small town. People ran to the bus, hoisted all sorts of things to eat at the window and got onto the bus to sell things. Very different to what we were used to. The women wore traditional clothing and strange hats, but oh no, this was not just for the tourists, this was the real thing.

Arequipa is a good place with some great things to see. Rebecca, no doubt, will provide more insight than I care to but over two days we have seen La Recoleta (a Franciscan monastery—well worth seeing) and the Santa Catalina Convent (an amazing city within a city of winding streets, dormitories etc.) We also took a taxi to the Molino de Sabandia which was an incredible mill. The owners directed the water so we could see it work. It was a wonderful afternoon spent there, sharing the grounds with three llamas, some water and the sun.

But enough of that because what I really want to write about are the prices. Argentina and Chile were cheaper than the UK. However, they were not cheap enough for two unemployed travellers, hoping to spend a year seeing the best sites the world can offer. Well Peru seems to be a little cheaper. On our first day our suspicions were aroused when we paid 10p for our bread for breakfast. Confirmation that things were cheap came at lunchtime. A strange starter of popcorn and bacon rolls, followed by a massive stew was a tasty combination. We then had the main course. I had a steak and pasta dish. Rebecca had spicy beef in peppers. We also had a drink each. The bill came to £2.04 for both of us. Instantly I wanted another meal!

Today, calamity struck us with the postal system. Arequipa was our second postal pick up place. Now either we are seriously unpopular, or the Post Office staff here are a bunch of thieves. One letter, cheers Tim. Pleased with the news that the birth went OK and you now have a beautiful new baby (Katie). Cheers. Fantastic news.

Rebecca

Arequipa, Peru
Sat 21st June 1997. 8.15 p.m.

Back in Arequipa for one night, after Colca Canyon and before we head to Pisco early in the morning, more of all that later!

As I said, the first place we got to in Iquique, was open and the owner very nice. He must have thought we would find his place too expensive and sent us elsewhere. To cut a long story short, we turned down a room in a shed and chose a place on a main street owned by a couple who were about thirty years apart, in age! A strange place with most rooms facing inwards with no windows for fresh air and very particular owners who liked to do things by the book! We even had to pay up front for the first time since we set off! We were both now really tired and decided to sleep for a couple of hours before heading off to buy our camera.

It was great to feel some warm sunshine again and it seemed a shame to be going shopping in such weather but it meant we could do whatever we wanted once the big task was out of the way. ZOFRI, a huge tax-free shopping centre, wasn't far from the centre and the taxi/collectivo was quite cheap. It was a huge shopping centre with independent shops row after row. It was difficult to know where to start but we just had a good wander round. There were more cameras to choose from than I imagined and the prices were amazing. We had two to choose from, one the same make and newer model of Vivitar (our old camera) and a Samsung with much more to offer by way of zoom and gadgets taking you into the realms of more than just shoot and press. The Vivitar was about £40 and the Samsung was double that. However, in England we decided it would probably cost about £150–£200. The bigger zoom won the day and it was bought. We then had the onerous task of finding a couple of sleeping bags. Simon and I had had some long discussions over the need for a sleeping bag and we had agreed that the Peruvian Andes would be pretty chilly, not only the hotel rooms but when sleeping under the stars—a definite in Machu Picchu, but unsure where else. Anyway, we ended up having a choice of one sleeping bag which we bought, but were quite aware that the quality was not like ours back home.

Simon

Chivay at the Colca Canyon—South Peru
20th to 21st June 1997

Something happened on the evening of the 19th and the early hours of the morning of the 20th. It was June, but it felt like Christmas. We lay in bed, aware that we had an early start the next morning to go to the Colca Canyon. We chatted, we laughed, we had in depth discussions, we laughed again and we pinched ourselves. The whole trip was a calendar of dreams and we knew it and we were buzzing accordingly. We couldn't wait for the Colca Canyon, and then the Paracas Reserve, and then Bolivia and India and New Zealand and the toilet and… It was not easy to calm down, far less go to sleep.

We took a tour to the Colca Canyon, but were not overly happy about the decision. Up to now, we had avoided excursions like the plague. The very name 'excursion' made us break out into cold sweats and conjured up images of coachloads of American tourists saying, "I love yourrr little country, it's sooo cute." However, we got a good deal and it appeared to be far less hassle than going by ourselves. Besides, we were bound to meet fellow backpackers like ourselves.

On the tour, we were the first to be picked up. Next came five Spanish people, then two Peruvian girls and then another couple of Peruvian girls. All looked absolutely super and ready for an adventure in the Andes. One couple even had hiking boots, brand new no dust, price tag intact.

It took about five hours in a van to get to the Canyon (more preciously the village of Chivay, near the Canyon). The van went for mile upon mile upwards on the customary path through the desert that is laughably called a road. Higher and higher we went as we listened to warnings from the guide on altitude sickness. She told us she hoped we would be OK. Very reassuring.

We stopped at the services (shack) for a mug of coco tea (cocaine tea). It tasted great. A dog chewed on some chicken feet. Not seen this at the Little Chef back home. Nothing goes to waste here. The guide purchased a bag of coco leaves and advised us to suck one leaf for the altitude, but chew more if we wanted an altogether different sensation. I plumped for just the one this time; finally, we arrived in Chivay.

I'll now resort to quoting word for word from the South American handbook. "The Indigenous population of Peru is put at about three million Quecha and Aymara Indians in the Andean region. Their literacy rate is the lowest of any comparable group in South America and their diet is 50% below acceptable levels."

Yes, we had our first taste of indigenous people on our trip to the Colca. Chivay was celebrating its anniversary and I mean celebrate. The tour took a trip to some local thermal baths. Rebecca and I stayed to have a look around. As we are accustomed to doing, we stumbled on their celebrations. Not in the town itself, but in a natural amphitheatre in a combe on the valley sides. Inca terracing completed a perfect arena for dancing. We found ourselves a spot on the hillside and watched the celebrations. The women all wore traditional dress and hats. Most carried a baby in a blanket strapped across their backs. We couldn't believe it. Did this still really exist?

As we looked around, we were the only 'gringos' there. It was excellent. Celebrations continued into the night in the main town. People were dancing. Laughing, drinking, parading and eating. Eating… yes. Food was being served everywhere. We had read the warnings about food in Peru. We talked about it, and we ate.

In fact, we had a plateful of salad, rice, chips noodles and chicken for £1.50 each from a street vendor. We selected our own meat carefully avoiding the pieces that looked like guinea pigs. We ate at the table where the food was being served and cooked, illuminated by a gas lamp and I have to say it was one of my great all-time meals.

In the Andes, it gets freezing at night. We kept warm by wandering around and drinking tea a lot. Tea was also served on the street. It consisted of boiled water served from a vat with leaves and branches in it, with numerous other ingredients added. It was great. I'll not forget my experiences there. I hope our photos will do the occasion some justice but I doubt it.

Onto the Canyon itself. Once again, I must resort to quoting from the handbook. "The Colca Canyon, said to be twice as deep as the Grand Canyon, was mentioned in the 1934 edition of the National Geographic magazine by Robert Shippee, although there is a claim that it was first discovered from the air by Gonzalo de Reparaz in 1954. The roads on either side of the canyon are at around 4,000m and Nevado Ampato, a short distance to the south rises to 6,288m. Unspoiled, picturesque Andean villages lie on both sides of the canyon and some of the extensive Inca stone-terraced fields are still in use."

The canyon was so deep the camera could not fit the whole scene in. The scenery is beautiful and spectacular. It is very different to the Grand Canyon. It is nowhere near as wide, but its shear depth is incredible. The terracing is still very much in use. I was expecting a couple of fields, but huge areas of land on both sides were given over to the active cultivation of the canyon.

If this wasn't enough, we saw many, many condors and at very close range. They were huge and they literally swooped only yards above our heads. With wing spans of two or three metres it was awesome. The guide informed us that we were lucky. Rebecca and I agreed!

Rebecca

Carhuaz, Peruvian Andes
Tues 24th June 1997

We have come a long way since Arequipa and so much to write about. Having bought our wares from Iquipue we were happy to get back to our hostel and head for the beach. We had also taken our first disposable camera to be developed and we were both pleasantly surprised at the quality! Luckily, we had used them in places with warm sunshine and deep blue skies. The only other thing we had to sort out was posting a package home including our old camera for Irene (Simon's mum) to try her hand at getting our money back. It all had to go in a box with brown paper and string tied around it and at first it was going to cost us about £20 until we convinced her that surface mail was adequate. She couldn't believe we were happy for it to take three months!

We had thought about going to see a place called "Humberstone" a large abandoned nitrate town but, when we got to the beach, we changed our minds! It was clean, soft sand, blue sky, sunshine, not commercialised, a few palm trees and the rolling and crashing waves of the Pacific. We decided there and then that a few days on this beach would do us the world of good, as well as save us a few pennies!

That first evening, we had also considered eating bread and cheese, but we came to the conclusion that bits of food bought can come to as much as a cheap meal, if not more. We were also sick of bread and decided to hunt around for some cheaper places to eat. A few doors away from us was a Chinese restaurant serving a two-course meal for two at about £8 it was absolutely delicious; a Chinese meal for the first time in nearly two months. There was so much and I could see from where I was sitting into the kitchen and it was obvious, they were making it all fresh. After the meal, we sauntered down to the Plaza de Armas where everyone seems to congregate in these towns. The "Theatre Municipal" was all lit up and what looked like a display of some sort just outside it. On closer inspection, it was a publicity stunt by the forensic police! A strange mixture of photos of suicides, murders, displays of weapons used, clothes worn and an even stranger display of different aged foetuses in jars! Couldn't understand Spanish enough to know why on earth they were showing all that. I then headed towards the theatre where there was a small display of modern, colourful paintings. There were also quite a few people mingling in the hallway as if they were waiting to go and see something. On the board outside, I noticed a poster with that evening's events, some kind of music recital by a bunch of ex-university men. The thing that caught my attention was 'gratis', meaning free! We were in luck; the chance to see some live Chilean music free in the main theatre! Although not really dressed for such an event, we queued up and went inside. Again, another theatre that was circular and beautifully decorated. We took our seats in the ground floor circle having been handed a delicious chocolate by a lady as we entered the theatre. It started late (10 p.m.) as everything seems to in South America. It was really good music, all men dressed in old fashioned Spanish style black pantaloons and jackets with capes. They all played a type of guitar which made a wonderful rhythmic sound and so talented. They sang and danced and even made jokes in between which of course we didn't have a clue about. It was another real-life experience, a packed theatre full of Chileans, no other gringos in sight!

Our bedroom was right on the main street with the window looking out. It was actually very noisy but we were so exhausted every day that sleeping wasn't a problem. We also preferred a window looking out rather than one looking in. The owners spent a lot of time watching TV and when we asked about a local laundrette, they informed us there was one downstairs! Easy-peasy, they did it for us.

As I said earlier, we spent the next three days on the beach getting some sun protection for Peru which would be warmer! The sea was so warm and the waves really good fun, frighteningly strong and you had to be careful they didn't suck you under too much. Simon especially enjoyed the ocean, the kid that he is, and the beach was very quiet by English standards and so clean. Between 12–3 p.m., we tried to stay out of the sun and, on the Saturday, we walked to the harbour and managed to get a small boat trip around it. It was really relaxing to be bobbing up and down on the water. It took about forty-five minutes passing the sight where a famous Chilean sea battle took place and some navy boats moored. The best bit was right at the end when they passed by what looked like some big rocks sticking out of the water. On closer inspection, they were rocks but teaming with sea-lions! They were all over each other and all sorts of sizes. We were gobsmacked—all in their natural environment! Some of them were huge, wrinkly and hairy and some were just little babies.

Lunch times at the beach became a traditional 'completos' or hot dog at a nearby small cafe. They were really good, similar to our first one in Santiago and an ice cream.

Our time on the beach was spent reading, writing, sleeping, swimming and sunning ourselves! At four o'clock each day, there was a man selling delicious doughnuts with the infamous caramel/chocolate sauce inside—stopping there became a daily ritual!

One day, we passed a shop called *Ropa Europa* which Charlie from Chonchi had informed us of a while back— second-hand clothes stores. Simon had realised we needed another T-shirt and I liked the look of a pink one with a collar, so got that. Simon chose a purple plain T-shirt that really suits him; our first foreign bought clothing!

Other than that, there was a Chinese restaurant we went to twice and we also found a small Bolivian restaurant that did a really cheap but good two course meal. They did different food every day and all the locals would eat from this menu too. "Eat what the locals eat," was advice we have had and we did. As with a lot of other restaurants, they had football showing on TV with a divide of who supported who.

Iquique was to be our last Chilean town and, although we were ready to move on, it was also quite sad to leave a country we both felt very fond of. On the Sunday evening whilst in Iquique, I decided to phone Oliver (one of my two brothers); it was his birthday and I had been thinking about him finishing his exams and graduating from university. I left it until it would be midnight in England, so people would be back from pubs etc. I got through immediately and spoke to a girl, not sure who it was although there sounded to be loads of people there! Oliver was so chuffed to hear from me and it was really strange talking to him 1,000's of miles away. From what he said, they were half naked from playing a drinking game and they all sounded worse for wear. Bless him, he asked some questions about where I was etc. The phone call probably sobered him up a bit. I felt as if I was muscling in on a bit of England and then zooming out again very fast. I felt quite choked to hear his voice and know he was okay.

So, on Tuesday morning, we got an early 7.20 a.m. bus to Peru, heading for Arequipa. Hopefully it would be in daylight as we had read the advice about trying not to travel at night. We had a bit of a nightmare getting the bakery next door to sell us their morning bread. They had assured us they opened at 7 a.m. and of course we were there at seven. They were not ready and wouldn't have been for ages if Simon hadn't made it very obvious why we were standing staring at them! It turned out to be lovely warm, fresh bread.

The first leg of the journey was to Arica, the next major seaside town near Peru. This lasted about five hours and was uneventful. We expected all our bags to get searched as the book assured us, they would be coming away from ZOFRI. Apparently, there is a limit on how much you can buy there and it's less for Chileans than foreigners. ZOFRI is a free trade port. Not quite sure how it all works, but it means we can buy great stuff really cheap. We didn't get searched at all and arrived in Arica to get another bus across the border to Tacna. Arica was really hot and we boarded a very old rickety bus heaving with locals. Hot, sweaty and smelly was the fragrant air and all crossings and customs went smoothly with lots of smiles and positive body language. Tacna was another story that I know Simon has already told! I made the mistake of asking our bus driver where we would get a bus to Arequipa! Bad mistake; the next thirty minutes was a complete whirlwind that we would regret and never forget. A very clever man made out he was genuinely helping us, but all the time was accepting backhanders from everyone. We let him do everything for us and both Simon and I were almost dumbstruck! Entering a new country isn't easy, especially when you are unaware of the new customs and culture and you like to feel your way and see how far you can go! I really didn't know whether this was acceptable or not and it was only later when Simon and I talked about it I realised how naive I had been! Making a mistake taught me a big lesson about trusting people too much. This is a value I have in England which I obviously cannot use in Peru, however small. I can't assume someone is innocent until proven guilty because by then I may have lost everything. On a scale of things, we were not hurt and what we lost was a few pounds, but our pride was hurt. Our common sense hadn't kicked in and we allowed someone to do this to us and get away with it.

Our bus journey to Arequipa, thereafter, was marked by the recollection of what had happened to us. We met a couple of English girls going to the same place who must have thought us most unsociable and unhelpful. We didn't really talk to them much, though. We were thinking too much ourselves and of course we were a little stressed when we got to Arequipa through fear of it happening again and determination that we wouldn't let it.

The journey to Arequipa was, however, quite interesting—seeing PERU for the first time. A lot more greenery than I imagined in places and more backward-looking towns. Houses are not finished off, with metal sticking out of them, and a lot of the women wearing odd 'A' line skirts and what looked like bowler hats! Whenever the bus stopped, there were hordes of locals sticking food and drink up at the windows on long poles in the hope of one of us wanting something. There were also loads of them cramming onto the bus with passengers and barging up and down the aisle show casing their goods, shoving them in your face, to try and tempt you. This has happened a lot since travelling through Peru and sadly a lot of them are children who look like they rely on you to buy their goods! Seeing women in colourful traditional dresses milking a cow in a field was a new sight.

We didn't manage to get to Arequipa before dark, but we didn't panic too much about this and chose a hostel from the book that sounded ideal. The other two girls wanted to come too and the idea of four of us walking around seemed easier but the hostel didn't have room for us all so we had to find somewhere else. We were convinced we would have got in just the two of us, but never mind. We found another place that was beautiful, colonial style and with a courtyard in the middle with the rooms all around it. We thought the man was offering us a room for about £1.50 a night, but when we realised, we had made a mistake and he actually wanted £14, we left as unembarrassed as we could. Disheartened and very tired, we set off to find another and got picked up again by the two English girls who were in a van with a bloke who owned a hostel; he offered us all accommodation for £3.30 each a night! We couldn't say "no" as we needed to find somewhere fast and so piled in the van. The accommodation was fine, quite central and clean, with a big en-suite room that had a very dodgy shower connected to the electricity. If you turned the water tap before turning off the electricity, it would give you an electric shock! It was literally deadly. We were very tired and a little fed up of our earlier escapade so we went to bed without a meal inside of us.

The next day, we were still going over the previous day's escapades and decided it was probably our worst travelling day yet. We were obviously a little nervous of Arequipa, but we had been told the security had been stepped up and in fact it had. There were police on nearly every street corner making Arequipa quite safe.

Simon

Pisco and Carhuaz
22nd June to 25th June 1997

I was not looking forward to these few days. Why? Firstly, we had heard so much about Peruvian transport for the worse. Bus terminals are notoriously dangerous in Peru. Also finding your way about a new place in Peru with your world strapped to your back makes you a sitting target for the thieves you hear about. Backpack slashing is not uncommon. We knew we had a lot of travelling to do to get to the parts of the country that we really wanted to see i.e., Northern Peru, Qosqo and the sacred valley, the central highlands, the Amazon Basin and the Cordillera Blanca. The problem with Peru is that there is just so much diversity and so much to see. That's great, but the road system is laughable, which makes covering a huge country (it must be twice the size of Spain) harder than expected. So we have uncomfortable buses, boiling days, freezing nights, dirt roads in the main, a road system that is determined to take you to the coast wherever you want to go, and the thought of thieves awaiting your every move at the bus terminal. If this wasn't enough, our book advises travel only by day to reduce the threat of bus hijackings or even muggings on the bus. But we really want to see Peru!

These thoughts buzzed around my head as we approached what I knew would be a "ball breaking" few days.

We decided to travel by day to Pisco. This would take twelve hours. We planned to see the Paracas Nature Reserve or the famous Ballestas Islands and then continue our journey to the Cordillera Blanca. The journey to Pisco was atrocious. By day it was hot, cramped and very boring. At the bus terminal, we were asked if we wanted to travel via "Pacifico" or "Montaghe" (the Pacific or mountains). Mountains sounded good so we chose this route, but "mountains" turned out to be a grey desert. The Pacific coast that we didn't see, by all accounts, was superb. A little boy threw up behind me and this put me off my lunch.

We got to Pisco and it looked rough. There were loads of people about—a Peruvian version of Millwall away to West Ham. True to form, someone tried to snatch my watch. My lightening reaction saved the day. Lucky for him, I controlled my temper; otherwise, he really would have been sorry. No, I didn't like Pisco very much.

The next day, we made our way to the launch place for boat trips to the Ballastas Islands. We were told we would see flamingos, pelicans, sea-lions etc. The most concentrated area of marine life in the world. We were not told the sea would be so rough it was impossible to set off. Hmm, things were not going to plan.

However, it was possible to go to the Paracas reserve, but the excursion tour had already left (Paracas is a huge desert coastal peninsula with lots of marine life). This didn't stop the tour company from commissioning a taxi to take us on the tour. There were four of us in the taxi, plus the cab driver. The company introduced the cabby as our guide. Yeah right, who are they trying to kid? Four in a taxi turned out to be great. He took us all over the peninsula and did his best at explaining what we were seeing.

I'll now skip the rest of the thirteen hours of coach journeys and waiting at Lima bus terminal. Safe to say, we didn't get mugged at Lima.

In the Cordillera Blanca, we targeted the town of Carhuaz. The main towns in the area are Huaraz and Coraz. We imagined them to be big and touristy so we thought we would try an alternative. Alternative it has been. There are only a couple of hostels in the town. By looking through the visitors' book, the score-line reads something like visitors from Peru 1,000, visitors not from Peru nil. As a result, people have stared at us, but on the whole the locals seem a friendly bunch. I reckon we have set the town alight with talk of, "Have you seen the Danish lad and his friend in town? Throughout our trip many people assumed I was either Danish or German for some reason. Strange days are these!" Well, we did want to get off the beaten track and there is a price to pay for it.

Yesterday, we walked to the village of Chancos. It was great to be in the country again. The costumes are not as colourful as those of Chivay, but there is not a lot in it. From staying here, it is obvious the country is very poor. The farms seem to be the size of a large back garden and people till the earth with their hands. The women wash the clothes in the rivers and dry them in the sun on cacti. They haven't even got washing lines.

Today, we walked to the village of Hualcan. The altitude makes progress slow, but it really is beautiful. The locals are fascinating to us and indeed are fascinated by us. "Hey, Gringo!" will be a cry that I will not forget in a hurry.

Rebecca

Carhuaz, Peru.
9.45 p.m. Wed 25th June 1997

Our first day in Arequipa was spent seeing an old monastery, called *Recoleta*, and visiting an old mill in the countryside— oh yes, and having a delicious cheap meal in a tacky sounding restaurant *El Jumbo Jet*!

Recoleta was a beautiful old monastery with quaint colonial squares and little museums, plus a fascinating old library. The books looked ancient and any manuscripts were all behind glass. The English brochure had a translation that left a little to be desired, but we understood most of it!

El Jumbo Jet became our lunch stop and we stumbled across it by accident. They were offering two courses for £1 each; we couldn't believe how cheap!

Anyway, we scanned through our books to try and recognise what was on the menu and chose some really good stuff. Cazuela, of course, is a favourite starter and our main dishes were a stuffed red pepper with spicy beef and veg and Simon had a steak on a pile of pesto noodles. We were stuffed and decided to go to the Molino de Sabandia (an old mill) to relax!

We managed to hail a taxi that was an extremely old Datsun and hurtled along the roads to the countryside. Neither of us would dream of driving in this country, their driving is manic and usually takes the form of driving on the other side of the road and hooting horns nearly every minute!

The mill was beautiful. Our driver dropped us off at the end of the dirt tract leading out into the country and the mill. As soon as we went through the gates, the lady pulled up the barriers in the water runs to get the mill working for us. It was an old mill warehouse with steps leading down in a lovely open garden, complete with goats and llamas! It also had a mud fire in the garden where they obviously bake bread outdoors on the odd occasion. We sat and relaxed in the garden for over an hour and then headed back to the main road where we hoped our taxi driver had come back for us as promised. Of course he hadn't, but there was another guy in a Beetle that happened to pass by and picked us up.

Back in the centre, we had a wander round the main huge Plaza de Armas and just got our bearings on this beautiful colonial style city. By night, it is absolutely dead as we discovered that evening! Any bars we came across looked dodgy or dead and coming from Chile, where every street had two or three, this was most disappointing! We even tried to buy some beer in a shop, but it was really expensive so didn't bother! In the end, we bought two bottles of Peru's favourite drink—INCA KOLA! A wee coloured drink and we expected something great as it was flashed around everywhere. It was disgusting, very much like VIMTO which I hated.

Rebecca

Carhauz, Peru.
3.45 p.m. Thurs 26th June 1997

The next day was another glorious day and we decided we would visit the famous Santa Catalina convent. Before that we had to sort out what we were going to do about seeing the Colca Canyon. We had debated long and hard about how to see it, by tour or on our own. The day before, we had enquired a little at some of the agencies, all offering a basic package of two days, one night, guide and breakfast. None were offering inclusive meals at a decent price and all offers start at $17 per person. The agencies didn't hassle us as much as we thought they might; maybe we made it obvious our enquiries were information only! The handbook recommended a guy who does more adventurous trips and, intrigued to know what he would offer, we tried to see him. The place looked deserted as if no one worked there anymore. Our last chance was the hostel that offered a trip and would look after any baggage. We came to the conclusion we would take a trip, it would save time, we would learn more and it would be nice to rely on others for a change to ensure a certain level of service. We negotiated our landlady down to $16 and bought our tickets.

To save even more time, we went to enquire about getting to Pisco—our planned next stop after the Cola Canyon. We found some dodgy looking bus companies down a dodgy street, all offering the same price and all travelling at night. The handbook had specifically advised us to travel by day in Peru so we searched further. The recommended company was "Armeno" who had loads of buses going to Pisco; one at 7 a.m.

to arrive about twelve hrs later. We plumped for that! In Chile we had got used to a new computer system of booking tickets and seats but not in Peru! All handwritten tickets and 'radios' used to radio through any out of the way bookings! The other advantage of taking this bus with this bus company was that we didn't need to go to the main bus terminal on the edge of town, as this one had their own central terminal. It was going to be a tight schedule—Colca Canyon Friday to Saturday finishing at 6 p.m. and then off to Pisco Sunday morning at 7 a.m.!

Santa Catalina was not disappointing.

Rebecca

Cajamarca, Peru.
Sat 28th June 97—5 p.m.

I am sitting downstairs from our hostel in a courtyard restaurant called El Real Plaza, made entirely of dark wood. Simon is trying to sleep off Soroche, an illness brought on by changes in the altitude and boy have we had plenty of that. We are now 2,800 m above sea level and have caught a bus from the coast where it was SO hot and humid! He says he feels dizzy. Headaches, bad cold and generally tired. Bless him. I do feel sorry for him. We managed to get out today and had a lovely day, tell you about that later.

Santa Catalina in Arequipa was open to the public in 1970 having been closed to anyone but Nuns for over two hundred years! It is a city in itself with everything from a laundrette to kitchens and vegetable gardens. Girls could go from the age of three and basically be brought up in the convent, if the families wished. Many arrived at six and were kept in one cloister with about ten "cells", very basic living and only a teacher nun each to talk to through a shutter in the window. At the age of eighteen, they moved to other cloisters where for a while they all had a maid cooking and cleaning for them while they prayed for seven hours a day. Later, maids were abandoned and they had to fend for themselves as a community. The maids were allowed outside the walls of the two-hectare convent to buy whatever the nuns needed and wanted. The nuns were never allowed out and will have never seen outside those walls all their lives! The possessions held by the nuns and the luxury of their lifestyles inside the convent was dictated by how much their families were prepared to pay for them. Some had huge accommodation with nice bed and wonderful crockery and big gardens. They had a bath once a month and were never allowed to bathe nude as they shared it with another nun. At one time, there were 300–400 nuns living in the convent. It was a beautiful place adorned with flowers and painted bright colours. A lot of wood and stone floors everywhere. There was a dining room with long trestle tables and a beautiful basic church that is open for a service at 7 a.m. each day. There are still about one hundred nuns living in the convent and are shut away in one area. The girl who showed us around spoke very good English and was very knowledgeable; the only problem was that we were with a bunch of American businessmen on a day trip. They did make stupid comments sometimes and ask some daft questions! At the end of the tour, we were free to have a look around on our own, and we found the cafe (of course!) and had some empanadas and apple tart baked by the resident nuns. It was a very strange feeling walking around a convent that used to have quiet nuns dressed in white with black headdresses walking around and praying, thirty years earlier! And what a life they led—no thanks!

It was another warm sunny day and we both felt like going to a park, sitting in the sun and reading. There was a small park just up from our hostel so we headed there. It was a very strange park, lots of levels, not very well looked after, quite scraggy-looking, but a good view over the city and the river. There was a man by the stream running through it, washing himself and the clothes on his back. There were also a few schoolboys and single men passing through! We didn't feel particularly safe and only stayed about thirty minutes. You just know when you can't relax and you are constantly watching people to make sure they are not going to pounce! We decided to go and have a look at the "Artesania" markets and see if they had anything that took our fancy by way of souvenirs. This was housed in a beautiful old prison block on two floors. Lots of stalls selling bracelets, rings, necklaces, jumpers and ornaments. The only thing we fancied was a colourful rug displaying a scene from a street in Chivay (Colca Canyon). It was really unusual, but it caught both our eyes. We vowed that if we saw the same thing again in Bolivia, we would probably take it to New Zealand and ship it home. That evening we ate in a vegetarian restaurant called Lachschunivan. It was a set meal, veg soup that was delicious although not hot enough, so we sent it back for a re-heat. It was then a delicious veg sauce and rice. We had some great brown bread and a small bowl of yoghurt for dessert. We ordered lemonade and regretted it as it was fresh, but probably tap water! It was about 25p so we didn't worry too much about leaving it. On leaving, we bought a fresh vegetarian short bread biscuit that we had seen people coming in specially to buy and it was very tasty!

The next day, we were up early to get our bus to Colca Canyon. Simon went out and bought bread for breakfast and at about 8.20 a.m. they arrived to pick us up. We were picked up in a big van with seats inside for about twelve people, quite comfy actually and windows to open. We only took Simon's rucksack of stuff as we didn't need everything and left mine locked away in a room for our return the following evening.

The next hour was a bit of a pain as we were hunting around the streets of Arequipa looking for addresses to pick people up. In the end, there were five Spaniards (three girls, girls lads) and two sets of two Peruvian girls, two about thirty and two about eighteen or nineteen. We didn't expect any Peruvians at all on the trip so that was a bit of a surprise. There were no other tourists who had a problem with the language so we had English translations throughout the trip just for ourselves!

Clariss was our guide and Jose the driver, both very nice. Clariss knew her stuff, but it was delivered in a rather rehearsed fashion and at times I felt she could have taped it and played it to us without being there! She was okay when we asked other questions though.

It was a fascinating journey over sand dune hills and flat desert along dirt tracks and going up to altitudes of 4,000m. We stopped to see strange animals, a type of vicuna apparently that looked like a cross between a deer and a kangaroo. We also stopped at a shed looking road side cafe for a drink of coca tea, to help the altitude adjustments. This was a mug of water stuffed with coca leaves and tasted quite nice. The indigenous tribes also chew the leaves and use them for medical purposes stuck to their foreheads for headaches etc.! Clariss told us it would take quite a few coca leaves to feel high but we tried one for the experience! Whether it helped or not I don't know, but it helped Simon's stuffy nose like nobody's business; however, he received a headache as well!

The journey took five hours and eventually we could see down to the village of Chivay at the start of the Colca Canyon. All the companies taking parties of people go here and generally stay in the same hostels. Ours was fine, quite basic with our own bathroom. It was very cold being over 3000 metres above sea level, but lovely in the sun. We had lunch when we arrived (3pm!) a set meal of cazuela and the first time we ate alpaca meat, a type of llama! It was actually really nice. The trip was then taking everyone to the local hot springs for a dip, but we didn't fancy it and wanted to see more of Chivay and the surrounding country. We didn't have a lot of time before dark, but Clariss told us of some local dancing happening at the next village to celebrate Chivay's anniversary which was taking place that weekend.

We headed off over the only bridge over the canyon. At this stage, the canyon was very small and we walked over the hill following the direction of others as we went. It was the first time we experienced seeing locals wearing traditional costumes, well the women anyway! They seem to wear about three different coloured skirts (often bright pink!) and they hoist the first one in the belt to show the others underneath. They also wear hats—in Chivay they looked like bowler hats—signifying which Indian tribe they originate from. Quechua was the main language they speak and most women have a baby strapped to their backs in a multi-coloured blanket.

We walked through a village with buildings made of mud,

following people and the sound of music. The sight we saw was amazing it was a natural open-air stadium with terracing all around for people to stand or sit, and watch what's happening below. There were hordes of locals watching and below about three different groups of dancers waiting to go on, all dressed alike in their costumes. We hiked a little up a terrace and perched ourselves on a rock each and sat with our mouths open for about an hour. This is what we had come travelling to see, a local celebration/culture/tradition. We were the only "gringos" in sight and I felt sorry for the others who had gone to the hot springs which were supposed to be quite touristy! The music was made up of trumpets, drums, recorders, really anything anyone could find that sounded musical with a beat. It turned out to be a competition and one of the teams won a silver cup. There was also a Miss Chivay crowned and the procession then headed for more partying in the centre of Chivay. We tried to take some subtle photos as the whole scene was amazing. As the sun went down, we walked a little way alongside the canyon and watched the sky change colour to a light mauve before heading back to our hostel.

That evening, we were supposed to have a local folklore band playing in the hotel and dinner there, but because of the celebrations the band was not playing. All the others had also decided not to eat there and although I was a little disappointed that we weren't really going to have a knees-up there, we wanted to go and see what was happening at the Plaza de Armas.

The whole town and villages around were there. You could tell they had all been planning and preparing it for weeks. There were stalls everywhere and even candlelit gambling tables! We spied some women selling what looked like hot tea and feeling quite chilly we had some. It was served in a pint glass and was a concoction of different spicy liquids and hot water that was boiling with some tea leaves in it. It was absolutely delicious and we found out later supposedly very good for your liver and stomach! We weren't sure whether our bodies would react, but we didn't care, it was all part of the experience.

There was also one street laden with food stalls. Women were cooking in the streets and they had picnic tables attached for you to sit and eat their food. All lit by lamps, we had to try some. It was heaving, but we found a spot and had a big plate of rice, noodles, chips, salad and a piece of chicken in a delicious sauce—all for a £1. We weren't that hungry at 8 p.m. having had a big lunch, but we weren't going to miss out and we loved every mouthful.

We wandered around the Plaza taking in the ambience, had a beer in a cafe and then more hot tea to warm up! It was actually very cold and many of the locals had blankets wrapped round themselves and their babies. We found out the next day that the party was still going on at 5.30 a.m.! They really know how to celebrate!

The next day (Sunday), we were up for breakfast by 6.30 a.m. as we were due to see the flight of the condors (hopefully!) at '9 a.m.-ish. It was so nice to have a cup of coffee again! Peru doesn't seem to have breakfast included in a hostel and Iquique didn't have it either so this was a treat. We stuffed ourselves with fresh bread and jam and rejected a glass of what smelt and tasted like puke! It was actually a very common Peruvian drink from what looks like a "squash" yuck!

The trip to the highest and deepest point on the canyon was magnificent. Having never seen a canyon before I wasn't too sure what I would find, but it was beautiful. The land suddenly disappears to form a huge gorge/canyon and up again the other side. Huge hills surrounded it, Inca terracing farmland was obvious and you could hear the waterway down below. Before arriving there, we stopped off at a couple of villages steeped in history and many badly affected by recent earthquakes and not rebuilt.

At the canyon, we perched ourselves as near to the edge as comfortable and waited, the sun was warm, the air was cool and we were told to be quiet, although I think the German tourists visiting misheard that bit!

It took a while for any condors to be seen at close range and none were going above our heads as people had explained they would.

Rebecca

Cajamarca, Peru.
Tues 1st July 1997

They eventually did and we moved closer to the edge to get even better views. They were so graceful with a huge wing span of up to three metres. We were told that the babies are always brown and the older condors black with white chests. We also found out that that particular spot where we were viewing the condors used to be where a local meat company came to shed its waste and hence the condors came to eat! This is where they decided to stay.

Before heading back to Arequipa, we had lunch in Chivay amongst the marching of locals on their anniversary procession. We even tried some local ice cream which instead of a blob of cream on top had some whipped egg white! Perhaps we shouldn't have eaten it, but it was good. The journey back was uneventful, only stopping once for the toilet and mainly being a chance to catch up on a bit of sleep.

Back at Arequipa we had to buy a few supplies for the following day's journey and re-pack our bags.

7 a.m. sharp the next day, we got a bus to Pisco which took about twelve hours. Probably one of the worst journeys for us as it was a day long trip twisting in and out of the mountains and sea coasts. The driver (as usual!) was a maniac on the roads and it was such a roller coaster ride that a little boy behind Simon threw up on the floor! Great! We decided we much preferred night journeys; it doesn't seem such a waste as driving during the day.

We arrived in the dark and had to get a "kombi" to the centre of Pisco. We had seen loads of "kombi" vans in Arequipa carrying piles of people and have a bloke hanging out of the side shouting something to everyone. We didn't have a clue what kombis were until now, local busses that are privately run and therefore have to rustle up business as they go along! Bizarre, but quite efficient and very cheap.

Pisco was extremely busy for a Sunday evening, the Plaza de Armas was heaving with youngsters and we felt a little conspicuous walking through the crowds with backpacks on. As quickly as we could, we found the hostel that was recommended in the book—very basic, but clean and a window looking out onto a plaza. We were both very hungry and having negotiated a lower price because they had no hot water due to a faulty boiler, we chucked our bags in our room and went in search of a restaurant. We made the unfortunate error of taking the handbook with us and thereby looking like travellers. Pisco was also very warm, much more than we had been used to as it was by the coast and we had gone out in our short sleeves and watches showing! As warned a bloke tried to snatch Simon's watch on the Plaza outside our hostel! There were loads of people around and many saw it happen. Simon's quick action stopped him by snatching his hands away. We were both so pleased he hadn't got away with, not that it is worth anything but that he was foiled! I was really shaken up by it, but Simon was very philosophical and of course was right: we were both okay, no one was hurt and petty theft and crime is really all we need to worry about in Peru. If we were in Mexico, we may have to be wary of people getting a gun out on you and shooting! Anyway, we were fine and having taken the book back to the hostel and hidden our watches in our pockets we found a nice little restaurant for a meal.

Neither of us liked Pisco as a place as it did seem quite unfriendly and threatening whenever we stepped out of the hostel. We didn't intend on being there very long as it was the Paracas National Reserve we had come to see, and a break from bus journeys. On arrival in Pisco, a lady had shoved a leaflet at me regarding trips to Paracas National Reserve and the Ballestas Islands. Both were supposed to provide views of the largest amount of marine bird life in the world and fantastic desert coastline. The leaflet quite clearly stated to turn up outside the office at the five times listed and a tour would be going. Our time was precious as our next bus out of Pisco was leaving at 3.30 p.m., the shortest visit we have done so far in two months!

At 9.30 a.m., the tour had not arrived and the office wasn't even open! We were getting suspicious and when they did open, we were told you had to book the day before! I was really annoyed and tried to explain my frustrations to the lady, but she didn't care. We decided to go on our own and hailed a taxi to El Chalo, the fishing village/beach at Paracas where the boats leave for Isla Bellastas. Pisco produces a lot of fishmeal and we passed all the main companies along the sea front causing a real fishy smell! It was a beautiful day and El Chalo was a nice small fishing port.

Trips to Isla Bellastas were off as the red flag was up, meaning the sea was too dangerous to go out in a boat! What else could go wrong?! However, trips were being organised to Paracas National Reserve up the road but at a price! Why do these sales people always look a little dodgy! We haggled and ummed and arred and decided that we would go for it and spend the £12 on the three-hour tour! The tour party included us, two Peruvians and the driver in his little Daewoo car!

Paracas National Reserve was a desert as I had always perceived one! Flat, hot, dusty and goes on for miles! It was incredible and so beautiful. We saw crashing waves at the junction between a Lawrence of Arabia desert and the deep blue of the pacific. Beautiful and mesmerising.

Rebecca

Cajabamba, Peru.
Wed 2nd July 1997

Our driver/guide couldn't speak a word of English, but somehow, we were able to understand his slow, deliberated Spanish and it worked well. He also took us to a small fishing village where they can only fish in the middle of the night. Again, in the middle of nowhere. When we turned up, there were some other tourists all having a dip in what looked like a beautiful lapping seashore. It was a shame we hadn't brought our swimming gear as the sun was hot. I think they were Danish as they immediately latched onto Simon and asked if he was Danish too! His blonde hair and now beard are giveaways, but he says it happens whenever he wears shorts too—maybe it's the knees! Our guide took us to another inlet of sea where pink flamingos were amongst other sea birds wading in shallow water and feeding. Amazing! They were on the horizon again with blue sky and desert all around, what a place. Our guide finally took us to the museum in the park that is currently being extended for an archaeological laboratory. Although fairly small, the museums there were excellent with English translations. It showed how Paracas was discovered in the 1950's by a man called Tello. Obviously there had been and still are, a lot of digs to discover its history and it goes way back! The museum tried to show us what the life-story of the inhabitants of Paracas would be like 1,000s of year ago. There were even some real "funeral bundles" that had been dug up showing how they buried their dead—a very basic, simple existence living by the sea in a hot desert, but producing some amazing materials and woven clothes. One simple thing we are learning is that people adapt to their means and, with nothing, you seem to be more creative with what you've got and use your common sense about nature to allow it to work for you. We have become far to use to technology and western methods to really think about how nature could help us. We also don't make time for the simple things in life like making things and hand to mouth living. It can be very tough, but it's all they have known.

The only thing we didn't manage to see were sea-lions,

but having seen loads at Iquique we didn't feel too cheated. We also weren't expert enough to know about the sea life we witnessed and know which animals were rare. Overall, the trip was superb, an eye opener and again something so very different. It also wasn't laden with crowds of tourists which makes a huge difference.

Back in Pisco, we had enough time to have a good lunch to set us on our way for the next leg of our journey. Our aim was to get to Northern Peru and as with all journeys in this country they take forever by bus and have to go up the coast in order to go inland. This meant going through Lima which we had hoped to avoid. We were lucky that buses coincided and we were able to get a night bus to a place called Carhauz. However, the journey was four hours to Lima, two hours wait and ten hours to Carhauz. We were also lucky that the same bus company did both legs meaning we didn't have to move bus terminals and it was their own and not the horrendous sounding main Lima bus terminal! Phew!

Rebecca

Cajabamba, Peru.
9.30 a.m. Thurs 3rd July 1997.

Our next bus to Carhuaz goes at 11.30 a.m. so I have a little time to write more of the diary and catch up on Carhuaz.

What we saw of Lima looked a little grotty although we passed a couple of nice-looking buildings. The bus set off late for some unknown reason, other than typical Peruanos! The bus was comfortable but very hot and the guy in front kept shutting our window whenever we wanted it open because it was blowing on his hair! As we got up into the mountains it went cold and all our layers came in handy. Another twisting and turning journey up in the hills and early morning we stopped at Huaraz where hostel owners tried to persuade us to stay there. We bought a delicious hot empanada from a guy who came on the bus and then had another hour on the bus to Carhauz.

The scenery was fantastic, snow all over the Cordillera Blanca and some greenery around which made a change from the dusty desert.

Carhauz was a lovely small town nestled below the hills and surrounded by valleys. The air was fresh and the sun lovely and warm. The book recommended a place supposedly one kilometre away that was in a country setting and included all meals. We tried to find a taxi to take us, but no joy at 8.15 a.m. So we decided to walk, asking locals, who were very friendly. W soon began to regret walking, it as it was all uphill. It was our first proper trek with our backpacks! The altitude meant we had to take it steady and we cursed the book for being so wrong on distance. We eventually found it and it really was beautiful. Wind and solar powered, the whole place was made of wood, the lady spoke good English and the setting was glorious. Unfortunately, she was asking for a lot of money and, although she brought it down to include just breakfast, it was still at our daily budget limit and we weren't travelling for the luxuries! They grew a lot of their food and we knew it would have been fantastic, but we couldn't justify it. We had come all that way and we now had to go all the way back! Fortunately, it was all downhill. The lady said she would take us down in her car as she was going but things suddenly changed and she had to supervise felling a tree at the bottom of the garden! Her son walked us down into town, an odd boy who seemed a little hostile but would suddenly strike up a conversation about something. He told us about a bike race he had done at the weekend around Lima going up and down some incredible mountains.

We got back to Carhauz and found just what we were looking for, a hostel that was clean, spacious and friendly oh and a lot cheaper! We had a small balcony looking out onto the town and the hills beyond. They also had laundry facilities out on the roof. What a location to do your washing. We managed to do a whole load, including our very dirty trousers and they even had a washing line and pegs in the sun! They were all dry by the end of the day!

One of the only problems with the place was the water supply. In the evening, the water seemed to go off and whenever we wanted a shower, we had to give him an hour's notice so that it would heat up. Then he might forget to open the water supply to our room so we had no water at all! We managed okay and the room was one of the best we have had, with towels!

The same day, we arrived we decided to go and explore a place called Chancos where there are some thermal baths. We had a good lunch in a basic restaurant, infamous soup and then meat and rice. This place did however serve a nice little salad of beans and corn that hasn't popped, which we love. We then got a kombi bus from Carhauz to Marcara and did a lovely six kilometres walk up to Chancos. It was another dirt track road into the country, following a river. It was a glorious day and a fascinating walk out of town and amongst the country folk. "Gringos" became the popular word flying around as we walked, as it seems to be all over Peru!

Simon

Carhauz, Cajamarca and Huamachuco
26th June 1997 to 5th July 1997

In Argentina, I used the phrase "nothing is as it seems" to describe the travelling experience in that particular country. For Peru the phrases, "Seems is nothing as it" or even "It seems as nothing is" would perhaps be better suited. You can rely on nothing here, save apparent confusion, stupidity and downright inefficiency.

We left Carhauz in good spirits. We had had an exhilarating walk and we had a bus to catch at 8.00 p.m. We even had plenty of time to get ready. We even had our room as the hostel owners had kindly allowed us to remain there.

Our showers took about an hour, and during this time, we planned and re-planned our pre-departure details. You see we hadn't realised that to get 'agua caliente' (hot water) we had to order in advance. OK, we hadn't realised, so we ordered the agua caliente. Twenty minutes we were told and it would be ready. This presented much discussion i.e., should we: 1) wait for the shower, then have dinner and come back for our bags, or 2) have dinner then come back for a shower and our bags, or 3) wait for the shower, then take our bags to the restaurant.

Not much of a problem, but think about this: will it really be twenty minutes? From past experience in Peru, twenty minutes could mean two hours. We could hang about for ages for the agua caliente and miss out on a shower and or meal altogether. The bus leaves in two hours and we are due on it for the next twenty-four. What if we were to go for option (2)?

We could have our meal and then miss out on the agua caliente. You see agua caliente is not on nonstop supply. Once on, agua caliente is not indefinite. You see there is a window of opportunity with agua caliente. After twenty minutes of agua caliente, the roof top tank fills to maximum and spills four floors onto the street below, and when agua caliente empties onto the street below, the hostel owners turn off the water system.

Enough of these ramblings. The point is that in Peru nothing is straight forward.

All ended well in the end. We went for option (1) with some success. The shower was hot, the meal was great and we caught the bus feeling clean, fresh and ready for the journey. I was on top of the world and ready for anything. The bus was only fifteen minutes late, it was clean and we had ample leg room.

The euphoria and feeling of cleanliness lasted three hours. We started the journey with spare jumpers and coats as it was an overnight trip. However, as the bus headed lower and lower towards the coast the bus got hotter and hotter. This was absurd. I remember seeing sweat trickle down the windows, as I unzipped the bottoms of my travelling trousers. It was the most unpleasant journey we have had so far. It came unexpectedly upon us. Here, you can take nothing for granted and any plans made are almost certainly bound to change as often as the hour hand moves to another number on the clock.

Northern Peru has been great for us. It is without doubt the area that I have most enjoyed so far in the country. The Andes here are reasonably green and somehow look more accessible. The people here also are very welcoming and friendly.

Our first port of call was the beautiful colonial town of Cajamarca. There was plenty to do here. On the first day, we didn't see the town. The town looked nice enough but I had to get out into the country. At the time, I wondered if I was clearly forming my ideas on life style wants and preferences. For some time, I believed that I prefer the village and country life. But was this preference becoming an obsession, a phobia even of town life? Perhaps I was becoming allergic to all things civilisation. I felt most peculiar.

We got the bus to the Ventanillas de Otusco. We sat in front next to the driver and it felt like I was six years old, being allowed to sit in the front seat next to Dad. The Ventanillas de Otusco is part of an old pre-Inca cemetery and has a gallery of secondary burial niches. It was great. I had been itching to see some ancient ruins in Peru and up to now we hadn't seen any. The view from the burial niches, situated as they were on top of a hill, was fascinating. We were in the Andes and life was going on as normal for the local folk. A man was ploughing his field with the help of a couple of cows. People waited by their bus that had got stuck in the river, whilst attempting to cross it.

We had planned to do an all-day walk from here. We tried to but within ten minutes of setting off I found myself yelling at Rebecca. I did feel most peculiar, dizzy, stuffy nose, headache etc.; the exact description given in our book for soroche or altitude sickness. We got as far as some thermal baths known as Los Banos Del Inca. From here, we paid a premium rate for our own private thermally heated bath. It was just what I needed. By the evening, more symptoms of soroche had developed including diarrhoea. The cure apparently is plenty of rest and water, no alcohol!

Anyway, Cajamarca is probably one of the better places to be ill. It is a beautiful city with a pleasant climate in lovely surroundings. I'd recommend anyone to be ill there. My illness didn't last long and over the next few days we looked around the town, did some hikes and went to the thermal baths again.

Hiking in the area has been one of the great pleasures of our trip. The countryside is beautiful, but the people here seem far friendlier than in other parts of Peru. We are definitely as much a curiosity to them as they are to us. Reactions to us have been mixed in Peru ranging from hostility, to arrogance, jealousy, sarcasm, timidity and friendliness, but hardly ever indifference. However, here people are curious but friendly with it. It is amazing how far a smile and a "hola", on our part, go.

Great though Cajamarca was, after five days, we were ready to move on. My carefully laid plans on which towns we would visit rapidly fell apart when it became apparent that distances as short as forty-eight kilometres would take three hours by bus. There were so many ruins we wanted to see. Our plan was to bus hop from one base to another. After we realised a bus hop was more like a bus marathon, our plans became somewhat more realistic.

Before we left Cajamarca, there was time for one last bout of soroche for me. A three-hour return excursion by van up to 3,100m from 2750m was enough to ensure of that. Cumbe Mayo is a pampa on a mountain range. It is famous for its extraordinary, well-engineered pre-Inca channels, running for several kilometres across the mountain tops with the huge rock formations all around help to create an impressive atmosphere.

Our tour guide was excellent at pointing out rock formations that represented or looked like other things. A frequent and popular one was that "Which resembles a penis." Not mine, they didn't. The whole thing reminded me of a Blackadder sketch where Baldrick had grown a turnip that looked like a thingy.

Great fun though it was, I suffered afterwards. At the bus terminal, I was in gringo hell as I clutched my backpack, a huddled mess on the floor. The toilets offered the usual delights for someone feeling decidedly worse for wear. I didn't and couldn't bring myself to throw up in such delightful surroundings, but I still had to pay for the privilege of rushing in and out again.

That afternoon, we got the bus to Cajabamba. We stayed one night in order to get a bus to Huamachuco. I won't bother to go into excessive detail on Cajabamba; safe to say, our accommodation was surprisingly good and our meal out that evening was surprisingly bad. I had chicken without meat. "That's the bird," protested the owner. A very thin bird, indeed!

The bus to Huamachuco was amazing. The bus was small and had precious little legroom, whilst tight for the average Peruvian, was gut crampingly ridiculous for a six-footer. It could have been very grim, but we were saved. The driver's assistant offered us the seats next to the driver. This is getting a bit of a habit for us, but we accepted with glee.

We had a great view from the front and they were definitely the most comfortable seats on the bus, especially as they were packed in the aisles behind us. It was a nice gesture to give us those seats.

Huamachuco is a very nice town. On the bus coming here, I was a bit worried about what we would find here. Huamachuco is described very briefly in our guide book. That tends to mean nobody ever goes there, especially tourists and especially gringos. Huamachuco has turned out to be one of those places. People are surprised to see us and we have been the focus of much attention.

Yesterday, we did a fabulous walk to some pre-Inca ruins named Marcahuamachuco. The surprise was that we found them. They are the remains of a hilltop fortress, now just lying amid the farmland that surrounds it. There are no signs, brochures, postcards or people. The farmer who has claimed the ruins has a fine place to grow his wheat. The views were spectacular and the walk must rank alongside Arrays Lopez and the Pacific coast at Corrall.

Today, we went to some other pre-Inca ruins named Viracochabamba. Once again, no signs, people around etc. What was once probably a hive of activity with an important village elder is now a lonely place in impressive Andean surroundings.

This trip never ceases to amaze me. Since we have been here at Huamachuco, mothers have taken their shy children up to us so they can speak to real life gringos like the ones on TV. Some kids shout out "Rrr-ebecca" as we walk past. At our hostel the owners are very proud of the TV room which we are free to use, but to their amazement don't. As far as we could work out, the TV has three channels with the light switched off, but infinitely more with the light on.

It looked like something from an X-rated film. It was a huge tool, but not shiny. It had obviously been used a lot. If the lady hadn't looked so friendly, we may have been a bit wary of this massive machete in her hand. She introduced herself as Maria and showed us the way to Viracochabamba. She asked where we were from, but hadn't heard of

"Inglaterra." Oh well, it must be our accent. I added "Londoners," but she was still perplexed. "Was this place over an hour away?" She remarked questioningly. Yes, I think it probably is, I thought.

Post diary note. We have since found out that Huamachuco is at an altitude of 3,200 not 2,300 as the book records. This explains the superb views from Marcahuamachuco and the cold evenings here.

Rebecca

7 p.m. Qosqo, Peru.
Mon 7th July 1997

The infamous Qosqo and we have arrived at last, safe and sound!

The rest of Carhauz was spent exploring the lower hills and local villages doing a great walk to a place called Hualcan in search of ruins that we never found. The scenery was breath-taking and we bumped into a couple of guys that had all the gear preparing for some climbs of the true mountains around; one was Swiss and the other Belgian and it was obvious that they always use up whatever holiday they get climbing mountains with pickaxes and snow boots. They managed to get a guide from the village to take them up for the first two days and were organising a mule for them to carry their equipment. No tourist companies have yet reached such sites; the locals are all you can rely on. Having said that, experiences we have had in Peru have shown that the locals often don't know for sure the way and can give you misleading and opposing directions.

The food in Carhauz was good, especially when we found "Los Pinos" restaurant that was recommended in the book and turned out to be excellent. We ate there on our last night before getting our next bus and we had a delicious plate of a Paella mix without fish.

Due to the bus times, we had to leave Carhauz sooner than we both expected and wanted, but with a bus to Trujillo at 7 p.m. each day we decided we didn't want to hang around another day. We were heading for further North, and we realised it would be a long trip!

Trujillo was so humid we could hardly breathe. We headed straight for the bus company that could take us to Cajamarca and had about four hours to wait before setting off again at 10.30 a.m. arriving in Cajamarca at 5.30 p.m. Whilst at Trujillo, we decided to look into flying to Qosqo from Lima as by now the bus journeys were becoming a bit of a pain and neither of us would be looking forward to a journey down south of about three days constantly on the bus! The other reason for looking into it was that whilst in Carhauz, we decided not to go through the central highlands area as there seemed to be some misgivings about security and safety whilst travelling and in some towns, we decided it wasn't worth the risk. We were also thinking it would be very difficult to get to and it would extend our time in Peru, eating into our time in Bolivia. Anyway, unfortunately any cheap flight deals that had been around from Lima to Qosqo had gone. It was now high season and the prices were back to $70. We paid it anyway and chose a date nine days in advance forcing us to see Northern Peru properly and with plenty of time for any long journeys. We both felt really relieved that we would get a slight respite from bus journeys. It was also quite exciting knowing we would again be flying before our big journey to New Zealand.

We decided to celebrate with a decent breakfast. Simon chose a greasy cafe looking place which could have been really good considering the good food that we have experienced out of dodgy looking places! Anyway, we did the daring thing of choosing something we didn't understand and of all things it could have been it had to be fried liver and onions! Simon said my face was a picture as my jaw dropped to the floor! We were both really hungry and to be honest I did have some of it. I did enjoy the coffee though, a treat we hadn't had for a long time.

The journey to Cajamarca was okay considering the heat and the views up over the hills were spectacular. Buses really do drive along the edge of cliffs here with no real barriers to make you feel safe that we wouldn't go over the edge! We stopped at a Peruvian refreshment station which was a greasy restaurant with holes in the ground as toilets. It was too hot and too busy to eat a full meal so we just had our fruit and bread we had brought.

On arrival in Cajamarca, which was so well situated amongst the Andes, we decided to walk to the hostel we chose from the book. As usual, we weren't as close to the centre as we thought but a couple of friendly girls walked us to the Plaza De Armas where "Hostal Plaza" awaited us.

The hostel was a fantastic wood-work building around a courtyard. It was actually very big and although the book had recommended two specific rooms, we knew they would be very expensive. At first, our room didn't seem too bad, but after a few days it became a little claustrophobic. It didn't have a window and the lighting was bad. It had three beds, one kind of double (for dwarfs) and a table and chairs.

Cajamarca looked beautiful and indeed it was; an old colonial town that had maintained its age very well by not adding any real monstrous modern tower blocks. There were cobbled streets and loads of history. That first evening, we were looking forward to a good meal and searched around for a cheap deal. There weren't really many decent looking places around and again not taking restaurants at face value we chose one that was grotty looking but had locals inside. "El Carlo" turned out to be the worst meal we had abroad to date! We should have walked out as soon as I realised the tables were dirty, but we didn't. The soup was probably three days old and the steak (although in itself okay) was served with some disgusting tasting beans! It is so disappointing when you look forward to your main meal of the day and its rubbish!

Cajamarca was the start of the midge bites which we actually got in Carhauz on our walks, but which grew in abundance all over my body. By the end of our time in Cajamarca, I decided there must be some biting insects in the beds, as each morning I was finding fresh bites in odd places like my backside and boobs! Although Simon suffered a little with them on his legs, he didn't get many on his body. To this day, I am not entirely sure why we stuck that place/room out as we weren't happy with it and the water supply was somewhat dodgy.

Just to get all the groans out of the way, it was also the start of Simon's soroche suffering. The different altitudes had given him a stuffy nose but this grew into a cold and a lot more. He had headache, dizziness, nausea, diarrhoea and on reading about altitude sickness we deduced that was what he had got. On our first full day, he felt he couldn't stay in bed, couldn't manage to walk around town and really longed to be in the country. We decided to do a portion of a walk from the Ventanillas de Otuzco to Banos del Inca having got a bus to Ventanillas. The bus was the usual combi and sitting in the front we had a great thirty-mile journey.

Ventanillas de Otuzco is a pre-Inca wall of burial niches high on a hill—a strange but interesting ruin showing how the bodies were buried horizontally into the wall. The views around were superb, patchwork quilt of different farmlands, hills and valleys. All the locals were once again in traditional costumes. It was a perfect day for walking as it was cloudy/a little cooler, but nice when the sun came out. Simon felt quite rough at times, but really couldn't face going back and the walk was lovely. It wound round the river and then over a small hill and through a village down to Banos del Inca. This is a place where thermal water provides bathing for locals and tourists. There are different situations you can bathe in, shinning pool or different qualities of private baths. We decided to go for top of the range costing us about £2.60 and walked through what looked a bit like a holiday camp with the different baths looking like chalets. It was just what we both needed, a relaxing hour in a natural hot bath. We could choose the temperature ourselves and pretend to be Inca people bathing hundreds of years ago. My bites were soothed and Simon's soroche wasn't as prominent. We came out hot and refreshed and treated ourselves to a 17p ice lolly which became a daily treat for Cajamarca!

That evening, as with all the rest, we decided to eat at the restaurant which was downstairs from the hostel. They changed the menu of the day at lunch and then dinner, and we found the food good, plentiful, cheap and a clean and pleasant courtyard setting. We also had a cheap breakfast there most mornings and thoroughly enjoyed the coffee we had. It was convenient to eat there and always good quality.

Rebecca

Qosqo, Peru.
1.20 p.m. Tues 8th July 1997

Simon's diarrhoea has taken a turn for the worse and he is laid up in bed, poor thing! I feel so sorry for him. He woke up with really bad stomach pains and felt really sick. He managed to get to the toilet and has had about four bouts of diarrhoea since (no sickness!).

We decided that as with the rehydration sachets we should start him on the Imodium tablets. He is slightly better and I am hoping he will be a lot better by tomorrow. It gives me a chance to catch up on the diary, letters and reading. I may even go and phone Mum later, so looking forward to speaking to her but kind of wish it was when we were both on the up rather than when Simon feels ill. I also wouldn't want her to worry so I don't know yet. It is so grim being ill anywhere, but especially away from home. It must be awful if you are on your own, at least we have each other and he has quite enjoyed me reading parts of the diary and reliving memories of our trip. He is also craving news of QPR. Funny what you want when you are ill! Anyway, let's hope he feels better soon and I shall continue writing about Cajamarca.

On the Sunday, we decided to explore the town itself and what it had to offer. Santa Apollonia is a hill overlooking the town where Atahualpa (King of the Incas) was supposed to place an alter and pray. There is one cobbled street leading up to it from the Plaza da Armas with steps leading all the way to the top. The sun was hot, but with a cool breeze, and the views were superb all around the town and the Andes. There were locals trying to sell their handicrafts including some really nice pottery.

Rebecca

Qosqo, Peru.
4.45 p.m. Wed 9th July 1997

I didn't get as much diary done as I thought I would. At one stage in the afternoon, I was trying to get a doctor to see Simon, but our saviours Sarah and Jonathan turned up and were able to supply a few antibiotics and a tonic of a three-hour chat!

Back to Cajamarca, that same Sunday, we decided to have our meal at lunchtime and strayed away from our restaurant downstairs. The place we went to was okay, but we wished we had stuck with "El Real." Banos del Inca was also pulling us back so we went for another bathe in the afternoon. It was so busy; all the locals were having their family weekly bath and even the tourist park was really packed.

On Monday, we did the other half of the walk from Saturday starting early at the "Banos del Inca" and walking to a small village nearby. The route was beautiful in a valley and the weather was quite hot. The village was described in the book as a typical Andean village, nestled amongst the hills. We sat in the Plaza, watched the village life go on around us and drank a bottle of coke. A man and his son were parading around the square with a stall trying to sell wellington boots over a microphone! They really weren't the kind of footwear people around there would want!

From there we walked around a hill towards a hacienda (large farm) called "La Copa". It was in the middle of nowhere and we bust our gut to try and get there for 2 p.m. as the book said that was the time we would be able to see them hand milking cows. The place was fascinating but dead and no hand milking to be seen anywhere. As well as all the cowsheds and the church they had small gardens and a small lake that really had not been looked after very well. It was really pleasant sitting in the peace and quiet of the farm, by the lake and after about twenty minutes a small black calf decided to come and investigate us. It immediately took a shine to Simon and went straight for his fingers. Simon had always refrained from allowing an animal to suck his fingers, right now he had no choice and he loved it! His face was a picture as the calf slavered all over his hand. The calf then turned to me, but I wasn't keen to nurse a calf licked hand all the way back to Cajamarca so I firmly refused. We then walked back to the marked road past "La Copa" and managed to pick up a kombi back to town. Here we enquired about buses to Huamachuco which we found out was going to be much more difficult and lengthier than we thought. We would have to get a bus to Cajabamba and then to Huamachuco and probably over two days and not just one!

Again, that evening, we ate downstairs and I can't remember whether it was that day or the day after that we went to see El Regresso del Jedi (the Return of the Jedi)! What a flee pit of a cinema, but it was subtitled so we understood everything apart from Jabba! It was such good fun going to see a film here, a treat that was cheap and a definite must again sometime. On the Tuesday, we did a walk the other side of town up a hill to another nearby village where there is a pottery school for children. The views once again were amazing and the pottery lovely. So tempted to buy something, but not really keen to cart it around.

We booked our bus ticket that day and a tour to Cumbe Mayo which we managed to negotiate down a bit. We organised it so that we did the trip in the morning and the bus at 2 p.m. It was also either Monday or Tuesday that we both decided to try and have a haircut! We found a unisex place and were told it would be about £1.70 each! I thought I had made it quite clear to the lady that I really only wanted a little bit off and the layers remaining. She cut off so much and made me look like a sixty-year-old woman. I have never been so devastated about a haircut before, but this was the first time! I was so upset I got back to the hostel and washed it myself and by the time it had dried it did look a bit better, but I really didn't want such short hair again! I had just got it so that it could go up in a ponytail easily with no bits hanging down and now I had to start all over again!

We also managed to change some money from street changers and get some photos developed which were really good. Two of them we had blown up bigger, free of charge.

Our last day in Cajamarca and we were up early to pack our stuff and get to the tour office by 9 a.m. Of course, the trip set off late and we shared a van with a Peruano couple (living in Switzerland) and an older man. It took about one hour to get up to Cumbe Mayo, high above Cajamarca on another infamous winding mountain pass. It was quite cool and windy at the top and we then set off on a ninety-minute guide around some fantastic rock formations. They were all odd shapes and sizes from hundreds of years ago and he pointed out all the rocks that looked like certain animals and birds. We went through a narrow cave and witnessed an irrigation channel that was an amazing find from so long ago. Cumbe Mayo was beautiful and we even had some corn with the locals and photos of us with their daughter!

It didn't take as long back down and when we got to the bus terminal to catch our bus to Cajamarca, I suddenly realised Simon was not very well! The sudden change in altitude over the last three hours had knocked him again and all the soroche symptoms came flooding back! It was such a shame but we were lucky that we were there in plenty of time and that the bus was late, due to a change of tyre. He huddled on the floor amongst our packs and coats and wavered between sickness, diarrhoea, dizziness and headache. The locals were most amused and their stares really didn't help, but in time it subsided, and by the time we got the bus he felt much better. An ice cream, a few crisps and water and biscuits helped to perk him up and the symptoms went. I had packed some chopped raw carrot which I really enjoyed. I do miss fresh crunchy vegetables and these were delicious.

The trip was amazing over more incredible mountain passes and we arrived in Cajamarca at about 8 p.m. Of course it was dark and we immediately enquired about getting to Huamachuco. 4 a.m. or 11.30 a.m. were the times and not wanting to risk our health again we plumped for 11.30 a.m. the next day and set off to find a hostel. Again, we were a fascination and looking round the Plaza we couldn't see a hostel in sight. Simon went to ask a local chemist and from down the street a boy appeared and took us to a superb place called "La Posada". Wood everywhere and beautiful pictures the lady told us to treat it as our home, help ourselves to coffee/tea etc., whenever we wanted. We negotiated a good price and went out in search of a restaurant that she recommended. We found it quite quickly and although they did not have a "menu" the food looked good and we thought it would make a change just to have a good main course. Clueless about what we were choosing the man brought us a plate of nice potatoes and a piece of chicken and sauce. Mine was small, but it had meat on it; Simon's was a wing bone and skin!

Simon

Huamachuco & Qosqo
6th July to 7th July 1997

Huamachuco ended on a sore note at the time, hilarious in retrospect. The hotel on our last day had no electricity or water. This mild inconvenience was intensified to a matter of life and death as we knew we had a forty-eight-hour marathon journey ahead to Qosqo.

We kept asking when the water would be ready. Promises were continually made and continually broken. "La Tarde became "cinqo (5 p.m.) then seize (6 p.m.) and then nueve (9 p.m.)". Our bus was due to depart at nine!

The hostel owners told us it was not their fault and that the whole of the town had no water or electricity.

Strange then that when Rebecca asked the public 'shower shop' next door, they were experiencing no difficulties at all. Their whole attitude was awful. They laughed and shrugged shoulders to an irritating degree. We had already paid as we kept telling them for the room, with hot water and electricity.

"It's a problem," was the response. To cut a long argument short, after they refused to give us the money for a shower at the public shower shop, we stormed out promising them revenge in the form of a stroppy letter to the South American Handbook.

Meanwhile, in the public shower shop with hot water but without electric light, we got into the chicken and egg situation of not being able to find our torch in the dark because we couldn't find our torch. Safe to say, it ended in a heated debate with me blaming Rebecca for not putting the torch back in the correct place in the back pack. I then left the public shower shop for some fresh air in the plaza.

Before doing this, I still had time to rip my rucksack whilst rather heavy-handedly, tightening the cords around the sleeping bag!

We then met up later in the plaza just in time to venture to the bus station, me without food or a shower, Rebecca without food.

I love Peruvian roadworks. No lights, no cones, no signs, just large holes in the road ready and waiting for the odd stray gringo. I remember us crawling across the road, anticipating certain death at any moment, fully laden with back packs. "Be all right if we had a torch!" I remarked.

Huamachuco was generally perplexed by our arrival. I think it was gob smacked by what happened next. The bus station was full. My bag had a rip in it, albeit a small one. It needed fixing and it needed fixing now. I proceeded to attempt to sew the hole using tooth floss. A good plan; somewhat with room for improvement in its execution. It took me ten minutes to thread the needle. I steadfastly refused the help on offer from various members of the Huamachuco public. I dread to think what they thought of me when I used our handbook to hammer the needle into the bag.

The journey after that was generally pretty hellish. The road to Trujillo was like a bridal way, clinging desperately to the mountain sides of the Andes. Trujillo was hot and humid. We did go to the largest adobe city in the world whilst waiting for our bus. Chan Chan the pre-Inca Chimu city was so impressive. It was massive. Most of it looked unexcavated.

Skipping lots of other details, we arrived in Lima airport at 10.30 p.m. By this time, we had been on the move for over twenty-four hours.

Immediately, we learnt that our airline was on strike. Soon after, we learnt that only two flights on that airline were leaving and ours was one at 6.00 a.m. to Qosqo. We could rest easy.

We didn't rest easy. Resting, let alone sleeping at Lima airport is anything but relaxing. Call me sensitive, but trying to sleep on a cold marble floor in the theft capital of the world are not the ideal ingredients for a peaceful night. I did sleep though, for at least one hour. Add this to the half hour we had the previous night and you get the picture.

It was probably a good job we didn't rest easy. Not resting easy ensured we were almost first in the queue at 5.00 a.m. We later found out that having a ticket for the 7.00 a.m. flight from Lima to Qosqo didn't necessarily ensure a seat on the plane. You see many other people also had tickets from two days previous and they were also keen to get to Qosqo. It came down to first in the queue first on the plane. We were lucky.

We got to the swinging capital of Latin America absolutely exhausted. In true party animal fashion, we got to bed at 9.00 a.m., minus a hangover or embarrassing memories of the night before.

I woke up at about lunchtime to go to the toilet. I noticed the toilet didn't have a seat. Strange how small details can play a major role in life's unfolding adventure. I was to notice the absence of that toilet seat many, many times over the next two days.

I had chronic diarrhoea of the worst kind. On the Monday, it was more of an embarrassing inconvenience. There was no way I could venture more than a fifteen second sprint from the toilet without a seat. I didn't feel rough but more a little self-conscious as I regularly dashed by—roll in hand—across the courtyard to the offending toilet.

Qosqo and the Incas

Simon

Qosqo and The Sacred Valley
8th July 1997

More inconvenience and self-consciousness turned to pain and agony the next day. I had acute stomach cramp and I couldn't believe there was so much water in me. I know us humans are made up of something like 90% water, but the way I was going I would end up only with the other 10%. If only that toilet had a seat.

It wasn't a pleasant experience, but Rebecca was superb. She steadfastly refused to go out, and spent the time with me reading extras from our diary. Oh, happy days!

My pains became worse and worse. We deciphered from our hand book that I had the "onset of dysentery". DYSENTERY! That felt serious and sounded worse. "In this case treat it seriously and seek urgent medical attention" recommended our trusted travel companion Ben Box (author of the travel guide we were using). All sorts of things went through my mind.

Rebecca went downstairs to phone for the doctor. Then one of these strange co-incidences occurred. Our trusted friends from Pucon in Chile, Sarah and Jonathan, had heard where we were staying and popped into see us. I'm sure Rebecca's account of this will be better than mine, but can you believe it? Not only this, Sarah had been feeling rough and had taken some special antibiotics. They gave these to me. This and the sheer joy and amazement at having visitors to my sick bed in darkest Peru. They stayed for about three hours and it was superb. Rebecca couldn't get her words out quick enough and gabbled for three hours. Jonathan, pulling up his chair did a great doctor impersonation. Sarah couldn't stop laughing at the exploits Rebecca and I had landed ourselves in. I just lay there, slowly recovering whilst this pandemonium went on around me.

I felt better within four hours and by 10pm, I was ready to eat a horse. Egg, chips and rice brought to my bedside sufficed. I scoffed the lot.

Simon

Qosqo and The Sacred Valley
9th July 1997

At the time of writing this, I'm more than a week behind on the dairy; apologies for the brief description of the next few days.

The day after I almost had DYSENTERY, I felt better, but tired. We had a good look around Qosqo. I don't remember all the places we went to but safe to say that Qosqo is an interesting place. Inca stonework, now the foundation of more modern buildings is everywhere. As are gringos. Thousands of them. A real shock to us after a month of solitude.

Simon

Qosqo and The Sacred Valley
10th July 1997 to 14th July 1997

Today, we saw our first Inca ruins. Not the famous pre-Inca ruins, but actual Inca ruins. There are a few of them on the road from Pisac to Qosqo. We caught a taxi to the last one and walked back into town, exploring them all along the way.

In the evening, we had a meal with Jonathan. It was a pleasant evening but also a sad affair. Sarah had fallen ill again and it had become apparent that they would not be going on the Inca trail with us after all. Strange, last time we said goodbye, Jonathan said, "If you are looking to form a group for the Inca trail, count us in." We met up in Qosqo, by mistake. We both planned to go on the Inca trail with the same company on the same day. All the signs pointed in the same direction, until fate intervened. I felt very sorry for them. Jonathan in particular looked gutted.

Rebecca

Cusco Inca Trail Section
7th to 14th July 1997

Simon had described our departure from Huamachuco that turned out to be a disaster, one thing after the other went wrong for us including the loss of our beloved Maglite torch and small useful calculator. We were gutted! I had had a shower, Simon had not and we hadn't eaten a proper meal so my fruit and bits had to suffice and we boarded the bus to Trujillo. It was really cold high up and the journey so bumpy that sleep wasn't really an option. We arrived in the early hours of the morning to a warm, sticky Trujillo and sat waiting until it was light and a decent hour before searching for bus tickets to Lima. The best result would have been a bus in the evening that got us into Lima in the early hours. We caught a few taxis to various bus companies and found out that most buses go at the same time, morning and early afternoon. A bit of toing and froing and we deduced that the "Royal Class" of Ormeno buses at 1.30 p.m. was our best option. Double the price of a normal service but still quite cheap and a chance for perhaps a bit of luxury.

With a few hours to wait we decided to find somewhere for breakfast and then head to the ruins of Chan Chan just outside the city. Sunday mornings are quiet wherever you are and this was no exception. Knowing that markets often sell food early we headed in that direction and sure enough it was buzzing. We sat at a cafe stall and ordered hot empanadas, a big glass of fresh orange juice and a big piece of cake to share. It was delicious and so cheap being in the market. All the stalls compete for business and request your company at their cafe. They all look alike and it is sometimes difficult to choose which one to go to. It can be down to the look of the food others are eating or even the nice way they entice you. Although markets can be dirty the eating stalls are generally very clean, colourful and inviting.

We then headed for a street where a minibus would take us to Chan Chan. The South American handbook did have a warning regarding this road to Chan Chan, not walking it alone but in groups etc. We didn't have much choice and walked the twenty minutes with no problems. We were in the desert again, what seemed miles away from a town. The sand dunes covered a lot of the views and walls around the old city were obvious and strange to see. We were there by the time it opened, all the guides dressed in khaki coloured trousers, shirts or shorts and cream blouses/shirts and all with a hat. They tried to persuade us to pay £5 for a guide but this was beyond our budget and we were happy just to look around ourselves.

Chan Chan is an old Chimu Empire City (Pre-Inca) who were conquered by the Incas. Surrounded by huge walls and hidden until you walk through corridors and alleyways and quite a bit of it restored, it extends to the sea. It reminded us a lot of what Egypt would look like with hieroglyphics on the walls making patterns and throne places in big squares for the leaders to sit and ceremonies to take place. It was pretty impressive, especially from a tower built to give you a panoramic view. Digs are still being made all around there to discover the whole city but the taste we had was enough and well worth it.

It was by now very hot and we trudged back along the road to get a bus back into town and back to the bus terminal. We both longed for a refreshing wash and knowing they had decent toilets this would be a possibility. A small cafe down the road gave us shade and a place for a great cold coca cola before we went back into the bus terminal.

We both washed and felt much better, especially Simon who hadn't had a shower for a couple of days. There was a TV on in the terminal showing scenes of the recent handover of Hong Kong and Prince Charles doing a speech about Britain not forgetting Hong Kong! We had seen some other TV pictures in Cajamarca but neither of us feel as if we know how it all went.

The bus was incredibly posh, so much more than we expected. All the seats were at the top of the bus and with heaps of leg room. They all reclined really far back and it was air-conditioned plus having a small TV screen, every few seats back, for when they showed videos. There was a man's and a lady's toilet downstairs and buttons for service (like in an aeroplane) as well as light buttons overhead, which actually worked! The ride was incredibly smooth with no stops until Lima and no locals let on to sell their goods! Apart from foreigners the clientele, were obviously rich. Peruanos - none of them had traditional costumes on. They provided a light lunch and horrible orange juice. I was expecting a few more refreshments throughout the trip but this was not the case! It was incredibly relaxing and just what we needed. They showed three movies, can't even remember what they were except a film by Jim Carrey which was absolutely horrendous. Anyway, we arrived in Lima at about 8.30pm – 9pm. Again, it was at their own bus terminal so it was protected and safe. There were taxi drivers outside and we negotiated a realistic price with one and headed off for the airport. A boy racer at heart this taxi driver was mad and on route stopped for some petrol. We both agreed we didn't seem to have missed much in Lima and arrived at Lima airport all in one piece. As a foreigner coming into the airport you don't get half as much hassle as when you are leaving but getting to know your way round an airport can take time.

Our flight was at 6 a.m. the following morning with "FAUCETT PERU" and on looking at the departures board it wasn't up there. We decided to go and find out from a FAUCETT desk but they were all empty, assuming they had no flights going out at present. Looking a little bewildered and lost a man came up to us and in excellent English asked if he could help. He asked who we were flying with and where to and on responding he then told us that FAUCETT were on strike and had been for a few days! What a bolt of lightning! No flights were going to Qosqo with FAUCETT and he pointed to an information desk nearby who may be able to give us a bit more details. Our minds were spinning, why didn't we know about the strike and everyone else seemed to? The lady at the info desk got hold of the main info centre and I spoke to a lady who took ages in getting back to me. In the end she asked which flight we were booked on and it turned out ours was one of twelve flights going out by FAUCETT the following morning! She also said we were extremely lucky! The lady at the info desk didn't seem to know this news and the man who was still hovering over us (apparently from Tourist Info in the airport!) was also surprised. They phoned to check and sure enough the information was correct. The man tried to get us to stay overnight somewhere in Lima but we explained we didn't need it and we were staying put at the airport, he realised he wasn't going to get any further!

The book told us that we would be able to sleep above the departure lounge and we made our way upstairs and sat down. I headed off to look for somewhere to eat. We kind of regretted we hadn't had our main meal at Trujillo but to be honest it was far too hot to think about a hot meal at that time, so we had to make do with hamburger and chips at a ridiculous price.

I find airports quite exciting places. Being the start or end of a new adventure somewhere. When people watching I wonder why they are there, if they are waiting for someone, waiting to catch a flight etc. It was great to be in one again as it made us feel as if we were really travelling and going on holiday. I honestly didn't mind staying overnight there, it was warm and quiet with a sense of something to come....

We treated ourselves to a can of beer each and then tried to get some sleep. The seats were singular and really quite uncomfortable but being smallish I managed to grab an hour or two. Simon ended up sleeping on the floor which he said wasn't actually too bad but it wasn't for long. The cleaners were working all night and at one point annoyed everyone by demanding we all stand whilst they moved the seats to clean.

At about 3.30 a.m. we were awake and on having a quick wash, by 4.00 a.m. we went down to queue up for our boarding passes. There were already a few people in the queue and as the queue got bigger and no staff seemed to be around a nervous feeling seemed to wash over everyone. There was a definite sense of "will this flight really go" and another feeling of "will we get on it". Groups of travellers turned up and had leaders who tried to push in but this was forbidden as far as everyone was concerned. The queue had become sacred and we soon found out why. It turned out there were a lot of people queuing who had missed flights from the last two days. The policy that day was going to be "first come first served" regardless of whether you had a booked ticket or not! We were pretty glad to be near the front of the queue and delighted when we were handed boarding cards! We then had to queue to pay tax, which we hadn't considered but turned out to be more important than checking our passports. We then headed straight through to the gate and almost immediately onto the plane. It took off about half an hour late but we knew that we were now on our way.

The flight really wasn't that long and they served breakfast, a small sandwich and cake, juice and coffee. By now

Simon was feeling a bit queasy but the guy next to him was a good distraction. He was Greek but is living in England and had only arrived a couple of days previously. We found out that Pete Sampras had won Wimbledon again and Tim Henman had got through to the semi-finals. We also found out the name of the new Conservative leader but for the life of me I can't remember! Anyway, it felt good to be next to someone who had just come from England. He also informed us it had rained for the whole of June!

The views from the plane were amazing of all the surrounding mountains. We weren't sitting on the right side for Machu Picchu views but I wasn't that bothered as I wanted to see it for myself.

We landed within an hour and went to pick up our bags marvelling at how fast planes are and how glad we were at not taking a forty-hour bus journey. Outside the small airport there were a host of agents with placards and names on them, as well as taxi drivers. We negotiated a price with a non-taxi driver and were a little suspicious when he got in the taxi with us and seemed to be paying a little of the taxi fare we had negotiated! We had chosen a hostel from the book and headed in that direction. Qosqo is built high up but surrounded by loads of mountains. A beautiful situation which we loved at first sight. We arrived at Hostal Union by about 8 – 8.30 a.m. and there was a room free but the beds not made so we had to wait a while. It was built around an attractive courtyard and the owners seemed really friendly. The "agent" came in with us and sat down in the courtyard with us as he explained about the Inca Trail and what he could offer. Surprisingly he wasn't pushy at all and left us the information to ponder over and a telephone number to call if we wanted to know more or book up. He then left! Bizarre! We weren't used to such things, no strings attached.

The owners could see we were tired and when I explained we had come all the way from Huamachuco he took pity on us and said we could lie on the beds and rest although they weren't clean yet. We were so tired we agreed and slept for about two to three hours.

They moved us to another/bigger better room upstairs and by now we realised Simon was not very well with diarrhoea, more of an inconvenience and having showered and changed we hung out in the sun in the courtyard reading and writing. It was a very relaxing afternoon. We met Thomas the Danish guy who was travelling on his own for a month and had got mugged up the road from the hostel the previous evening! Silly that he was out at night on his own but such a shame. There were a lot of Israelis in the hostel and even a lot of notices up in Hebrew! Sometime in the afternoon we had a little wander around Qosqo and the Plaza, just getting our bearings but Simon's bottom was calling and I was quite breathless so we headed back.

Having not seen any "gringos" for a few weeks it was amazing to come face to face with so many in one town. A quaint town with lots of cobbled streets and Inca remains down each street. Again, traditional costumes were the name of the game but there were a lot of foreigners wearing obvious travelling gear.

On the way back to the hostel we bumped into Dave, from Pucon in Chile! I couldn't believe it as I was convinced that we wouldn't bump into people again. Simon wasn't that surprised but delighted to see him. We stood chatting in the street for about fifteen minutes. He had just done the Inca Trail, loved it and had gone with an agency he couldn't remember the name of and couldn't exactly show us where it was! So Dave! The couple he was with had been with United Mice, excellent and highly recommended. He had already seen some of Bolivia and was now cruising through Peru. He was fascinated to hear about our adventures and felt we had had the true experience up in Northern Peru. He then told us he had bumped into Jonathan and Sarah the day before and had had breakfast with them. I was delighted to hear they were there too and gob smacked if we managed to see them too. However, I decided to tell Dave where we were staying and to pass it onto Jonathan and Sarah if he saw them again. We left Dave and went back to the hostel to rest.

Simon

The Inca Trail to Machu Picchu
10th to 13th July 1997

Yes, the day had arrived: the first day of the Inca Trail. Surely the biggest tourist attraction in South America. The Inca Trail to Machu Picchu is what everyone talks about. Why? There is a certain mystical appeal about it. An ancient trail, still in use to a lost city whose use nobody knows. Whatever their reasons, it has a huge appeal to a great many people. Touristy it might be but not spoiled none the less. I'll come back to this point.

The first day includes a cold shower at 5.00 a.m. followed by a pick up from the bus to the hostel at 5.30 a.m. We met the rest of our group of fourteen. They seemed like a good bunch and our guide appeared to be switched on.

For me, the first day and supposedly the easiest, was not

easy at all. It was my first experience of carrying a heavy backpack over a long distance in tough terrain. I found the first night in the tent cold. At 2,800m, I was worried by this as the next day we were due to camp at 3,950m!

The second day is supposedly the longest. It involves a climb to a pass at 4,200m then down and up to a pass at 4,000m where we camp. I paid a porter £5 to carry the backpack up to the first pass and it was money well spent. At lunchtime, I had a cold-water shower in the open. It was cold but hey, how often do you get the chance to shower in such amazing surroundings? The evening saw the arrival of the dreaded camp at 4,000m. Like everyone said it was freezing—minus three degrees to be exact. We sat huddled in a group playing games that I couldn't get the hang of just to keep warm. We went to bed early. Funnily enough, I was warmer that night than the previous night. The secret? Two pairs of socks and to make full use of the draw string around the hood of the sleeping bag.

The third day was hugely enjoyable. There was flatter than the previous day and the scenery was stupendous. I found the final stretch downhill to our camp site very hard though. Those Incas loved steep steps.

Well what can I say about the fourth day? We set off before sunrise to see the sun rise on Machu Picchu. Our first sight of Machu Picchu was quite emotional. Without words, we both knew what the other was thinking. We were there, overlooking Machu Picchu. We were living a long-awaited dream. In our small scale of things, we had taken risks, saved, scrimped, worried, planned and dreamt, but now we were here. This was one element, albeit a significant element, of our trip and we loved it. Every moment. How many people can write a statement like that?

Machu Picchu is amazing. The postcards make it look so, but still can't do it complete justice. For me, the best view was after we had seen the ruins and had walked down to the valley floor. I remember looking up and seeing the terracing on one side of the ruins. A city in the sky, what more can I say?

The food on the trip was excellent. I couldn't believe that other people were not as keen as we were. We even had fresh vegetables, a first for us in Latin America. The cooks did a great job and so did the porters who carried it.

The variety of scenery on the hike is incredible. It ranges from woodland to semi desolate moorland to jungle. The mountains are incredible looking like huge stalagmites sprung themselves through the Earth's crust. They don't look real, but the beauty is real enough. It was here that we had our first experience of jungle. I couldn't believe the variety of plant life and the range of colours. In the valley after Machu Picchu itself, we saw parrots flying overhead.

We were lucky with the group we had. Most groups totalled between twenty to over thirty. We had fourteen originally, but it dropped down to twelve after the first day. We got on with most people in the group.

I found the history of the Incas the most interesting part of the hike. There were ruins all along the trial. Inca service stations, post offices, messenger points, small towns etc. I'm convinced there are more to be found that are hidden by the jungle. The Incas built the trails for trade and for communication links. It was possible for them to transmit messages from Qosqo to Lima in two days by stationing messengers every seven miles. They would run for seven miles and pass the message onto the next person. Today it takes forty hours from Lima to Qosqo by bus.

They built their buildings with walls facing inwards. Was this merely the fashion or was it to protect them from the many earthquakes the area still suffers today?

They built their cities in the sky so they could be nearer the spirits of the mountains. Their towns and cities were brilliantly situated for trade, religious festivals and security.

The Incas remind me of the Borg in Star Trek. They assimilated other cultures. Resistance really was futile as they always seemed to win. However, they were very pragmatic in everything they did. They would take the best parts of the cultures they assimilated, learn from them, and incorporate them where appropriate and beneficial. The leaders of the people they assimilated were given powerful posts in the new society, a superb method of preventing rebellion.

They ran the economy by statistics. They knew exactly how much produce was needed, and they produced accordingly. The common man gave up certain freedoms in return for a guaranteed income. All this and more we learnt from Mairo, our guide. He was superb. It was obvious he was totally enthralled by the whole subject. He said that the name "Inca" is a misnomer. The leader of the society was the Inca, but the people he led were the Quechas. Today, the people around the Qosqo area consider themselves to be first and foremost Quecha and Peruano second. They speak Quecha and many cannot speak Spanish.

Mairo told us about spirits, good and bad, he had encountered on the trail and it was obvious to him it was true. He told us that one of the teachers told him that there was a reason that people from all over the world flock to Machu Picchu. People see it as the place to go to in Latin America. Non-hikers pay good money to hike for four days to the city. Why? Because they had been there before in another life.

Could it really be that behind the tourist gloss of Machu Picchu, something else is shining beneath the surface, pulling the strings, drawing people to its web?

Moving on, the city itself is every bit as good as the hype suggests. The only down side for us was that Mairo was not our guide to the city itself. We had Francisco who was nowhere near as inspiring. Perhaps the city was using its secret defensive mechanism to prevent us from discovering too much about it. Who knows?

We finished the trip by hiking down to the village of Aguas Calientes where we washed and bathed in the hot thermal baths there. After we caught our first train in Latin America to the village of Ollantaytombo, the word chaos springs to mind. We had seats, we lost them; we stood, we sat on the floor. The carriage was packed, not only with locals and tourists, but with people selling things as well. An experience, but three hours of it was enough and so ended our Inca Trial experience.

Rebecca

The Inca Trail—Macchu Picchu
10th to 13th July 1997

Simon recovered remarkably from his two-day illness and we did indeed book to do the Inca Trail with United Mice. We were devastated that Sarah and Jonathan were not able to join us but when we went to book it we met another nice Aussie couple and with a number of about 14 of us and a guaranteed English speaking guide we were so looking forward to it.

It was strange and quite sad to say goodbye to Sarah and Jonathan for the last time but we swapped addresses and we said we would write and let them know all about the trail. Before we left, they were discussing using the money they got back on a helicopter ride to Macchu Picchu. This was going to cost them $160 one way instead of $150 for 4 days and 3 nights trekking. They were going to see it before us!

Anyway, the following day (11 July) we got picked up at 5.30 a.m. from our hostel and piled into a minibus which took us to the start of the trek for about 10.30 a.m. We had packed Simon's rucksack for both of us to try and save on weight but it really was quite heavy! Part of the weight were our warmer coats we had been advised to take as it gets very cold at night in the mountains.

The whole four days was magical, touching, exhilarating and a true experience. The walking was extremely varied over high mountain passes, through forested jungle, down steep Inca steps and gentle slopes. The second day was the hardest for walking due to us ascending from 2600m to over 4000m but we all made it—somewhat exhausted. One of the hardest things is the altitude where you get breathless quite quickly. You have to take it slowly and steadily. The third days walking was my favourite due to the variety of paths we walked along and of course the scenery—this was immense and nothing like I had seen before. Huge mountains coming out of the earth and soaring to the sky, some farmland, some jungle, some snow-capped. When it is constantly around you, above, below and as far as the eye can see, it feels amazing!

Our whole group was excellent starting at 14 people and reducing to 12 after the first day, as an American became ill and she and her brother went back. It was such a shame for him as he was a true climber, had been in South America for over a year and was so looking forward to it. The rest of the group consisted of ourselves, 3 Aussies, 3 Danish people, 2

Swiss and 2 American girls. We all got along really well and thoroughly enjoyed finding out about each other with the one thing we had in common—travelling. The evenings were spent huddling together to keep warm and telling stories of our recent adventures.

Our guide was a Peruano bloke called Mauru—his English was excellent and he was a real treat for the four days. He was very clear on basic instructions about where we were going, for how long and what we should or shouldn't do—he brought the whole trip to life. He told us lots of stories and taught us a lot about the Inca people and their way of life with excellent descriptions and theories of all the ruins that we came across over the four days.

United Mice provided all the tenting equipment and 9 meals, carried by about four porters for the whole trail. The porters would ensure they were well ahead of us so that everything was ready for when we arrived for either lunch or the campsite in the evening. The food was excellent, as good as any restaurant and plenty of it. Breakfasts were bread, jam, pancakes, porridge, coffee, tea, chocolate. Lunches were home-made soup and then usually hot pasta, fresh veg, salads, tea, coffee and fruit. Dinners were a range of trout, roast chicken, pasta with veg and home-made soups to start. They also gave us hot toddies each night to ward off the cold!

The second night was freezing, camping at 3950m but the other nights were not too bad. We ended up sleeping in our clothes to keep warm. Showers were out of the question but a good wash in cold water was always available and I am now a dab hand at toileting outdoors!! Toilet paper is an essential item for a western traveller, wherever you go. Even if you find a toilet here it may not flush and it probably won't have a seat.

On the last day we had to be up at 4am, as we were due to

see the sunrise over Macchu Picchu—'The Lost City'. When the Spaniards invaded and decided to destroy everything the Incas built and believed in, they never actually found Macchu Picchu, hence the excellent condition it is in. We arrived at the 'Sungate' overlooking Macchu Picchu at about 7 a.m. and there it was below us. This old city perched on the top of a mountain. The Incas worshipped the mountains, the sun and the moon hence the reason why a lot of the towns and cities are built so high up.

Both Simon and I felt quite emotional, having arrived at a point in our trip that we had dreamt about and had strived for over the last few days. We always knew it could be a highlight of our trip which we never imagined coming true and there we were in South America on the top of a mountain looking down at a beautiful Inca ruin. It was truly breath-taking and a moment neither of us would ever forget. The trek had been hard and trying but we had made it!

We spent until about lunchtime looking all around the ruins and taking in the atmosphere. We then made our way down to a small town at the bottom of the mountain called 'Aquas Clientes' meaning hot waters. It houses thermal baths, which of course by then we were dying for. We were dirty, sticky, smelly and very tired, so a hot soak was perfect in the open air.

Simon

Ollantaytambo. The Scared Valley
13th July 1997 to 16th July 1997

As time has progressed, Rebecca and I have been keener and keener to stay in towns outside the main tourist areas or main towns. Following this train of thought, we disembarked from the train from Machu Picchu at the village of Ollantaytambo. It is beautifully situated in the picturesque Urubamba valley. Waking up on our first morning there (it was night when we arrived), I lay in bed looking out of the window at the amazing mountains which surrounded and dwarfed the town.

We had two great days there exploring and relaxing after the Inca Trail. There are spectacular ruins on the edge of the town and Inca terracing in the valley behind. In terms of scale, they can't be much smaller or less impressive than Machu Picchu itself.

It was great to be alone again after the intense group experience of the Inca Trial.

Simon

Qosqo and The Scared Valley.
17th July 1997

After two days at Ollantaytambo, I was ready to face the chaos of Qosqo once more. Ready to face the chaos from a distance perhaps, but certainly not ready enough to partake in it.

Having had a sneaking suspicion that that would be our state of mind, we had cunningly arranged for a couple of the people we met on the Inca Trial (Mark and Julie—Aussies) to purchase our train tickets to Puno. To do anything in Peru involves time, hassle and frustration. To buy a train ticket in the height of holiday season is sheer hell.

We planned, therefore a relaxing hassle-free day, involving the consumption of nothing more than good food, strong coffee and a healthy quantity of alcohol.

Our plans soon resembled something like an Inca ruin when Rebecca met up with Mark and Julie and they told us they hadn't bought our tickets. They needed our passport numbers and didn't have them. The ensuing frustrations of the Qosqo rail terminal ticket office completely shattered our dreams of a hassle-free day. We queued for an hour despite being fourth in the line. Don't ask me why.

Frustrations aside, the rest of the day was superb. We drank our coffee, wrote our postcards and even watched a film (Carlito's Way) at a video bar. We spent the evening at Mancunian birdwatcher Barry Walker's Cross Keys pub and then ate vast quantities of food from a street seller. For the first time since travelling, I was well and truly pissed. We even met up with Mark and he agreed to buy our car when he arrives in England in a months' time. If that pays off, it will be the first drunken pub plan that I've had the pleasure to be involved in. We could certainly do with the cash right now.

Simon

Puno—Lake Titicaca.
18th July 1997

We spent the day travelling by train from Qosqo to Puno. In summary a fantastic ride across the Andes with views of mountains, llamas and empty space. We sat opposite a strange man who had steel bars in his ears. This may explain the perpetual look of anger on his face. If I'd had one too many and my mates had done that to me in my drunken stupor, I would probably have had an attitude like his. Maybe not.

We had the pleasure of spending the night in Puno.

Rebecca

Copacabana, Bolivia.
6.25 p.m. 20th July 1997

I am so behind on this diary it's frightening so I shall start here and work back.

On Friday, we set off from Qosqo at 8 a.m. to arrive in Puno by about 7 p.m. Sarah and Jonathan had done the trip by bus and hated it so we had decided to invest in a train ticket. Buying it was fun, queued for half an hour the day before amidst other European travellers and stroppy Peruanos. We did worry that not having passports with us could cause problems, but as usual they only wanted a name and a passport number that was never checked. The same day was our "veg" day in Qosqo, a day of recuperation and somewhat luxurious. We hadn't anticipated having to buy our tickets as we had hoped Mark and Julie would have been able to do this for us. We arrived at their hostel at about 9 a.m. having showered and breakfasted on banana, bread and cheese empanadas! It turned out they had a change of plan and were now going to fly to La Paz on a cheap $55 flight excluding airport tax which turned out to be $25 each! What a rip off! Anyway, they also didn't have our passport numbers or last names so they had been unable to do the deed.

I wasn't feeling on top form as a cold was forming, but determined to relax and take it easy we headed for purchasing a torch from a lady who was more intent on chatting to her male friend than sell anything from her shop! We then made our way across Qosqo Plaza de Armas to a great cafe that allowed us to sit and sip coffee whilst reading or writing. We felt like rich travellers for the day, but so relaxed. By now, it was lunch time and we decided that our main meal that day would be "Almuzero". Having had my eye on a vegetarian restaurant called "Naturalia" for a little while up "gringo" alley, we enquired about a set meal and found one for five sols. The place was down a small alley and seats were under a canopy in the open. Both tables and chairs were made of chunky tree pieces and we sat on our own and had a delicious meal. "Quinua" soup to start with fresh parmesan cheese and then pumpkin and spring onion omelette with rice and salad. We then had a strange jam/sauce dessert with some lumps of fruit and a strange dark red juice to drink. It was exactly what we wanted: a great meal to say goodbye to Peru!

All our clothes were being washed back at our hostel so we decided to go back and try and put on our trousers as walking around Qosqo wasn't too conducive to shorts! However, they weren't quite ready but I persuaded them to part with damp trousers knowing how good they are at drying when on! We then headed to a small cafe/video bar where you can choose a film out of about 350 films to watch all on your own. We chose "Carlito's Way" and sat in front of a big screen TV, in big chairs, in the dark eating free popcorn! It was great just to sit and mindlessly watch a rather good film starring Al Pacino. Coming out was a strain in the bright light of day. We felt as if we had been wakened from a dream. Back to the cafe heading for the "Cross Keys Pub" at opening time 6 p.m.! By this time, my throat was so dry and sore, but I was determined to have our planned couple of drinks; it was happy hour and Mark and Julie said they would probably meet us for a drink.

Such a cool pub in South America, we felt quite at home

drinking red wine, Pisco Sour & beer. Completely gorged out, but a great place for a drink and a chat overlooking the Plaza. Mark turned up and told Simon that Julie had turned sick, was in bed and please could we wait another twenty minutes until he had been to the Post office. True to his word, he came and was a real laugh, better company in many ways than with Julie. A friend he had met in Huaraz called Jono also turned up unexpectedly and what an intrigue he was! A twenty-one-year-old bleached-blonde snowboard instructor from France, he was travelling with his thirty-two-year-old girlfriend Steph, who apparently was acting a "bit weird". It turned out, she was feeling odd just meeting people in their early twenties and they weren't getting on. Jono was really concerned about it. They were going on the Inca Trail the following day and I am unsure how much he was really looking forward to it.

We were in the pub from six to nine and realised that really, we should try and find something to eat. The previous evening, we had found some wonderful street food up "gringo alley" that a restaurant owner was eating and persuaded us to try! It was fantastic, deep tried yuca and pastry balls filled with veg and an olive! It was served in a piece of paper with hot chilli sauce all over and it was yummy. Our descriptions of it tempted Mark and we headed back there in the hope she was a regular seller! She was and we stood on the pavement stuffing our faces with about five of her delights. She was as thrilled as us and so was Mark. He wished he had found it earlier and hoped to drag Julie out the next day to have some if she was feeling better! The woman also made some stuffed peppers that night that were spicy and yummy. After my fifth, I realised I had eaten too many and started to feel a bit queasy. A cold, alcohol and spicy food were catching up on me so we went back to the hostel and went to bed.

Friday, as I said earlier, was our train journey to Puno and my stomach really wasn't up to much. We bought fresh bread and on arriving at the train early we ate breakfast in our "pew like" seats! They were so hard and straight backed. The train was full but, having chosen the more expensive tourist class, we didn't have hordes of people all over us and the aisles like the train back from Aguas Calientes!

The journey was through some beautiful mountainous areas and past thermal waters reaching up as far as 4,000m in places. The whole time my stomach wasn't happy and I went through phases of nausea and diarrhoea. I got to know the train toilet very well and had some great views out of the toilet window! The guys opposite us didn't help. They were so weird and never said one word to us. One of them was Indian and the other I think from England with strange silver posts through his ears. He was so rude to his friend telling him he didn't know what he was talking about and choosing to talk at him all the time and not once showing any interest in his views. He used to go off for ages wandering around the train and getting off at every stop. He chose to have the set lunch on the train which was horrendously expensive and looked nothing much. Unfortunately, he only got two courses instead of about five and I expected him to have a stand-up row with the waitress but instead I think he altered the bill himself so he didn't have to pay the full 18.50 sols. It was a shame they weren't sitting in some seats a little distance from us as we noticed an older couple from England who looked really cool and from eavesdropping it sounded like they too were doing things on the cheap. It would have been good to chat to them but it wasn't to be!

We arrived at Juliaca at about 5.30 p.m. and we ummed and arred about getting off and getting a bus to Puno or waiting for the train to re-align itself, half to Arequipa and half to Puno. The guy opposite us spoke for the first time and said it had taken an hour coming. That was enough to help us decide and we promptly hopped off the train with our luggage and headed for a collectivo/kombi. Two American girls who we met at Qosqo, Melissa and Tessa, were also on our train and we persuaded them to come with us. They had done the wise thing and booked accommodation knowing that when a train arrives the place gets full. The bus was cheap and took about an hour.

Puno looked a real dump and we were glad we were only staying one night before getting a bus to Copacabana. The bus took us pretty centrally and on getting out the hassle started. We had chosen our hostel from the book and one of the guys touting for business had their card, we negotiated a good deal with bathroom and hopped on his bicycle taxi! He tried to persuade us to buy our bus tickets on the way, but our experience in Tacna had taught us to go alone so we refused. On arriving at the hostel that looked okay, they had no rooms except a four bed with bathroom and it was far more than we had negotiated! We left and decided to go alone! Another guy saw us wandering and offered us what we were looking for guaranteed! I know Simon wasn't keen, but it was dark, the guy seemed genuine and he was saying it was guaranteed. Not far to walk and he took us to a brand-new small hotel which turned out to be exactly what we were looking for, clean, a bed, hot shower and safe. Unfortunately, our original bicycle taxi man followed us and stood in our bedroom doorway demanding money for his taxi service. We were livid and no way were we paying for someone who guaranteed us a room and did not deliver. It was only fear of him getting his mates onto us that we reluctantly gave him one sol, but made it very clear we weren't happy!

Rebecca

Isla del Sol, Bolivia.
5.35 p.m. Mon 21st July 1997

We then headed out for something to eat and on the way booked our bus tickets to Copacabana for 8 a.m. the next morning and changed a bit more cash to tide us over until Bolivia. We found a great meal in an ordinary looking restaurant called "Restaurant Trujillo" for a decent four sols. Simon had lamb (grilled) as his main course and I had a delicious Chinese chicken noodle dish, really tasty with some crunchy veg and garlic-soaked chicken. There were a lot of touristy restaurants around the centre of Puno offering ridiculous prices for western foods, ours was typical and delicious. Puno was cold (as we expected) and we decided to head back and get a good night's sleep.

We caught the bus, no problem, the following day and spent some of our last sol coins on bread and empanadas for breakfast and our first shoe shine which wasn't spectacular! The bus was pretty busy but quite comfy for Peru and it even had a toilet at the back. Coming out of Puno, something went into the side of the bus causing some disruption/shouting and hassle as they just drove off! The views all along the lakeside were great and the bus journey went without hiccups. My stomach had stopped playing up and I was feeling much better.

We arrived at the border town of Yunguyo and stopped for

all to change a bit of cash for Bolivia. Bolivianos look like monopoly money and feel it too, plasticky coins and thick notes. Passport controls were hassle free being stamped out of Peru at one office then a short walk across the border passed women selling last minute sweets etc., to the Bolivian office. The amusing part was an Israelian bloke who had outstayed his welcome in Peru by about two days and was told he had to pay a $20 dollar fine. He was really unhappy about it, but what a twit to mess with Peruvian law! He could have been shot; instead, he had no choice and had to pay!

The Bolivian office had pictures all-around of politicians and their old president and as a token a picture of a topless woman! So typical of South America. We thought we had to change buses, but our bus was to take us all the way. All the way was only another twenty mins and at the entrance to the town, the bus stopped and we were all told we would have to pay three Boliviano to the policeman coming on the bus. Suspicious, everyone delved in their pocket as the man walked up the bus and took the money in exchange for a ticket. Also, at two-thirds up the bus he ran out of tickets and promptly left the bus satisfied he had enough money for lunch! The bus was in uproar and laughed out loud at this typical South American antic! Even the bus assistant said it was the crazy Bolivianos! The South American handbook actually outlined this activity and said it was to go towards the Sanctuary. Whatever that is. The Lonely Planet book said quite clearly it was money to line their pockets! We were fortunately near the back of the bus and therefore got away with it. Funny how people just pay it and don't question why or wherefore or even refuse!

Copacabana is described in the handbook as attractive but to be honest it is quite dreary in places. Although we had been recommended a hostel call "La Cupula" at $6 pp a night we decided Bolivia was a chance to really save some cash so we headed for a cheaper place called Emperador and was pleasantly surprised. Behind a huge white cathedral down a little alley, the hostel was around a courtyard: basic, clean, bright and very friendly helpful people. We had probably the only room with a window facing the lake. We even had a hat stand which amused Simon, and he promptly made good use of it!

Simon
(NB. It didn't amuse me. I used it and Rebecca fell about laughing saying, I quote, "It's just typical you!" What does that mean?)

Part Four
Chile
19 July – 14 August 1997

Time
by Pink Floyd

Down by the Lake

Simon

Bolivia, Copacabana and Isla de Sol, Lake Titicaca
19th July to 23 July 1997

The border crossing into Bolivia was relatively hassle free. For the first time (Royal Class to Lima apart) in Peru, we had a reasonably comfy bus, without chickens and people crammed in the aisles and without a boy being sick. Trust Peru to save the best till last.

Something did crash into the bus at out point, but the post-accident formalities, i.e. lots of shouting, were completed within a minute or two.

The Bolivian immigration office was professionally staffed by people in jeans and nude girlie calendars on the wall. They did have a picture of a president on the wall to make things seem more professional, but that president wasn't the current one. General Banzer is in power again now. He was in power in the 1970s when he killed and repressed lots of people. However, this time, he has promised to act within the law, so that's OK then.

Our destination was Copacabana, on the shores of Lake Titicaca. Our guidebook warned us about police charging tourists entry to the town illegally. Sure enough, a policeman did board our bus. The people at the front paid. However, halfway down the bus, he ran out of tickets. This meant half the bus didn't pay. Welcome to Bolivia.

Our guidebook described Copacabana as an attractive town. Goodness knows what other Bolivian towns are like. It's not to say the Copacabana is ugly just that it reflects the state of the Bolivian economy.

We had a good time at Copacabana. We have sat by the lake, explored the town, and hired a kayak. The best thing we have done is pay not a lot for living i.e. £3 a meal for both of us, three courses and £3.33 for accommodation. This is particularly important to me as I want month three to have an annual daily spend below our daily budget of £27.50. It is approaching month end. I feel like an accountant. I sound like my accountant friend Nick and I came travelling to find myself!

Moving on from Copacabana, Lake Titicaca looked beautiful. A huge inland sea of gorgeous blue. What has struck me is the lack of commercial exploitation here. Sure, the boat keepers want gringos' money and they cannot afford to eat the trout they catch but there are very few towns on the lake and hardly any boat traffic. It really is very tranquil.

Moving on from the Isla del Sol, Lake Titicaca is indescribable. We took a boat trip to the island of Inca legend. It was from here that the sun created the Inca dynasty. It is situated in a calm sea of deep blue, glass or light blue depending on the time of day. There are no waves on Lake Titicaca and the water is a clear as it can possibly be.

We got off the boat at the north end of the island and hiked steadily towards the south. The views were amazing. Picture a combination of the following and you may start to get near to what we experienced:

1) Amazing plant life.
2) Fascinating bird life.
3) Quiet villages.
4) The locals and their animals.
5) The huge inland sea of Lake Titicaca.
6) The rolling hills on the shore.
7) Secluded beaches.
8) Snow-capped Andean mountains in the distance.

Safe to say, we were gobsmacked.

We knew that we wanted to stay on the island. It has no running water or electricity, but that made it all the better as far as we were concerned. We even knew where we wanted to stay. The Casa Blanca in our book scored well. Some boys wanted to show us to a hostel, which they did, but we were adamant that we wanted to see the Casa Blanca. The boys did show us to a Casa Blanca, and in hindsight, called very softly for someone to come to the door. Nobody did and we went back to their preferred choice. The hostel has been great for us, but we have subsequently on our travels seen the Casa Blanca.

On the island, we have felt like we have been in paradise. It has no roads and wherever you go the views are amazing. We have seen beautiful sunsets. Last night, we saw a full moon shimmering on the lake, lighting up the hills in the background.

Today, we got up to see the sunrise. The sun came up over the snow-capped distant mountains, lighting up the sky with a variety of colours, purple, orange and red. It was one of those beautiful moments; one I will not forget in a long, long time.

It sounds sentimental and American soap opera-esque, but Rebecca and I have talked about deep and meaningful things.

What is important to us is how we want to live and how we are going to achieve it. Rebecca is bound to correct me on this, but basically it is important to try and live the values that you believe in; for us, a happy life can only result by a combination of hard work and luck. We think it is important to continually question if things are going in the right direction and to always try and view things from the other person view point.

At the moment, we know that our ambitions are to be happy and fulfilled. We think a small village life would be great to try. We believe life outside work is important but also it is crucially important to enjoy what we do. The main question missing an answer is what to do at work? Perhaps investing in writing a book is worth a go. It would be a gamble, but it might pay off. We shall see, but this missing answer does trouble me, if only occasionally.

On our final night on the island, we sat and chatted to another couple named Santiago and Anne. He is Argentinian, she is Swedish. They are lively people full of life, interest and a love of nature.

We talked a lot about Argentina and he shed some light on some of the history we read about, such as the 20,000% inflation.

Today (23/7/97), we planned to catch the 10.30 a.m. boat back to Copacabana. We originally wanted to charter a boat from the island to the nearby village of Yampupata. From there, it would be a fifteen kilometre walk back to Copacabana. I really want to do this as I now have a bit of a thing about mind blowing walks from one point to another. I have the Inca trail to blame for this.

I wasn't very happy when we were told that the first charterable boat back would be in the afternoon, leaving us no time to complete the walk back in daylight. So we waited for our 10.30 a.m. boat. We went to get it, but stumbled upon a boat just leaving for Yampupata. We agreed a price of ten bolivianos "por los dos" (which means, for the two of us) only for the two people already in the boat to kick up a stink with the boatman.

We merrily clambered in, not quite believing our luck only to find out that the two passengers had chartered the boat for twenty-five bolivianos. They didn't seem as particularly overwhelmed at our luck as we were. They thought we were paying ten bolivianos each. We didn't say a lot, but justice was done. They were the same people who had kept Rebecca waiting in the freezing cold for her shower. I've always said this, but don't mess with Rebecca; she will always win in the end.

The walk back to Copacabana was excellent but long. It took four-and-a-half-hours. We have been back three hours now and I'm nicely knackered. It's been a superb, few days and we have both loved it. Roll on La Paz tomorrow.

Rebecca

Copacabana, Bolivia
6.20 p.m. Wed. 23rd July 1997

Our first day here we had a wander around, specifically by the lake where boats and canoes are lined up for rental and small cafe huts with chairs outside manned by the local Bolivian women. Warm sunshine, but cool air we headed around the lake and found a quiet spot on the beach for a read and a snooze. "Far From The Madding Crowd" has proved superb, so much so I can't put it down! Simon has also been reading "A Tale of Two Cities" with avid attention!

Lake Titicaca is huge and such a deep blue and sitting by it was so peaceful and relaxing. As the sun faded, we headed back and sat with a bottle of coke by the beach watching the world go by. You can even hire little motorbikes here, much to the delight of foreign men! We were still trying to weigh up how much cheaper Bolivia was going to be and that evening we ate a meal (two courses and coffee) for £2! It was in a restaurant called "Snack 6 de Agosto" which was recommended in the South American handbook. The following day, we realised there was another one down the road with a similar name; we had gone to the wrong one! The meal was very good, highly amused by three western girls one of whom demanded more chips than rice, a tomato salad and a glass of wine. Didn't she realise she was in a Bolivian cafe, not an English restaurant?!

Sunday, we did Copacabana as much as possible; we were both feeling under the weather with colds and coughs, but we really enjoyed an hour on the lake in a kayak. We both got soaked, but it was really peaceful and the water so clear. We walked up one of the hills overlooking the town where there are a series of crosses. I didn't quite make it to the top as my chest got the better of me so I perched myself on a rock and sat looking out over Lake Titicaca and the islands beyond. Simon ventured to the top and was amazed at the families who went to pray at each cross in turn!

Off our food a little, we had rubbish for lunch and then went to look inside the cathedral which dominates the town. A strange huge and beautiful building, mainly white with coloured small tiles forming patterns on the towers. It also houses a convent and a beautiful cloister. Nuns in their brown outfits wandered all around and there was a kiosk to buy holy water. The cathedral itself wasn't as big as we expected, but had loads of religious paintings all around and behind the altar. Outside the cathedral, women sit and sell all sizes of candles to take inside and light. We actually purchased some ready for the Isla de Sol, knowing there would be no electricity and organised tickets, food and our bags for the proposed next couple of days.

That evening, we ate at the right recommended restaurant which was better. We sat next to a Dutch couple we had met in Qosqo when buying our train tickets to Puno. We said an enthusiastic 'hello' and received blank greetings back with obvious no recollections of who we were. We ascertained they obviously were not people-oriented people like we aspire to be and as they were deep in Dutch conversations with another couple, we allowed them some peace! Similar to Peru, the set meals are soup and then meat, rice, chops and salad and then coffee.

The next morning, we were up early for our breakfast we had arranged for 7.15 a.m. (it arrived at 7.45 a.m.!) and a shower. This came later than expected as, coming out of our room, I bumped into a Belgian woman who wanted to know where the shower was. Being kind hearted, I allowed her to go first but made it quite clear there was only one. I waited a good ten mins! God knows what she was doing, but she obviously didn't care I was waiting and there was only one shower! Breakfast was good, bread, butter, jam, coffee and the fried eggs never appeared as the gas was playing up! We got the minibus outside the hostel on time and they placed our two "Mochillas" (rucksacks) on the top of the van, with no ropes to strap them down. We then bumped and swerved all the way down to the lakeside expecting to see our bags flying off the top!

The boat was busy and we managed to sit on the roof hoping the sun would be strong enough to keep us warm. It was a beautiful scene at that time of day; the lake looked like a mill pond and the islands looking as if they had been placed on the water very carefully. The two-hour boat ride was great and we arrived at the north end of the Isla del Sol at about 10.30 a.m. A lot of people were doing a day tour that took them to Isla de la Luna and the south of Isla del Sol. Hardly time to see it all properly. Anyway, our plan was to be there a couple of days in the hope it was a beautiful place. It was magnificent.

We set off for the south of the island and for most of the way we saw the lake and the snow-capped mountains in the distance near La Paz. From above the lake was magnificent and the walk took us through small villages, up over hills and down onto deserted white sandy beaches. It was paradise and the walk was perfect. By 3 p.m., we were outside a hostel that two boys had taken us to. It was high on the hill with the lake either side—what a view. We had tried to find a local recommended hostel, but the boys didn't take us to the right place; anyway, this hostel we stayed at was cheaper for us because the landlord knew we were looking elsewhere. They would also provide a meal in the evening for us so we were happy. We drank a bottle of his coke out on his veranda and then decided to find the "Fuente del Inca", Inca steps and water spring. About twenty mins walk from the hostel and a busy place on the island as it was the landing stage in the south for boats. We decided not to venture all the way down but instead perch ourselves on a small ledge overlooking the bay and the coming and goings. It was also a lovely spot to read some more of our great books. The boat that we had taken that morning came, and went with the "tour people" that included the older couple we had seen on the train to Puno!

Although Isla de Sol has not become a commercial/tourist island the locals are certainly aware of what they could get from "gringos". Children pester you for food/sweets and money to take photos of themselves in traditional dress and their Llamas! It can get quite annoying and firm "no's" have to be used if you want a quiet time. Children also seem to be used to entice you to the local hostels and I am sure they are paid a bit by the landlords if successful. It is sad but a way of life for them and a way to get a bit of extra money. We have been told that Bolivia isn't bad for being pestered so we will see if it continues or gets better.

By the time we got back to the hostel, having been the only ones staying there, we were suddenly inundated with loads of other people. In fact, for dinner, there turned out to be thirteen people, so much so that the owners had to get another table and more chairs to cater! Whilst standing on the roof watching the sun go down, the final couple arrived, an Argentinian called Santiago and "his girlfriend" Anne from Sweden. They too watched the sunset, took photos and wanted to know what we were doing, were we had been etc. It turned out they met whilst travelling around Australia and Fiji and hadn't seen each other for eight months! They were now in Bolivia and Argentina for about three weeks. She works in media and communications in Stockholm and he is a guide for tours around Salta, at present, although he is used to doing tours in South Argentina. He described where he came from as being near the Falkland Islands, how cool is that! They were a great couple who seemed to see eye to eye with us. Their beliefs on travelling were similar to ours, having a need to see the real countries, people, surroundings and food in as none touristy a way as possible. Santiago loved bird-watching and would go off for walks on his own to look around the island. Anne was feeling a bit rough, possibly altitude sickness, and stayed in bed most of yesterday. However, we had a couple of meals with them and thoroughly enjoyed their company. We even got chatting about our work which was a novelty as we haven't talked about it for weeks and it is over three months since we were there. It was fascinating talking to Santiago about Argentina and we all know "El Bolson" as Anne had also stayed there last October. We felt quite sorry for them being so far apart and obviously very fond of each other. It was difficult to see how it would work out for them, but Santiago was determined to continue travelling, possibly get into writing and photography more. Maybe he would be happy to see Europe or maybe Anne would be happy to travel with him! Strange to think we pass these people like ships in the night and we may never know the ending of their story.

With no electricity, our candles and new torch were invaluable and the new coke bottle became a great candle holder. Knowing there is no choice about having electricity you adapt very quickly. Over dinner, the owners had gas lights in each room, just enough to see what we were eating. Soup to start and then fried fish, chips, rice and salad. Very nice too considering they had two gas rings to cook on, a small kitchen in candlelight and thirteen people to cook for. Local men came in to help serve us all. The four of us grabbed the table for four by the entrance and all the others sat huddled in a separate room around a long table. We were extremely animated and next door were dead quiet. There were about six people I recognised from around Copacabana, some had eaten at the same restaurant the night before. They ate in silence and got up in silence! We just talked and laughed!

The moon was beautiful, pitch black skies with a full bright moon lighting up the lake and causing great shadows. Simon was ecstatic for at last there was a chance to use the bulb function on the camera. This is for night shots where a normal flash is not enough and you can expose the film for a longer period of time, allowing more light in to be able to take photos at night. We decided I perhaps had a steady hand having tried to find somewhere suitable to perch the camera. I pressed the button and counted to twenty-five hoping it would be enough. Goodness knows whether it will come out; hopefully, it will. We won't forget the scene though "Moonlight over the Island la Luna!"

Yesterday, we treated ourselves to breakfast and on asking for the continental breakfast with egg he said he would be a couple of minutes as he had to go and buy the eggs! Superb! Good breakfast of rolls, butter and delicious apricot jam. I have certainly changed my taste buds round, when it comes to jam; I really like it now and having had so many breakfasts of our own with just plain bread it tastes really good.

Another glorious sunny day (but cold wind), we decided to explore the island a bit more and set off full of breakfast, a pack of fruit, rolls, cheese and chocolate and our books and diary to look forward to. The views had not changed and were as spectacular as ever as we weaved our way north on small paths by housing and fields. We got down into a cave and found ourselves by the lake and rocks sitting reading our books in the sun whilst some locals sorted out their boats, fishing and produce. Again, so peaceful!

We then walked further north to a beautiful coastal bit we had seen the day before; this time, we sat in the shade under rocks and had our lunch looking out onto deep blue clear waters and white sand. Paradise!

We talked about all sorts of things and decided that we may invest in some good, light camping equipment for the rest of our trip. We agreed that over the last two months there had been occasions when we could have used it and felt we could have seen the countryside a bit more. We agreed to look into it in New Zealand or even La Paz as it could be cheaper. A potential hefty investment, but one we could plan for and ensure we used it to make it pay, as well as it giving us the choice in the future, which at present we don't have.

Last night, we decided to see the sunset from the hill above the hostel and having read a little in the sun on the roof we donned all our layers (as it was so cold!) and trooped up to see it. Santiago and Anne were already there and we were just in time to see the sun settle behind broken clouds. It gave off a beautiful deep pink at the sides and lit up the clouds at the front leaving great rays of sunshine like the ones we had seen at sunrise. This we planned to do and set the alarm for 6.30 a.m. to ensure we got up and witnessed it. It was magnificent as the sun came over the snow peaked mountains. We are hoping those photos will also come out!

Another full house for eating but to our surprise not all staying there. Maybe they were staying somewhere that couldn't offer food, but there was a whole group of Spanish speaking people and we four were quite happy to be anti-social again and revel in our own company. A strange meal followed the soup, chops, egg, fried cheese, rice and fried pieces of banana with tomato! For some reason, I had no rice and two eggs with the rest which to Simon's amusement meant I must have looked like a "chips and egg!" person.

They were cold nights and with hardly any lighting after dinner there wasn't much to do except go to bed, so a couple of early nights were in order.

This morning, we agreed to eat our own food for breakfast and save a few pennies for the trout we had planned as a treat for dinner. We were down at the landing stage by 9.40 a.m. eating our rolls and bananas and watching others turn up for the 10.30 boat back to Copacabana. We had originally planned getting a short crossing to Yampaputa and doing the fifteen kilometres lakeside walk back to Copacabana. We were told boats left at 1 p.m. so we abandoned the idea, disappointingly and planned to come back and do a short walk around the peninsular. Simon's explanations of the next events are quite adequate here so I won't re-write what happened. Safe to say, we have chuckled about the boat crossing all day and the fact that the couple (who are even staying here again!) still don't know what we really paid.

The walk was great with superb views again! It was longer and more up and down than we imagined and having set off at 10.30, we were sitting eating a plate of chips and drinking coke in a cafe at about three pm in Copacabana. They tasted so good, we were exhausted and starving.

The hostel owners, kind of recognised us as I told them how wonderful the Isla del Sol was. We half expected not to get a room at all and certainly did not expect us to get the same room back with the little hat stand! In the couple of days we were away, not only had the decorators painted part of the hostel deep pink they had changed our room number to 8 from

7!

The shower never felt so good and feeling refreshed, we went out to buy bus tickets to La Paz, post letters, and buy some bits. Simon had already booked our accommodation in La Paz which sounded great and said how popular it was: double the price of this place, but hopefully worth it. The bus tickets are actually the front seats of a minibus so goodness knows what the three-and-a-half-hour journey will be like!

The trout was delicious, as good as we expected in the popular gringo restaurant. It was grilled flat, filleted and served with chips, rice and salad. We washed it down with bubbly Bolivian beer and as we were leaving a group of girls came to take our table. Amongst them to my amazement was the stroppy Australian girl from Chonchi in Chile! I don't think she saw us, but she was the last person I expected to see again. Such a small world!

A Change of Plan

Simon

La Paz
24th to 25th July 1997

On our last night in Copacabana, we treated ourselves to trout. It was delicious. I say treated ourselves, but the whole meal (a massive portion of trout and beer) was just over £7. Heavens above! Up to now in Bolivia, our meals for both of us have been costing between £3 and £4. This is the beauty of the dilemma of travelling over an extended period of time on a budget. A trout meal all in for two people for £7 is an absolute give way. However, on a budget of £27.50 a day for both of us, the difference between £3 and £7 is a lot. It can take days of scrimping to stay under budget but just one bad day can blow two weeks scrimping.

The next day (24/7/97), I woke up regretting the trout meal. Sod the budgetary constraints, I was feeling very ill. We managed to brave the four-hour combi van journey to La Paz, but I don't know how. The journey involved climbing to even higher altitude on rough, mountain clinging roads. I had a headache, breathlessness and I was cream crackered. I couldn't sleep or shut my eyes, even though I was so tired, for fear of vomiting. It was like I was drunk. It was like I had soroche.

I had soroche and I collapsed in a heap on the hostel bed in La Paz. The most I saw of La Paz on my first day there was the hostel room and Rebecca. Once again Rebecca was great; she looked after me through my suffering. Does this all sound familiar?

The one bonus of my having soroche was that I had a great night's sleep and woke up the next day feeling full of energy and life. I needed it as our day in La Paz turned out to be mentally and physically shattering.

Why? Well basically, we realised we only had three weeks left in Bolivia and indeed in South America. We realised that we had less time in Bolivia than we had for Chile and Peru. We had reserved many things we could have done in other countries for Bolivia for reasons of time and money. We realised that Bolivia had loads to do and see in its own right and was not just a cheaper place to do it than say Peru and Chile. On top of this, we realised we were still over budget, even though we had been scrimping like mad. Bolivia, like Peru before it, was supposed to be our financial saviour. Bolivia was supposed to stop us from writing a post card to the Abbey National from New Zealand.

Panic set in. We are skint. We can't be leaving South America already; we've only just arrived. We haven't seen anything yet. Help! Mummy!

We spent the day roaming around the streets of La Paz trying to discover our options and throwing ourselves into even deeper confusion in the process. When are the flights to Rurrenabaque? How much? How much will a second-hand tent cost 1) here and 2) in New Zealand? Is it cheaper to hire one? What will our bank accounts say, when they arrive in the post in New Zealand, after three and a half months without seeing them? Could we successfully haggle the price of a single fare down? And if so, how much more could we save if we just sat in the Yungas instead and starved ourselves to death? More importantly, when would our laundry be ready? What is the meaning of life?

I'm unclear as to the upshot of these ramblings of yesterday apart from the following. Firstly, I had a brain ache. Secondly, we walked a lot and, in the process, saw much of La Paz.

La Paz is the perfect place to be driven mad with confusion because La Paz is madness and confusion personified. In La Paz, you have traffic lights with policeman standing under them directing the traffic in tune with the colour of the lights. All shops shut for the entire weekend in La Paz. La Paz is the political, economic, bureaucratic, legal and political heartbeat of Bolivia. La Paz is not the capital. Sucre is the capital, despite being a tenth the size of Bolivia's largest city. La Paz is the first place in South America where we have had to play hunt the taxi.

Funnily enough, I loved La Paz. It is built in a hollow and is amazing at night. You can see the lights of all the buildings rising up all around the sides of the hollow. We didn't go out to see La Paz. La Paz came to see us. La Paz is a great place to be confused.

Simon

Sorata—The Yungas.
26th to 28th July 1997

We are here in Sorata, deep in the Yungas. It is very beautiful here. Our hostel is amazing as well. It is the former mansion of a German rubber baron. It is a huge, tumble down ram shackle place with a maze of courtyards and passage ways. The gardens are brimming with wild flowers of all colours and near our room a pet parrot sits proudly outside his cage. The house has huge old pieces of furniture and has the atmosphere of family home. Last night I even watched the film "K2" in front of a roaring fire.

On top of this, we discovered an excellent restaurant, *La Tarraza* which does a superb set meal for just over £1.

Moreover, the walking opportunities are superb. The area very much reminds me of the Colca Canyon in Peru. The huge mountain of Illampu towers over the town and the valleys deep below.

We have done two great day walks and would have stayed longer had we not been so pressed for time. Yesterday (27/7/97), we did a ten hour walk from the town to the sacred lake of Laguna Chillata, an overall climb from 2,700m to 4,200m. We hired a guide as it is a sacred lake and we didn't want to induce the wrath of the locals. It was very tough indeed but well worth the effort, with stupendous views.

Today, we got up late. It was beyond 11.00 a.m. which is pretty unheard of for us recently. I washed our clothes and even did Rebecca's knickers. I think I deserve a medal for that. Then it was off to the underground lake in the caves of San Pedro. The walk was once again fantastic with magnificent views along the valley.

The cave was as touristy as you would expect of a South American country. We paid our five bolivianos which gave us fifteen minutes' worth of lighting. The lights were powered by a petrol generator that had seen better days. The cave was long, dark and very warm. Our descent to the lake involved scrambling under ceilings of a height of about three to four foot.

Once at the lake, the lights went out for a few seconds. Pitch black, we couldn't see anything even with our torch. Bats screeched and flew about our ears. It was a really weird experience. I didn't fancy a swim and I didn't fancy getting stuck down there with the lights out. Back we went and just in time. The generator spluttered to a halt. I think it had run out of petrol. Just so typical South America.

Simon

La Paz
29th to 30th July 1997

Back to La Paz to book up a flight to Rurrenabaque to see the Amazon jungle. I had that sinking feeling when the desk clerk at Transporte Aero Militar told us that all flights were sold out for the next week. Our carefully to the second, meticulously detailed fool proof plans had been made a fool of. It wouldn't have been so bad but our carefully laid, to the second time, meticulously detailed plans take ages to correct. We didn't have ages left in Bolivia.

After much soul searching and heartache, we scrapped Rurrenabaque. The only other way of getting to Rurrenabaque would be a gruelling and lengthy route by bus. I refused to allow us to go downhill, valley side on the track they term Death Road. Reports vary between one lost vehicle from once a day to once every three weeks. Whatever, I didn't like the odds, especially when you bear in mind how little traffic there is on these roads.

With the money we saved on going to the jungle and all that that entailed financially, we bought a tent, a stove and full dinner service. Not only would this give us even more weight to lug around the world, but would give us the opportunity to undertake some of the great long-distance hikes the globe has to offer.

Simon

La Cumbre to Coroico. The Yungas
31st July 1997

We planned to start our first great hike with the three day "Choro" or "La Cumbre to Coroico". We had heard it was a spectacular walk. I had heard it was mostly downhill.

We spent the day before in La Paz meticulously buying super light-weight camping gear. That now meant no more room for the coats we bought in Chile and no room for the cups bought in Argentina. This we gave to two of the staff at the Hostal Austria. I've never seen two grown men so pleased. They wore the coats throughout the night. One of them, Manuel, ceased to try to sell us a carved piece of stone. He gave it to us saying it was Pachamama or mother earth. All in all, it was very moving and for me will be a better souvenir than any ring or chess set that we buy on our travels.

So, on the 31st of July, we set off early, and were dropped off at 8.30 a.m. at La Cumbre on the summit of the Yungas.

Rebecca

Coroico, Bolivia.
Sunday 3rd August 1997

So much has happened that I haven't had a minute to write the diary! (Would help if Bolivian pens worked!)

We arrived in La Paz from Copacabana a week last Thursday; goodness knows how we got there without Simon throwing up. Soroche had taken hold again and for three hours he looked and felt really rough as we wound around hills and mountains and even crossed the lake at one point by boat. We had chosen a minibus, instead of a normal bus and once it was full of passengers the driver set off. Our first sighting of La Paz (through the outskirts) was quite shocking. Simon's words were, "It looks like Lebanon in the war!" not threatening just run down and people everywhere selling anything they could on the streets. We then rounded a corner and got our first sighting of the city from above, it was incredible. To the right of us this basin of buildings, quite a few high rises which surprised us as no other city so far had had such monstrosities. The bus took us into the heart of some market street where we expected to be bombarded by taxi drivers and hostel owners, but no such thing. This was Bolivia, we had heard it wasn't as pushy and the one day we desperately needed a taxi to get us quickly to a hostel and Simon to bed there were none around. It took us at least ten minutes to flag one down and he seemed reluctant to take us to Hostal Austria, which sounded good in the book. Calle Yanacoche is in the heart of La Paz, built on a hill. Lots of rooms which were quite clinical looking, cooking facilities, showers, TV, lounge area and a very friendly owner called Manuel. Simon's reservation paid off and he was in bed within minutes. Manuel decided he should have some coca tea and promptly shuffled me into the kitchen and gave me two steaming mugs of coca tea, delicious! It was just what we both needed and helped Simon who spent the rest of that day in bed (from about 3 p.m.). I went out on my own into big bad La Paz and felt extremely safe. I only went round the corner to buy two hot cheese empanadas and two doughnuts, in the hope that Simon might fancy one or other of them. I then spent about two hours writing the diary and reading up on La Paz in the lounge area. A German bloke and his dad came in to play chess, the cleaner was listening to her small radio and watching TV and people came and went. An English bloke called Martin, whom I had seen earlier, came and sat at my table and we got chatting. Having left an engineering job in Manchester and about to start a design course in September, he wanted to see South America before then. He had only been away a week and couldn't remember much news from England which was a little disappointing. He talked about going to do the La Cumbre to Coroico walk which at that point was still an option for us, although what we would do about equipment was another matter. That evening, I needed to eat reasonably decently even if Simon wasn't really up to it so I set off in search of a cheap little restaurant where I could hide away, eat some food and read my book. They all looked a bit seedy for a girl on her own. I ended up in a hamburger bar eating cheeseburger and chips! It tasted really good and walking back along the pedestrianised street round the corner from the hostel I spied all the night street sellers setting up! Amazing things you can buy at such hours! I munched a peanut nutty bar and made my way back to Simon's amazement at such speed!

The following day, Simon's health was back to normal and he had enough energy to see him through what was a gruelling day.

We headed off to Aerolineas Argentinas in the hope of changing one or other of our flights to avoid a huge amount of time in Buenos Aires. This was not possible as there was only one flight from La Pas to Buenos Aires each day and this one was the only one we could get in time. Never mind, we confirmed them both and resigned ourselves to spend hours in Buenos Aires airport! What fun!

Simon

La Combre to Coroico Walk, The Yungas
31st July (Cont...) to 2nd August

I've done some silly things in my time, but this felt by far the silliest. The air was thin, the wind was freezing, the scenery was one of desolation and as the bus pulled away it left us completely on our own with dead weights on our back. On top of this, we had to climb up through the snow line to cross the mountain pass.

We eventually did get to the top and the view was immense. We could see all around from the moonscape behind us to the view of the path to come.

The first day was hard but fair. The timings according to our instructions were reasonably accurate and we made good progress. The path was reasonably well used and we passed a number of Llama herders and their herds. We camped at the village of Achapalla Pampa. It was a beautiful campsite.

I personally found the next day very tough. I woke up tired and never quite recovered. The scenery, however, was like none I'd ever experienced before. Dense jungle as far as the eye could see, which was normally more than a few inches. Creepers crept into our hair, grass and plants clung to our ankles. The plant life was amazing and we saw all kinds of different plants at often uncomfortably close quarters. By the afternoon, I was feeling very tired, claustrophobic and frustrated at our apparent lack of progress. According to our book, we could have walked back to the UK on the second day. I knew the book was unrealistic in its expectations, but it didn't stop me from getting thoroughly pissed off. Rebecca was great though especially when our supposed campsite turned out to be a waterfall with as much spare land as Wimpey needed to build a home. We had to move on.

Eventually, we did get to a patch of free ground just before dark.

The next day, we made amazing progress. So much so that we reached our supposed campsite by 12.00 and the end of the walk by 3.30. A walk that was supposed to take four days, we completed in three just after we thought it would take five. The final day was beautiful.

Rebecca

Coroico, (Sol y Luna), Bolivia.
11.50 a.m. Mon 4th August 1997

I am sitting in a deck chair, on a veranda overlooking the Yungas, banana trees and other beautiful plants. The sun is shining, the rain clouds have been out and I have got some washing drying on the line! This is bliss! A well-earned rest!

Anyway, back to La Paz, having sorted our future flights we decided to look into the more immediate future and a trip to the jungle. A bus journey would be about twenty hours and we had been told the road was pretty treacherous. A flight to Rurrenabaque would be about double the cost of the bus and therefore worth investing in. The South America handbook said that the Bolivian airline LAB flew to Rurrenabaque, we waited in a queue for about twenty minutes to be told no they don't fly to Rurrenabaque, TAM do! Who the hell are they? Apparently, the military airline that flies about four times a week. The Tam office was the other side of La Paz, but we trudged our way over there and enquired. We could get a flight on Monday if we wished, but we still hadn't decided exactly what we were doing! Having sat down and worked out how many days we had left we realised we didn't have enough time to do everything before flying to New Zealand. We decided to go to Sorata for a few days, a beautiful place apparently, in the heart of the Yungas, with a few good walks to do. We would then go back to La Paz, book our flight and head off on a two-day trek to Tahesi, having bought or hired camping equipment. We could then go back to La Paz and our flight to the jungle before coming back to La Paz for our flight out to New Zealand! A hectic schedule but realistic, feasible and fitting in some essential Bolivian spots.

Hiring equipment was quite expensive (about £5–£10 a day) but we weren't convinced we would find cheap and good quality camping equipment in Bolivia so this probably wouldn't happen until New Zealand. Club Andino Boliviano was very helpful and they may have had some second-hand stuff to sell, but they would find out and leave a message at our Hostal. They never did! Another shop up Sagarnaga (the handicraft shop street), had a very nice gentleman who said he would take us through the walks if and when we wanted to hire his equipment. All the running around was exhausting and, in the evening, we were looking forward to a cena (set meal). Unfortunately, La Paz does not really do set meals for dinner as they tend to focus on cooking set lunches, called Alumerzo instead. We (again!) trudged around various recommended restaurants, and found relatively expensive food! In the end, we found a place selling half a portion (ample amount) of steak with a fried egg on top. It was delicious for £1 and we were happy. We vowed that day to eat cheap set lunches and the delicious looking street food in the evening which was always dirt cheap.

The next day, Saturday, we were up and on a bus to Sorata by 10 a.m. A taxi from the hostel to where the buses set off was quick and as soon as we stepped out of the taxi there was a bus and an assistant waving us onto the bus and herding our bags inside. Our first experience of a true Bolivian bus. All the locals were there donning hats and babies and rice sacks full of things. We sat right at the back with a good view all the way down and some great views outside. There was one other gringo on the bus, a German man (about forty) and very frustrated with the lack of leg room and the busy bus! He asked Simon at one point to shout out of the window at an ice-cream seller to get a couple of ice-creams for him. As with Peru when buses stop at prominent places, sellers show their goods and want you to buy through the windows. We have seen some strange looking brown drink in a plastic bag with a strange nut or piece of fruit at the bottom. All the locals drink it by biting a small hole into the bottom and sucking it out. Most of the time it spills everywhere, which was exactly what the woman next to me did! She also got her lunch box out at about 11.30 a.m. filled with spicy potato, rice and meat mixture, all eaten with her fingers! Not proud and so natural. Her money was tucked away in layers of clothing in a woollen small pouch. She kept getting it out and counting it up; obviously, afraid she would lose it.

The journey lasted five hours and was great. Always

fascinating watching who gets on and off. The views were spectacular starting outside La Paz, towards Lake Titicaca and then heading into the hills and taking mountain passes around the Yungas—luscious green hills and deep sided valleys and even snow-capped mountains.

Sorata is in a beautiful situation amongst the Yungas with a huge Plaza full of palm trees and banana trees—a sleepy town that tourists use as a base for walking, trekking, mountaineering and climbing. We headed for Residencial Sorata that sounded great and had been recommended. It was beautiful, a huge old German owned mansion that had been left as it was when the man from Quebec bought it. A beautiful tropical garden, pool (not filled) and courtyard with great rooms everywhere. We managed to get a room on the second patio which wasn't as spectacular, but cheaper and the view was immense! A sweet little room with a veranda and a shower/toilet downstairs. We had a bottle of coke, ate our lunch and then had a look around the place. There were loads of maps on the walls in the main big entrance room showing local walks/treks. We bumped into a local guide who takes groups and we chatted to him in his office across the street about walking to Laguna Chillata—a one day walk from about 2,600m to 4,200m taking you to a lake below the Illampu Mountain. As a sacred lake, you have to have a guide to take you. We decided to do it the following day and paid our guide money and agreed to be there at 7 a.m. the next day. We knew it would be tough but rewarding and we were both looking forward to it. We had a small look around Sorata and bought our food ready for the next day. In the evening we headed for a restaurant called La Terrazza which was recommended and looked good overlooking the main street. It was above the town's market which was a fascination in itself. Locals had fish, fresh, dried, whatever out on the floor and they were sitting amongst it trying to sell it. I had decided we needed to be brave when it comes to taking photos of such local scenes, and not be too concerned about what the locals might think. If they vehemently opposed it, I wouldn't do it, but taking a photo of Simon amongst it all couldn't be too bad and it wasn't. Anyway, La Terrazza proved a real find and we ended up eating there three times, each evening meal. Super food, all home-made and fresh and a choice of main course, usually pasta with/without meat (which was really tasty and garlicky) and then two nights it was fish and the third night a delicious veg omelette with yuca and salad. Instead of coffee/tea on the third night, the cena included a dessert which turned out to be a crème caramel! Really good stuff and all for £1! The soup starter was always excellent, served with infamous bread and hot/pepper sauce.

We were up with the larks the following day having organised breakfast at 6.30 a.m. Coming back from La Terrazza, we got chatting to a Dutch couple whom we had originally met in Qosqo when we bumped into Dave. Apparently, they had spent about five days with him! Anyway, they were only there for about two to three days and were keen to do a walk but unsure which one. We persuaded them to come with us the following morning and met them for breakfast too. Fresh orange juice, coffee, loads of bread and jam and a delicious pancake was on the menu: a really hearty feed for our walk.

Larissa and Jon were Dutch through and through, a very nice couple who have their opinions (pretty black and white) and like to stick to them, not bad English, friendly but slightly stand-offish (especially Larissa). Both had finished their jobs to travel for three months, but could go back to them if they wished and felt going for longer would be too far away from the realities of working and can be seen as escapism! They had just come back from Rurrenabaque and it was good to get some thoughts from them about the jungle and the Tampas trips, as well as a bottle of DEET that they had spare and we therefore bought!

Arriving in the office just after 7 a.m., we had another member of the party, an American guy called Jed from Colorado. Looked about forty-five he told us quite soon on he had dumped his life back in USA and had come to discover himself and find something new. What he had left behind exactly we never really got to the bottom of although, in the course of the day, he mentioned being in Paris at some point with his wife. I was intrigued and wondered whether he might have kids or some terrible things happening back home. He also mentioned looking for love out here so who knows...

Anyway, we all set off together with our guide who seemed fine at the beginning. The walk was very tough to say the least and of course mainly uphill, which is not my forte. The pace was quite fast and whilst everyone seemed to be able to hold conversations while climbing steep hills, I was trying to control my breathing and maintain a rhythm in my strides! The guide couldn't speak any English and didn't even seem to understand anybody's Spanish! He was pretty non-communicative and when asked questions seemed disinclined to answer. He didn't explain the route or tell us about any of the surroundings etc. He was just a local guy getting paid to show us the route. He was also quite keen to walk quickly and then stop periodically for ten mins at a time, but we all decided we preferred slower place and more frequent but shorter breaks. We explained this to him and he allowed us this luxury. Once above 3,000m, the altitude was obvious and nearing 4,000m made the going quite difficult. Larrisa started to struggle and about forty-five mins from the lake had to stop as she was feeling so rough. Going down to sea level for a few days had not helped coming back up and it was agreed that she would wait for us on the downhill track not far from where we were. Jon, however, came on with us as the guide said it wasn't much further. He was very vague all the way up about timings and distances, we realised later because he didn't have a clue, possibly due to lack of education more than anything else.

We continued to the lake but the steep inclines were really difficult and the stops more frequent. The views, however, were magnificent; ahead of us, the foreboding snow-capped Illampu Mountain and behind us the hills and valleys of the luscious Yungas. We couldn't see Sorata from such a distance. The sense of achievement at the lake was marvellous, both of us had found it very difficult and at times had wondered whether we would make it, but whatever lay ahead we had got to the top and we were delighted! The lake itself was quite small and nothing to show its sacredness, we just had to take their word for it.

Lunch never tasted so good and everyone seemed to share food around. Jed had brought a tin of tuna, a small packet of mayonnaise and tomatoes to make sandwiches. He allowed everyone to have some and Simon and I really enjoyed one between us. We had bread, bananas and chocolate and we all shared food with the guide as well, all part of the deal!

The walk could go further, but only Jed felt brave enough to face it and left the rest of us (except the guide) to go down and join Larissa. We watched Jed's figure go higher and higher and just as we reached Larissa, we heard the sound of his Qena (Kena), small recorder like, instrument. It was the same sound we heard from Mauro on the Inca Trail and it sounded beautiful.

The trail downhill was different to uphill and as with the way up I had the distinct impression that our guide was happy to take us on the shortest but most difficult and dangerous route! It was much harder than I expected or liked and as usual the downhill always takes longer than you think. I had quite an interesting discussion with Jed about believing in fate and he revealed quite a lot about his past disfigurement of his spine which with various healing and spiritual processes is now corrected, whereas at one time he could hardly walk. The need to find himself again was making more sense.

Near the end of the walk, Jed asked us all about tipping the guide and I made it quite clear everyone was welcome to do so, but I wouldn't partly because we had overpaid for him anyway and he did nothing for me to warrant a tip, unlike Mauro the Inca Trail. Jed felt he should as the guide had taken him further than us.

We arrived back in Sorata at about 6 p.m., relieved, tired but again with a sense of achievement. We had all got on quite well and on suggesting we all met for dinner we agreed to go to La Terrazza at about 7.15 p.m., in time to watch "K2" which they were showing that evening at our hostel.

A shower never felt so good and I had developed a slight headache which felt like hunger and exhaustion. All refreshed, we headed on down to the restaurant and although Larissa and Jon had enjoyed quite an expensive meal the night before everyone chose the Cena. The lady (who was a very good

South American waitress, seemed to be aware of service!) brought us a piece of the fish main course to try; good, but we all chose the spaghetti. A slight saga erupted when Jon had asked specifically for no cheese on his meal and of course they forgot and then tried to cover it up with more sauce. He said this trick happened all the time in South America and he eventually persuaded them to bring him a fresh plate of food with absolutely no cheese. It came.

By the time we had eaten our meal, I felt really tired and my headache hadn't gone away. I decided an early night was in order and I left Simon and the others to go and watch "K2". I really wanted to see the film, but my bed seemed more inviting and I didn't want to be suffering the next day.

I felt much better the following day, having had about fourteen hours in bed! We decided to go and see the San Pedro Caves, which were supposedly a couple of hours walk away. A four-hour walk, in relation to the previous day's eleven-hour walk seemed nothing. We set off after lunch, having said good-bye to Larissa and Jon and having eaten a couple of delicious tuna, mayo and tomato sandwiches. Another warm sunny day and we found the route quite easily along a track away from Sorata and along the road. The road hugged the hillsides and, at times, moving up hill was hard. It was also a lot further than we thought but, on reaching San Pedro, we stopped off for a bottle of coke to refresh ourselves and then carried on to the caves. The path up the cliff to the cave wasn't altogether obvious and the entrance a little makeshift! There were two French girls ahead of us and the lad manning the cave was keen that we all went in together, partly to save power costs on the lighting. He told us the lighting would be turned on for about 15 minutes so we went inside anticipating the cave would be just there. It was further than we thought, a good five-minute walk down slippery steps and bending low in the cave. As we got further into the cave, it became hotter and hotter, until it was really quite sweaty humid. The lake in the cave was really unusual to see, very low and quite small. Bats were flying around above us quite innocently, although I really wasn't too chuffed about having them around. We were only there about five minutes and we realised we would have to start back before the lamps went out, our torch would not have really helped us in such darkness. I am glad we saw the underground lake, but it was over so quickly. We had some chocolate to give us the energy for the way back and we set off again. The way back was mostly uphill and our legs were weary but we made it. The views (as usual) were wonderful and Sorata soon came back in view. It really was a very special place and it would have been good to stay there longer, but our schedule was calling and La Paz was our next stop. There were plenty of buses going back to the La Paz the next day so we decided to be ready in case the 7.30 a.m. decided to run.

Again, our meal was really good that night and we treated ourselves to two bottles of really good beer, Pilsner (tropical). Up with the larks again on Tuesday and we went out into the Plaza to get a bus. The 7.30 a.m. was not running, but we managed to get one at about 8 a.m., again at the back and soon full before too long along the route. We were both tired and dozed for most of the way, until we stopped and all the locals were eyeing us to get off and trying to explain something, which I thought meant we needed to get off and change buses. Another gringo was getting off too, but heading elsewhere and on asking the driver the bus was going to La Paz and we really did not have to get off at all! It was a chance for Simon to have a pee break and by the time I got to the back of the bus again our seats had been taken and there was no way we were getting them back. Much to the amusement of the locals we found a couple of separate seats and stayed there for the rest of the trip.

La Paz seemed a little quieter where we were dropped off, but we managed to pick up a taxi and back at Hostal Austria we got the same room back! Very lucky I'd call it as it is a very busy time of year with lots of students, mainly from England! Our intention that day was to buy our Rurrenabaque tickets for Saturday and find some camping equipment for our Tahesi walk starting either the next day or the day after.

We filled our bellies with lunch from next door (Fregata) and then headed off towards TAM. First of all, putting in another film, the fourth in a few days. Once we arrived at the TAM office, we really couldn't believe our eyes and ears when the woman said they were booked up until the following Wednesday 6th August! A bomb shell had dropped on us and I was gutted to say the least. I had been so looking forward to the jungle, it was a chance to see something very different and see something very new. We had also planned it all so carefully and it was now in tatters. Planning is important but expectations are raised and it is so disappointing when it doesn't/can't work out. We still decided against the bus, deciding not to rush it and spend the next two days debating our options over a bottle of coke in a seedy restaurant overlooking La Paz. We came to the conclusion that perhaps it wasn't meant to be and it was a sign telling us not to go. We changed our plans completely and decided to try the four-day La Cumbre, Coroico walk, having sorted out some equipment somehow. I wasn't sure if I was capable of such a hike, but I was willing to give it a go, especially as most of it is downhill.

We also decided that on completion of that we would head south to Potosi and see the mines, part of our original plan from way back. We had heard it was worth seeing and now we suddenly had time to fit it in.

The rest of Tuesday was spent looking for camping equipment. Jon had bought a tent recently in a shop in the market owned by a Chinese man. We had seen the tent, which felt lighter than others, but we weren't sure how light it would have been. We eventually found the shop and with some haggling managed to buy a two-man tent, roll mats and a chest strap for Simon's rucksack for about £70! A bargain especially when we then managed to buy a stove, cooking set, gas cylinders and cutlery for another £30! We had done it now, no going back; we had more stuff to carry and we would have to use it along our trip to pay off the investment! We knew we would be saving about £40 on not hiring equipment, but will we use it during the rest of the year? I can imagine we will and the good thing is it now gives us the choice and the flexibility to camp and to do overnight hikes. You can certainly see places that public transport cannot reach.

The following day would be too soon for us to get everything ready for a four-day hike. So, we resigned ourselves to another day in La Paz and ate that evening in the street, a delicious steak sandwich and chips and a chicken, rice and chips meal!

The following morning, I awoke to the sound of others in the hostel heading off to catch the Rurrenabaque flight and a French girl talking to her mother on the phone. Both things seemed to get to me and I got quite upset about our plans having changed etc. Simon was really understanding and reassuring but I managed to throw him into confusion too and we needed to sit down and go over our plans again to make sure it was what we both wanted and we were both happy with them.

The food shopping was actually quite fun and the market provided almost everything. It needed to be light in weight but filling in nourishment. We chose ravioli pasta with tomato puree, packet soups, sliced ham for sandwiches and pasta, sliced loaf of bread, Brazil nuts (so cheap!) prunes (for me!) dried/fried banana pieces and the fruit and tomatoes we already had. Really chuffed with our choices we then spent the rest of the day enjoying ourselves. We went back to the central park for another view of La Paz, this time by day. Tired, we caught a cheap taxi to the supposed Indian market.

What a minefield this was, hordes of people and food everywhere. It was really nice just to wander around the stalls. We also had a peek at some handicraft streets and found a huge rug that we may go back and buy as our South American souvenir.

A recommended restaurant (*El Lobo*) did a decent lunch set meal and we headed in that direction. Having ordered and prepared ourselves the waiter came with the coke and informed us he had no set lunch left. We just about stopped him opening the bottle and walked out, unprepared to spend a fortune and annoyed we had missed it. We searched for an Alumerzo after 1 p.m. and found one that turned out to be quite good.

Heading back to our hostel we bumped into a parade at the local Plaza where the Presidential offices stand next to the cathedral. The President and his wife were heading off somewhere with a full piece band and set of colourfully dressed soldiers to see them off. Talk about making it clear he was around! They had sealed off the Plaza from traffic and even had very heavily armed other soldiers guarding them from the crowd. All heavy stuff and really quite fascinating.

Simon

La Cumbre to Coroico Walk, The Yungas
2nd August 1997

As I was saying, the final day of the walk was superb. It was the perfect combination of jungle with amazing views. The day before the jungle had conquered all, views, included. Today, however, we made good progress and we could really appreciate the wilderness in which we had spent the last few days. We were due to reach our campsite by 4.00 p.m. We got there by 12.00.

So instead of sleeping there, we simply had lunch and moved on. It would have been a superb place to camp. Sandalliki is the mountain home of a Japanese man, who as far as I could see lived on his own. Heaven knows how he ended up there in the middle of nowhere but he certainly had found himself an impressive spot in which to live. Two hours on foot to the nearest village (no road); it could most definitely be called isolating. We signed his register of passing travellers and decided to move on to reach the end of the walk.

So, we finished the walk in three days instead of four, but the day was certainly not finished there. We nearly reached the end of the trail at the nowhere village of El Chairo by 3.00. We didn't want to stay there as we were keen to reach the town of Coroico. Tales of Coroico sounded promising. Apparently, it is a great place to hang out and 'relax' El Chairo by contrast didn't look like a great place to relax.

El Chairo doesn't have the most sophisticated public transport system in the world. Trucks leave at weekends at midday. We had missed the truck by 3 hours.

All was not lost. We had the option of "chartering" a pickup van for £30. Our daily budget blown in an instant. Hopes of sipping rum and coke by a pool in a fancy hotel in Coroico dissolved in an instant. We got the price down to £20 and ventured off in our own private truck.

The privacy didn't last long. The privacy lasted about fifty yards out of town. The privacy of our own specially chartered truck ended when the driver stopped to pick up an old man then an old woman, then their mother, then a dog etc. Five minutes into the journey, I had the feeling that this apparently simple journey, this apparently simple business transaction was going to end in tears.

The old man got off half way without paying. The old woman got off a few yards later and paid about 10p. Their mothers later got off and said gracias, smiling at us as they left. The dog jumped off and cocked his leg, either at us or the driver. I couldn't decipher which.

Then we stopped to pick up about fifteen kids. Not any old kids, but some kids that had hassled us at our first campsite.

Then we reached the end of the journey. OK, 1-2-3, deep breath. We had already given him £15 and we told him to get the rest from his friends, family and neighbours that he had picked up along the way. This, of course, was the trigger for absolute chaos all around us. He told our next pickup truck not to let us on and demanded the money or the police. This sparked me off to choose the police option at which point the driver immediately started lowering the amount of money he was demanding from us. Encouraged by his obvious reluctance to go the police, I was determined to go to them. So, go to them we did.

If, before we left the UK to go travelling, you had told me that I would end up in an out of the way police station in Bolivia I may have thought twice about my sanity.

South America, the land of some of the most corrupt, deprived and sadistic departments in the world. Here we were in a Bolivian police station.

The policeman on duty couldn't believe how much the truck driver had tried to charge us. However, he said that we had agreed the price and ought to pay it. By a mixture of our stubbornness and inability to understand in full what was being said, we held out and only paid another £1.50. Looking back, I'm still really pleased we did what we did. I can accept cultural differences, but this was gringo pricing on an outrageous scale. We saved ourselves £5, but more than this, we embarrassed the crook who stitched us up. I just hope the experience makes him think twice before he tries such a stint on someone else. When travelling or any other time for that matter, you do have a duty to stick up for yourself. If you don't, not only do you pay through the nose but so will other travellers later on. It cannot be good for any community to grow up believing in double standards or double pricing. If travellers don't help force this message home then nobody else will.

We finally arrived in Coroico that evening exhausted. The town was packed with gringos and weekenders from La Paz. Therefore, it took us six hostels and much walking around later, to find an OK hostel at a decent price.

Simon

Coroico, The Yungas.
3rd to 5th August 1997

We were desperate to relax. There were two obstacles hindering this. Firstly, we were skint. This meant our hostel was OK but was not the ideal place to hang out. Secondly the other hostels were all packed anyway. Lady luck (excuse the gambling speak, I'm currently reading the trashy novel *Casino* by Robert Kersch) intervened. We met a couple of English girls who told us about a hostel out of town. It sounded excellent and has been superb for us.

This is where the diary on Coroico should end because since we discovered the hostel Sol y Luna, we haven't done a lot except sit about, relax and enjoy the view. It seems to be a bit of a hippy joint. Judging from the visitors' book, more people arrive than leave. There is one guy here who has been here for two and a half months. He told us he would stay longer but his Bolivian visa runs out in two weeks.

Another guy, Mick, who is staying here, is a bit of a perpetual traveller. From what I can make out, he has been travelling for about six or seven years now. I feel like our plans are a bit of a whirlwind trip to him. For him, spending three months on an island off the coast of Thailand is nothing. In five months in India, he saw hardly anything. He has been held hostage in Vietnam and has almost been shot in Peru, and we wanted to write a book on travelling. Hope he doesn't write one first.

There is a giant map of the globe on the wall here. When

I look at it, I'd be surprised if we are covering 1% of the globe on our trip. One month in a country is nothing, but yet we only have a year, so that is usually all we have. At times like these, I wish we had more, but I know I couldn't travel year upon year. If we see all we plan to it will be more than most people do in a lifetime. For now, that will have to suffice and we have been up to now very fortunate indeed.

Rebecca

Coroico, Bolivia.
Tuesday 5th August 1997

Photos we have had developed in La Paz have been very good and each film you get developed comes with a free enlargement. The last ones had the experimental moonlight shots and Isla del Sol. Unfortunately, without a tripod, they weren't as good as they could have been, a bit of shaking over the various seconds that the camera was held and two photos are wobbly. Never mind, at least we know now what will come out and what won't.

For the two evenings where we had had the set lunches, we ate from street stalls and really enjoyed it. The second night, we found a man selling potato balls filled with meat and veg that had been deep fried, served with about ten different sauces. Really tasty and warming in the evening cool temperatures. He also had ones made of yuca and banana, really good. We also treated ourselves to a beer in the restaurant next door to the hostel and toasted the next few days hike, hoping we would see it through okay.

We arranged a taxi through a friend of the hostel owner

for 6.15 a.m., a really early start! We had handed over our coats the night before to delightful faces of two men in the hostel. They were so pleased with them and we were delighted they were received so gratefully. We also gave them our cups, both sets of things we had replaced with lighter things and in return Manuel gave us one of his Pachamama stones, carved in the shapes of Inca faces. Being 'Mother Earth' and so highly thought of here in Bolivia, this couldn't have been a better gift and a great souvenir.

The map for the walk that we had got from Tourist Info had told us to get a 7 a.m. or 8 a.m. minibus from Ville Fatima. The taxi driver took us there but wasn't sure where we got the bus to La Cumbre so we got out in the cold and stood around wondering where it would go from. The bus company across the road weren't immediately helpful, but turned out to be going in that direction at 7.30 a.m.; we paid and took their bus. I was never sure this was the bus the leaflet was talking about but about an hour later we were dropped off at La Cumbre.

It was freezing, the wind was bitter and it looked so isolated I was a bit scared. We set off across the "moonscape" along a path that seemed to be going in the right direction. We headed for the snow line and the summit hoping we would find the triangle shape formed stones at the top. The going was tricky, as we were so high up breathing wasn't easy and it was quite steep. At one point, we thought we may have to go through snow but it was really icy so we skirted around it. The view at the top was amazing, amongst snow-capped mountain and hill peaks and looking down a valley that the Pre-Colombian path would take us. We now knew the route was pretty much downhill and set off passing various farmers and families with alpacas and llamas with them. It was a steep descent with some slippy and stoney patches to contend with. We passed the ruins of a travellers' lodge and started walking through more grass and farmland. At about midday we came across a hut selling drinks and sat outside sipping cups of sweet, hot coca tea! It tasted really good and gave us the energy we needed to carry on another hour before lunch. There were about three very sweet children there who were pretty fascinated in us. Ranging from three to eight years old their clothes were ripped and holey, their feet were like snake skin, they were dirty and their teeth were already rotten! Such a shame, but not a lot we could do except give them a bit of attention.

Our lunch tasted really good: ham and tomato sandwiches amongst a herd of LLAMAS! The route was still all downhill, but the scenery was becoming less isolated, greener and we came upon our first village, Chucura. Still further downhill at about 4.30, we came to our first campsite at Challapampa, in a valley, next to a river and on the edge of "Exuberant sub-tropical vegetation". It was unbelievably much warmer by then than the start of the day and we had lots of time to set up camp. The tent was really easy to erect (having had a demo in the shop) and we sat down to make a cup of coffee and watch the scene. There was a small family who lived in small housing huts by the camping ground. The lady came over and asked for a bit of money, not knowing whether we officially paid or not we coughed up the 60p! Another couple arrived about an hour after us and set up camp too and then a whole host of school boys arrived much to our disappointment. As it turned out, they were going further on to camp, but for about an hour they caused us a slight headache. By now, we had started to cook our soup and they were intent on coming up and asking us questions and generally being a bit of a nuisance. We were so glad when they eventually went, but a bit worried we would have to put up with them for four days. As it turned out, we didn't see them again until Saturday.

Broccoli soup and ham and tomato cheese ravioli was on the menu and thoroughly enjoyed. Why does food taste so good outside?! The light was gone by about 7 p.m., but we sat it out until about 7.45 p.m. and then washed up in the dark and in bed by 8.30 p.m.! What party poopers, but with another hard walk ahead the next day, we knew it was sensible.

We were glad of the DEET we had bought for $10 from Larissa and Jon. The midges on that campsite were particularly bad and going through jungle areas for another two days produced quite a few bites. Friday morning was no exception and we refrained from making coffee to avoid bites! Breakfasts were biscuits, dried bananas, nuts, a piece of bread and prunes! We were packed away having washed in the river by 8.30 a.m., ahead of the other couple! The going was really good through beautiful flowers and plants. Simon had woken still very tired and never really recovered all day. So, we rested regularly and took it steady. About lunchtime, we came to a bridge over a river and stopped for a rest and a sit down in the sun. As with most pedestrian bridges over rivers, this was rickety and dodgy but we got across and came up against a really steep incline the other side that was completely unexpected and really hard! It was also really hot so at the top on a nice patch of grass we stopped for an hour's lunch break where Simon had a snooze which he said made him feel a lot better. By now, the other couple had caught up with us, quite a young French couple, she was quite giggly and he tried to be funny! Their footwear was really quite odd, she wore shoes with a few ridges and he wore trainers and they carried a couple of very small packs. They had a tent but no sleeping bags and mattresses and they didn't have anything to cook with and told us they didn't have much food! Really odd, but it didn't alter their jolly spirits.

As well as the map which outlined the route with distances and timings, we had the South American handbook that supposedly described the route. Neither of them was absolutely correct, the leaflet slightly more so but we never really knew how much further we had to go. The path became really dense that afternoon and therefore difficult to walk through and no chance of seeing the views! This actually made it quite difficult for us both, but Simon's tiredness was getting the better of him and he wondered how much further he could carry on. The leaflet stated we would come to a river where we could camp or another hour further on to a stream where we could camp. We came to the river at about 5 p.m. with great relief, which turned into despondency with no obvious place to camp. We were really disappointed and were quite confused about why it would say camp there with nowhere to go. At the most, we had another hour to go and another climb with no definite knowledge of a campsite. I became a woman with a mission and walked really fast to try and get to the campsite before dark. Simon did really well, considering his lethargic state, which given another day he would have rested altogether. After nearly an hour, I could hear water and I shouted back to Simon in glee. A little further on I could see the French couple's tent pitched near the stream. "Thank God," were my words and again I shouted back to Simon the good news. I was really relieved now and didn't care that the patch for camping wasn't very big and really quite stony and rocky. It was good enough and having pitched up Simon had a sleep whilst I cooked in the dark. Our torch was a saviour and dinner was meat ravioli, tomato and ham sauce and then biscuits for dessert. I was exhausted and in bed again early. Soon after getting some sleep, the rain started and was on and off all night. We hadn't expected this and in the distance at about 1.30 a.m. I could hear the rolls of thunder and hoped it wouldn't get nearer. At about 5 p.m. it arrived— not as violent as it could have been but very heavy rain and at 7 a.m. it was still pouring. I wasn't very happy about getting up and packing up in the rain so I was very relieved when it eventually stopped at about 7.30 a.m. We knew we wouldn't have such a hard walking day so we got up in no hurry and left by 9 a.m. It was very wet underfoot but warm and, walking through similar vegetation to the previous day, we got wet through from the rain on all the plants.

Some expected uphill paths on Saturday which were also tough, but the views were clearer and really spectacular. We arrived at a refresco hut at about 11 a.m. and treated ourselves to a relatively expensive bottle of coke next to a banana plantation and overlooking great hills. Carrying on further we arrived at the infamous Japanese man's house by lunchtime at Sandalliki. We originally thought this may be our overnight campsite, but having got there so early we decided to carry on to El Chairo, the end of the path.

The Japanese man was down in his garden and when he saw us, he trudged his bent body towards us and gave us a book to register our names in to show we had completed the walk. The house was perched on the hillside with a magnificent view and impressive gardens. The site would have been great for us but we ate lunch, dried the tent, found out the route from the Japanese man and carried on.

Rebecca

La Paz, Bolivia.
Wed 6th August 1997

The walk to El Chairo was much further than we expected in relation to the distance and timings we had covered so far. It was nearly all downhill and, when we eventually saw it below us, we were really pleased!

El Chairo was a frontier town of no special significance except the end of the Pre-Inca trail we had been following for three days. It did, however, have a little shop where we could sit and drink a bottle of coke! We asked the owner about trucks to Coroico and we were told one would arrive in about five minutes that we could get. Marvellous, we were going to get to Coroico a day earlier than expected! We wouldn't have to stay in El Chairo after all. True to his word, the man came back quite quickly and on asking about the price he told us we could charter it for about £30! It was only about twenty-seven miles and this seemed a lot of money. Realising it would be expensive, but happy to pay over the odds to get to Coroico earlier, we negotiated to pay about £23. His kids piled in the back, us in the front and we paid about £16 upfront and the rest we said he could get at Yolosa, where we would be able to pick up a truck to Coroico for less than £1 for the two of us. We set off and soon it became clear that "our" truck was going to be a pick-up service all the way to Yolosa as adults and children (including the annoying ones from our first campsite) hopped in the back and the driver shouted for about two or three bolivianos (50p) from each of them. Of course, we weren't happy about this at all and we decided that as he was getting more money from other passengers and as we were obviously paying for others to travel, we would not pay him anymore. We arrived at Yolosa and of course he was far more interested in getting our money than the other passengers and we know that plenty of them didn't pay a penny. We explained the situation to him, but of course he wasn't having it and demanded the money as well as saying he wouldn't allow us on the next truck to Coroico! Again, better Spanish would have really helped us and our basics had to suffice, but he knew what we were saying and was a little taken aback when we asked whether he was charging us so much and no one else because we were tourists. He tried to tell us that the kids didn't have any money to which I replied that we didn't have any money either and certainly none to pay for others! He then wanted to go to the police which we completely agreed to and, therefore, he backed down and asked we pay some of the money and he would give us some of what he got from the others. We disagreed and walked down the road and into the small police station where one policeman was guarding the office. By now, another truck driver had joined ours in support so there were four of us around the desk. Our driver told his side of the story at which I chipped in a little when he made out all the other passengers were children and of course this was untrue. The policeman listened incredulously at how much he had wanted to charge us and gave the truck driver a telling off for trying to get so much. He understood our position and was sympathetic, but he said that a contract had been agreed and we should therefore pay it. We also explained how the other two French people (whom we bumped into during the argument) had paid less than half of what we were supposed to pay and this also helped make them believe we were being ripped off. In the end, the policeman compromised and to end the matter we agreed to just pay about £1.60 more. By now, we were exhausted and felt he had been fair so we paid and left. I never thought for a minute we would end up in a South American police station and, throughout the episode, I remembered standing and thinking how crazy it all was. Another mad experience, but a very positive one. We felt quite proud to have stood up for ourselves and the gringo pricing that exists in these countries. We felt he would most certainly think twice about trying it again without checking with the people first. It caused quite a stir in Yolosa, all eyes were on us but we left with our heads held high and immediately got a cheap truck up the road to Coroico.

The warm sunshine was still around by now, about 4.30 p.m./5 p.m. and we got out and searched for a hostel that took much longer than anticipated. Everywhere seemed full and a little boy was trying to be our guide, not helping and we certainly weren't going to give him any money either!

We eventually found one at the Plaza called Residencial de la Torre. Built around a courtyard it was quite clean, basic and much cheaper than others. It was getting dark by then and we both headed straight for a shower that we desperately needed.

Coroico is built in an amazing situation, on the edge of a hill overlooking the valleys and luscious hills of the Yungas. The town itself probably wasn't as nice as Sorata, but still quaint with cobbled streets and a nice plaza with shops, cafes and even bars all around.

In the evening, we went to find somewhere cheap to eat and stumbled across a market with cafe stalls selling cena for less than £1 each. It was really tasty, soup and bread and chicken and rice and salad. Our hostel also had a little cafe attached and we treated ourselves to a beer there afterwards. Exhausted we tumbled into bed and slept for about ten hours.

The next day, I was still really tired and another cold and cough had started, probably due to the changes in temperatures during the walk. Simon did the washing and leaving it to dry we went to have a scout around Coroico. Breakfast was a hot cheese empanada, a veg saltena and a banana, eaten in the sun in the Plaza. We then walked down a stepped pathway slightly out of town and found quite a posh hotel overlooking such amazing views.

We sat there for a while admiring all the banana trees and orange trees all around.

Back at the hostel, we fell asleep for an hour unintentionally and when we awoke, we decided to try and find the waterfalls that the town gets its water supply from and take some lunch with us.

The walk (as usual) was much longer than we expected. We had not wanted another long hike and were looking to rest but the views were spectacular so we didn't mind the distance and we cherished our tuna and mayonnaise sandwiches when we arrived at the waterfall. The waterfall itself was very disappointing as it had loads of water pipes everywhere sending the water back to the town. Two English girls turned up and said they thought there was more than one, but we were content with our walk and headed back. Obviously, quite a slow pace as the two girls caught up with us back in town and on chatting to them, we found out they were staying in a really nice hostel a little out of town but as cheap as ours. We had been considering moving to the "Esmeralda" that was supposed to be really good and very popular but they told us it was double the price. We decided to investigate their hostel, "Sol y Luna" and although it was a good twenty mins out of town, some uphill, we decided to move there; it was lovely, peaceful, great views, veranda, deckchairs, lounge area, tables and chairs outside and really relaxing. The only problem was that Emma and Becky had been talking about Rurrenabaque and had used the bus system themselves which they said was fine. They made us think again and we headed back into town (having reserved a room for the next night) and sat and had a coke to think about it. In the end, we agreed we would continue with our plans, forget the jungle and save more money; we had come to accept we weren't going and couldn't face the mental anguish of going back on the plans again. Another couple of days at the great looking Sol y Luna to relax and then back to La Paz for a bus to Potosi.

We were out of our hostel the next day (Monday) by 9.45 a.m. and donning backpacks we headed up the hill and arrived at "Sol y Luna" to a hearty, delicious breakfast on the patio of fried egg, toast, jam and coffee. Monday and Tuesday this week were lazy relaxing days reading, writing the diary, writing letters and playing cards and chess. The weather was great and the atmosphere—a real hippy hang-out! There were quite a few Germans and one guy who had been camping there for two and a half months, and was considering leaving Bolivia as his visa expired soon! There was also a guy called Mick (Australian) who lives in La Paz as an English teacher and has lived here for two and a half years. When he has a break, he goes to Coroico to get away and always to Sol y Luna. Maria treats him like a son. She was the owner, a very sweet little Bolivian lady who was happy to oblige in anything but would never rush!

We found out that Emma had just got a 2:1 at Cambridge in French and Italian and her younger sister had just finished her first year at Bristol University studying French and Spanish. Both from Norwich, they were really nice girls heading also down south to Potosi/Sucre and eventually Santiago to fly home on 25th August. We did venture into the town in the afternoon and booked a bus back to La Paz for Wednesday morning. We also tried to phone Hostal Austria in La Paz to cancel our Tuesday reservation but it was a holiday and all the lines were down so we would have to do it the next day!

That evening, we really splashed out on the special meal they make for a minimum of ten people. There were fifteen of us and at about 8.15 p.m. we sat down to eat a huge plate of Indonesian food. One plate was mainly salad, delicious cabbage, beetroot, lettuce, tomato, egg, cucumber and the other plate, hot rice, peanut sauce, bananas, peppers and about six different sauces to go with it all. It was absolutely delicious and such a great change from the normal soup and main course. We chatted for ages and had a really good, sociable evening over a couple of bottles of beer. Mick revealed some interesting travel stories, including a two-day hostage situation in Vietnam about five years ago and a gun held to him in Lima! He made out he really didn't want to talk about it, but he loved talking about himself! Becky revealed her year's living in Cuba which Mick took a huge interest in as he wants to go around Christmas time. Mick and the two-and-a-half-month bloke spoke a bit about experiences in India and Thailand which for us was fascinating. The islands off Thailand seem a must but with only a month (instead of about six!) it wasn't in their league of hanging out! That evening, it rained a lot and all night so that yesterday morning was misty and very wet. It was also somewhat colder but the sun came through and we managed to sit in the deckchairs. Breakfast was a delicious bowl of home-made muesli, including banana and pieces of papaya that Simon picked out and gave to me.

About lunchtime, we went into town to phone La Paz and found they had no reservation anyway! We had seen them reserve a room, but we weren't too concerned as we wanted to cancel it anyway; I just hoped they still had our bags.

We had a coffee and a piece of coffee cake in the other hostels cafe and then headed back to our place for a banana pancake! It was yummy; we could have eaten the whole time at Sol y Luna! A lot of the original people left yesterday, but sure enough by the evening there were a total of about thirteen people again including a really cool older lady on her own. We got chatting to her as we awaited our dinner and it turned out she was travelling for three weeks from California. Having travelled a lot over the years, trekking in mountains is second nature to her and she loves to get away from it all. Altitude sickness prevented her from going off the beaten track too much this time and has had to resort to just sightseeing. She had decided she doesn't like just doing that and is unsure how her travelling trips will take off in the future. She reminded me in looks of Granny Mudd (my Granny from my mum's side) and such an interesting lady.

We had treated ourselves to a bottle of wine in town and really enjoyed it with our delicious homemade veg soup and fried broccoli, rice, tomato and onion main meal which was yummy! A coffee to finish and an early night from the cold finished off Sol y Luna just nicely.

Our bus was due to leave at 9 a.m. this morning so we

were away by 8.15 a.m. with plenty of time to eat a couple of hot cheese empanadas and say good-bye to Coroico. It was a minibus and we had chosen front seats for the view. The driver was very careful on the winding cliff road and misty weather, but we did it in almost exactly three hours, passing our original La Cumbre starting point.

La Paz is celebrating Independence Day today and the inauguration of their new President Banzer. All shops are shut, the streets are quieter and we headed over to the bus terminal in another minibus (to save money!) to buy some tickets to Potosi. We hurled ourselves onto the minibus, Simon on a seat in front of me and myself and my backpack on a seat behind him. A fairly respectable-looking older couple got on and sat themselves down next to me. He moved my backpack nearer to me at one point and seemed a little odd. At one point my leg was touching hers and I felt a little prick which I assumed was her dress digging into me. I thought nothing of it, they got off and we found our way to the terminal and bought two tickets for a bus to Potosi at 8 p.m. I always put any bus tickets in the side pocket of my trousers and as my hand went in it came out the other side and to my absolute horror, I had a huge hole in the bottom of my pocket! Looking down my pocket had been cut and my wallet and bank receipts had gone! At first, I assumed it had happened in the bus station, but it needed to have been a longer time span than that and I suddenly remembered the couple on the minibus next to me! BASTARDS! I couldn't believe the nerve and I felt so angry that I hadn't noticed and caught them at it! I now have a rip in the bottom of my pocket which I still have to mend and am still annoyed that it has happened.

Simon

Potosi—Southern Highlands
6th to 8th August 1997

Not our first-choice destination for Bolivia but, when travelling on a budget, you don't always get to go to your preferred choice every time.

Potosi at 4,070m is the highest city of its size in the world. As a result, it is freezing. Last night (7/8/97), we got snowed in. Potosi was founded in 1545 after the Spaniards found Indian silver mines here. Ever since then, Potosi Mountain has been mined. Potosi is an attractive old colonial town and yesterday we spent the day wandering around looking at old mansions and churches. Interesting, but for me Potosi has been about three things.

Firstly, the town has something in common with most other towns in Bolivia and indeed Peru that I love. That is the central market. The central market is the life and soul of many towns. At the soul of the market, there is food and where there is food there is life, Bolivian life that is, because gringos seem to avoid eating at the markets like the plague. Due to budgeting constraints, we have little choice but even if we did, I'd like to think we would still frequent these haunts.

Over the past couple of days, these places have given us shelter from the snow and freezing cold for the price of 17p for a massive mug of coffee. We have had complete breakfasts for £1 for both of us.

Anyway, there is only one thing better than market food and that is street food. Last night, we had a delicious burger and chips for 25p each. Excellent!

The second thing about our time at Potosi has been the sense that we are here because we couldn't afford to go to the jungle. Yesterday, I was a bit fed up about this but it's good not to get everything you want all of the time. This trip, amongst other things, has been a complete orgy of fun, pleasure and excitement. We have, by rights of jacking in our lives back home, said, "Bollocks to it." Travelling is selfish, but I wouldn't change it for the world. It must be good that here we have had to put the brakes on and settle for second best.

The third thing about Potosi is the mines. Today, we saw one. In fact, today we went in one for about four hours. It was an amazing experience. Potosi Mountain has been mined now for about 450 years and the way the miners go about their jobs now can't be very much different to four centuries ago.

The government closed the state mines ten years ago in favour of privatisation. With this went any investment in the industry. Today, the mines are run by small co-operatives. The machines have gone save for the hammer, chisel and a few sticks of dynamite. The miners work in medieval conditions. They chew coca leaves constantly for medication and draw £5 a day in wages. 99% are very poor. The other 1% has become richer. If you find a seam of silver 75% of it is yours, 24% goes to the co-operative and 1% to the government.

We met one miner in the mines who is sixty-three and has been working there for thirty-six years. He says that the mountain only has enough deposits for another twenty years of mining. I dread to think what will become of the town then.

On our tour, we crawled around like rats in the mud. In the West, the tour would have been illegal on health and safety grounds. A tour only lasts for four hours. The miners live in those conditions all their lives. Seems like a long time to me.

Simon

Cochabamba. The Cochabamba Basin
9th and 10th August 1997.

Well it's all drawing to an end here in South America. However, no matter how little time you have here, there is always time for chaos and frustration.

Our supposed eight-hour bus journey from Potosi to Cochabamba took thirteen hours. I really do believe the people working for the bus companies don't know the expected arrival times. All they know is the price of the ticket and the departure times because that is all they need to know. A thirteen-hour bus journey is always uncomfortable, but normally OK. Mentally, we had prepared for an eight-hour journey so it is frustrating when the bus is rolling along five hours after we thought it would arrive.

The bus ran out of petrol at one point. The road surface was perfectly paved, a rare experience in Bolivia. So, all should have been well. We had a good road and a bus that worked as long as it had petrol in it. All we needed now was a half decent driver. Being fair and giving credit to the man, I have to say that our driver seemed idiotic. I've met people who could pedal a bike faster than our bus went. We were overtaken by every other vehicle. At one point a stop sign was making good ground on us. The final frustration came when the next bus (departure one hour later) from the same company overtook us within three hours. Nothing is as it seems in South America. At nothing it seems is!

Today, we did our final walk in the continent. A pleasant

uphill stroll with fine views all around the Cochabamba Basin. The walk should have taken us to some ruins within three to four hours. At three-and-a-half-hours, we gave up and turned around, satisfied with the views we had seen. On the way down, we met some follow gringos going up. We had been told by the locals it was an hour-long walk. Yeah right!

So, what is the best part about Cochabamba? The colonial architecture perhaps? Its youthful vibrant atmosphere that sets it apart from other cities on the altiplano? It's a beautiful mountain setting? How about its colourful Sunday carnival style market? Nope. The best part about Cochabamba is a restaurant called Papachin.

For once, we didn't have the cheap set meal. They didn't do one in the evening and we couldn't be bothered to look for anywhere else to eat. Our bus driver, speedy Gonzalez, ensured that. We opted for the churrasco at £2 a head, double what we would normally pay. We received the biggest steak I have ever seen. It tasted so good, that tonight we went back again and had the same meal. Tonight, it was even bigger. Tonight, our plates were carving dishes. Tonight, I ate like Desperate Dan.

Simon

La Paz
11th and 12th August 1997

On the 11th, we spent the day on a bus travelling from Cochabamba to La Paz. For me, it was a comfortable journey with a good bus, good driver and a paved road. I wasn't either too hot or too cold.

Rebecca wasn't very well at all. I still don't know what caused it but she felt very nauseas. Still, we had previously reserved a room at the hostel Austria. In Potosi, we met some Irish girls who told us about a hostel in La Paz that was half decent and a third of the price of the hostel Austria. Therefore, we also reserved a room there as well.

On arrival at the new hostel we were promptly informed that all the rooms were taken, but they had prepared "special" temporary accommodation for us. This "special" accommodation turned out to be the dining area and bar next to the kitchen. It was right at the front next to the pavement with no windows. At first, I thought it would be OK. After someone yelled, "Des bifstek a la probres," through the serving hatch from the kitchen I started to have my doubts. Within ten minutes, two lots of people pushed open our keyless door and asked for a room for the night. We finally decided to make a run for it when we discovered two more beds complete with baggage at the back of the bar. No problem but there was only one entrance, OURS!

No problem, at least we had a reservation at the hostel Austria. At the hostel Austria, we had a reservation for a matrimonial, but no matrimonial room. They gave us a double, but insisted we pay the extra for it. This resulted in the usual South American/gringo argument where logic had decided to go on the piss in Hawaii. The result was all too familiar. We were told we could always try the hostel from where we came.

I was pleased to get Rebecca to a room with some privacy at last. She really was feeling rough. I spent the evening doing "jobs" as well as rubbing Rebecca's back as she threw up.

The next day, she was feeling better. We spent the day around La Paz buying souvenirs. We bought a couple of rugs and a bag so we can carry even more gear across the globe.

Simon

In the Air

13th August 1997

We have spent the day (today actually) travelling from the hostel to La Paz airport and from there to Buenos Aires. As usual, the day was not without incident. The views of La Paz and the surrounding mountains were the best we had seen. Mount Illimani looked monstrously huge. It was a fitting end to our time here.

At the airport, we got into the usual mindless, logic-less, gringo shafting type argument with the official there. Despite more than adequate proof that we had already paid too much in airport taxes, we still had to pay once more. It cost us another US $40 and we have already paid US $100. Infuriating, corrupt and without logic, but nonetheless sadly very typical of South America.

Rebecca

Buenos Aires Airport. 10 p.m.

Wednesday 13th August 1997

A week of the diary to catch up on and about twelve hours sitting around to do it in!

After my pocket saga, we used Hostel Austria as a base for the day to sort our bags and hang around until our bus was leaving at about 8 p.m. Delicious street food did us proud before we bundled ourselves and our bags into a taxi and headed for the bus terminal. Another busy, noisy terminal with people shouting and touting for business. The usual Bolivian bus terminal tax had to be paid before boarding our bus *El Dorado*. A comfortable bus by all accounts of other people's Bolivian bus experiences, it was packed to the point of a family's two kids sleeping on blankets in the isle! At about 2 a.m., we stopped in some frontier town for about half an hour and oddly enough, for that time in the morning, we were both tempted by an egg sandwich being made by a boy of about twelve outside the cafe. They were absolutely delicious, free range egg sandwich, full of salad and a few fresh, crisp chips and mayonnaise! A quick pee in the shadows of the street and we were on our way again arriving in Potosi at about 7 a.m.

We were told that Potosi was cold, but not that it was bloody freezing! We got a taxi quite quickly and made our way to the Casa Maria Victoria, recommended by the South American Handbook. Down a really cool colonial street, the owners had not yet woken up and as the door into a really attractive courtyard was open, we let ourselves in and hung around. Another tourist turned up for the same reason, a French bloke who had come overnight from Villazon in Argentina. A year's trip had taken them to Chile for six months and, after nine months, they had to do about three countries really quickly.

Frozen, the owner eventually awoke and came out to say that we could have rooms from about 10 a.m. We left our bags in a little store room and went in search of some breakfast and at least a hot drink to warm us up! The book told us of the central market that opened to serve breakfast at 7 a.m. and fresh bread from 6 a.m. Very disappointed in the lack of info, and details about Potosi in the handbook we were pleased to find a map of the town and an obvious mark for the central market. By now it still wasn't 8 a.m. and on a "holiday" for the town we weren't convinced it would be open. We arrived at the crafts market and when we asked a passer-by it was clear our map had them the wrong way round, sending us to the wrong side of town! Cursing the Bolivian section, we got to the market and found some hive of activity upstairs. A section set aside by women complete with a small hob, boiling kettles, piles of bread and small benches and tables. A couple beckoned our custom and we sat down to a wonderful hot cup of coffee and two rolls with butter and jam, for a £1! It was just what we needed. Neither of us had a really decent night's sleep but for some reason we weren't prepared to go to bed in the day and managed to stay awake and see Potosi. We went to find and enquire about "Mike Tours" through a couple of companies recommended in the book. We obviously arrived at the wrong time as by 9 a.m. they had groups of people turning up to go off on tours. In both companies we got mistaken for being part of the groups and were offered tea and a sit down. In the end, we decided to go with a company called "Koala Tours" not "Mike Tours". They were supposed to be very good and we left our names.

Back at the hostel, we managed to get a "Matrimonial" by chance and put our things in the room. A quick shower proved to be a warm dribble and I then set to mending my trousers out in the courtyard in the sun as we both chatted to a couple of Irish girls.

They had both been travelling together for two years! At least six months of that was working in Australia, but they were both really looking forward to going home and sadly were not really enjoying South America as much as they could because they were so looking forward to getting back! Anyway, it turned out they had been to a lot of the countries we will be going to. We quizzed them for about an hour as my trousers started to look half decent again! Although sorry to hear about my incident in La Paz, one of the girls was interested to hear about it as she had recently had an expensive ring stolen off a bus, off her finger, without her noticing! We swapped stories and sympathised. They told us that New Zealand is beautiful, especially Lake Taupo, but very expensive. They hired a camper van as we hope to and thoroughly enjoyed the country. India is dirt cheap similar to Bolivia, but they only spent ten days there in the South! Bangkok is noisy, dirty and huge but worth seeing and the rest of Thailand is ACE. Hong Kong islands are superb. Sri Lanka was a really cool country and quite cheap too. It's funny how you meet these people for such a relatively short time and get loads of info out of them but end up never seeing them again.

Simon assured me you couldn't tell I had a scarred trouser pocket, but I knew it was stitched and we now had a true souvenir from South America!

For the rest of the day, we had a look around the town and what it had to offer. The two Irish girls also told us they had done the Mike Tour the day before, organised by our own hostel. It was good and about £3 cheaper so we changed our plans and decided to stay loyal to Casa Maria Victoria.

We found a tourist map from an agency and decided to follow a route taking us to the main tourist sites.

Rebecca

Buenos Aires Airport
6.45 a.m. Thursday 14th August 1997

This included "La Moneda" where money has been made in Bolivia and was built to increase the coinage in the country.

279

We walked around and saw various churches and found a good view point on the top of a hill to see Potosi as a whole. Altitude again made it difficult to walk around quickly. The main square was really quite attractive and the town had a lot of old, interesting colonial streets.

We found a cheap lunch and later in the day Simon had a sleep whilst I went to explore the market a little more. In the evening, we went back to the market areas and found a superb burger to eat at such a cheap price. By now, it was snowing and although it wasn't sticking it was so cold. We had experienced so much else, why not?

We awoke to snow having settled a little and prepared for our "Mike Tour" which was due to leave the hostel at 9am. I put all my layers on and had been promised a coat to wear and boots. We headed off to our Central Market for a good breakfast feed and were back in plenty of time. That day was Jonathan's birthday (my brother) and I was keen to phone him, but didn't want to rush the occasion so decided to ring him later.

There were about ten of us in the group, all from the hostel and our guide, Santos introduced himself and his lady assistant. We headed out into the street expecting to see some pre-arranged transport! NO such luck, he was trying to flag down a local kombi bus and did so eventually! On the way to the local mountain, that was obvious from the town and today sprinkled with snow, we stopped at what they call the miners market. They like to take small gifts to the miners and we were all kind of expected to buy them something, although it was supposedly voluntary! The basic mining gifts started to portray the basic mining existence in the mountain. We bought sticks of dynamite with wiring, bottles of 95% alcohol for them to drink, bundles of pure tobacco cigarettes unfiltered, and coca leaves! I have never seen a stick of dynamite before, an amazing sight! We then went round the corner and entered someone's home and courtyard to be given welly boots and rain coats to wear. It was really cold that morning and I knew my cold and cough would not take very kindly to the weather conditions. Both our welly boots were far too big and stupidly I had only worn a thin pair of socks so my feet were like ice! Simon's boots were such a sight, really falling apart and such thin soles. My coat was quite small and wouldn't fasten and wasn't half as long as I would have liked. I could see us getting dirty! Eventually, we went back out into the street and another local bus was hailed and took us directly to the mouth of the mine.

Another group had already arrived wearing similar clothing. The entrance was literally a gaping hole and outside it was a group of ordinarily dressed Bolivians who were miners. Some wore sandals some wore sensible shoes and all stood around chewing coca leaves which bulged in their cheeks.

Rebecca

The Coast of Argentina
3.40 p.m. In the Air—above

All miners come to work about an hour before it is necessary to stand and chew coca leaves as preparation for a day's work! On entering the mine, we soon became very aware of the basic conditions they work under—as Simon put it earlier in the diary, quite Victorian! We held lanterns lit by some coal and water mixture. They carry anything up to forty-five kilos of "stuff" on their backs along narrow, dark, wet tunnels that can go down very steeply and through very small holes! There were about forty-five companies working in the mountain, each having leaders who own various sections of the tunnels. They in turn have assistants who help them mine their section; we met one who had about twelve workers. They all have to buy and use their own tools. They work by hand and have no machinery to help. If any of them find a big load of silver, for example, they take a large cut of the profits themselves, a small % to the company and a small % to the government; hence, the reason why they are cooperatives. Recently, a miner had bought a whole load of coaches and set up a bus company for a long-distance journey from Potosi that was his investment from a lucky mining day at work.

We crawled through the same tunnels and literally passed men who were taking wheel barrow loads of minerals outside and up and down shafts—an incredible experience to see them at work, in such conditions. We met a miner who was about seventy-three and had been working there for about forty years. A handkerchief mask over his face he had a hammer and chisel to mine his patch. He had been working for about thirty-six hours as the previous day had been a holiday and he had opted to work extra hours to make up for it. Most of the miners earn about £5 a day, but always with the chance to earn more if they dig/strike lucky.

We were underground for about two–three hours where our guide, Santos, took pleasure in forcing us through some dangerous holes and over incredible drops! Scared was not the word in places, but only one of us dropped out due to an attack of claustrophobia. I found it hard going at times; my chest didn't really like the dust and rushing around, but it was fascinating.

Anyway, the mining experience was unforgettable and although Potosi was very cold, we really liked the hostel and thoroughly enjoyed eating from the night stalls around the market. We even treated ourselves to a beer in a trendy cafe that was so lovely and warm! Our next venture was supposedly Sucre but on reading about it there didn't seem much to do there and the bus journeys sounded long so when we got to the bus station to book our tickets Cochabamba suddenly became more attractive. The Cochabamba basin was supposedly fertile. Green and extremely beautiful with mountains all around. From memory our bus journey there started early with a good "Pasteles" and coffee breakfast at the station. The timings were completely up the spout and what was supposed to take about eight hours took all day with a rubbish driver going about twenty miles an hour to conserve petrol. We were tearing our hair out by the time we got to Cochabamba!

In itself Cochabamba was a big, busy town which we didn't really see a hell of a lot of but the situation amongst the mountains was nice, the hostel good but expensive and our steak dinners (as Simon has described!) were fantastic!

Our intention was to get to the countryside and for a final South American walk. So, the day after we arrived, we got a minibus to a small market town called Quillacollo. It was all happening there at the Sunday market and we managed to get another bus quite easily to the start of our walk. It was supposedly up to some ruins but for about the sixth time in three and a half months we never found them. The walk took us high above the valley and we saw some amazing views all around. It was warm and we were happy to get away from it all for the last time. It all seemed odd that a few days later we would have left South America altogether.

The morning we left for La Paz we went down to leave and pay our bill. For some reason there was no record of us having had a breakfast the 1st morning or having had some washing done. The man on the desk only charged us for accommodation and to be honest I wasn't going to tell him the truth! Sounds harsh but we have been diddled so much in South America that it made a change and saved us a few quid. I know Mummy would be horrified!

The bus to La Paz was fine except for some reason I felt really rough and on eventually having a pit stop and emptying some of my bowels I felt quite sick for the rest of the journey! The bus was comfy and the Bolivian scenery quite desolate and beautiful.

It was just about going dark in La Paz, it was also really cold and quite chilly. We immediately got a taxi to the hostel that we had been recommended and Simon had successfully booked over the phone the day before.

Slightly more out of town they were pleased to see us and promptly showed us a room they had prepared, due to the fact that previous occupants of a matrimonial room hadn't quite left! They took us to the dining room and kitchen where they had put in two beds! The cooking fat could still be smelt all around and we could have helped ourselves to drinks! No curtains, a cold draught, the kitchen hatch, another room where people would have to walk through ours and a few people coming into our room looking for someone, all added up to us deciding to go back to Hostal Austria, despite having to pay double. I was also still feeling rough and although I told Simon we shouldn't leave because of me he was really annoyed that they expected us to accept their offer and we therefore left quite quickly and with no explanation to the owners!

In the streets of wet La Paz we eventually found our trusty "Yanacocka" street and fell into Hostal Austria knowing we also had a reservation there from the previous week. Unbelievably we too had problems and a mindless argument occurred. We have a reservation but they haven't got a matrimonial room free, so if we aren't happy with what they can provide then we should go elsewhere! And yes, it will be more expensive! We were really hacked off but left with little option and as I didn't feel well enough to go searching the capital streets, we took it. The room was actually quieter than our usual one and considering I didn't feel well two single beds was probably better. Simon went off to find some food for himself and left me curled up in bed trying to read and take my mind off my belly!

At about 10 p.m. I was throwing up into a bag in our room with Simon rubbing my back and telling me how good I was being and how it was better out than in! I felt better and although in the middle of the night I rushed to the toilet thinking it would happen again (but didn't) I was fine by the next day!

We had been looking forward to buying a few souvenirs and our last day in La Paz was really enjoyable. We started by breakfasting on bread (not bad for South America) and headed to the post office to send our last few pieces of post. We bought a few typical postcards and sent a last one to Mummy and Daddy.

Souvenir buying was great fun and we managed to bargain down a couple of rugs from a lady on one of the streets. We decided against buying one big rug when these two smaller ones caught our eye. Really excited was not the word and we can quite easily see our house looking great when we get back, with all our gifts from around the world! I brought a jazzy bag and we managed to find a typical music tape and a bit of food for our next couple of days journey. Lunch we hoped would be a real treat and headed to "EL Lobo" for the second time in plenty of time for the set lunch. Once again, they really let us down, no set lunch with absolutely no explanation even when I asked why they have it on the menu. We decided to try another place that had been closed previously when we had been scouting for food and this time, we were lucky.

A vegetarian restaurant overlooking a courtyard and a set menu that served soup (what a surprise!), curried lentils and chapati bread, salad of carrots and radishes and then dried banana and yoghurt and a chocolate dessert! It was all served on a portioned off silver tray and made a really nice change. I had a glass of orange juice and Simon had a "lassy" which was a fruit yoghurt drink. Really nice!

Unfortunately, the weather turned that day and hail storms were not uncommon so we didn't shop till we dropped but had a couple of pit stops. The hostel had been very obliging in finding us a free matrimonial room for one night! We really enjoyed our hot spicy potatoes in the evening (on the street) and supped our last South American beer in the bar next door.

There was no rush the following morning as we had arranged a taxi for about 10.30 a.m. This was on time and it didn't take as long as we thought to get to the airport with a quick stop on route for great views across the city. The weather was superb that morning and the mountains all around La Paz were completely visible for the first time.

The airport was really nice and not very busy. We were there in plenty of time and as with most of these places I spent a lot of the time standing around with my mouth open, fascinated by the people, sights and sounds! We checked in early and then had to hang around further before our flight was called to go through to a departure lounge. We had fun with the tax situation when we argued our case for having paid it already. They emphatically denied we had paid it and told us we couldn't leave the country until we did! Good Old South America!

The plane journey to Buenos Aires had a stopover at Santo Cruz. Flat, hot and tropical with a group of British students getting on and complaining about no hand luggage space! Goodness knows why they couldn't put their stuff in the main compartments like everyone else! On the flight I realised I had left my pack towel on the back of the chair in the airport, drying off! I was gutted!

We were both hoping for a decent lunch that day but ended up with a sandwich and cake before Santo Cruz and then another sandwich and fruit for tea! We had bread, tuna and mayonnaise in our bags for dinner so we were literally sandwiched out. The good thing was we were able to collect a bit of wine along the way and relax!

Buenos Aires was much warmer than we anticipated. I was also a little worried about how the system would work at the airport, in relation to changing flights a day later than planned. We didn't have to fill in another visitor's card because we weren't staying any length of time. I was wondering if they would make us go out of the airport and pay through the nose for a hotel? I decided we should put the ball in their court and on leaving the plane we found an official who was directing "touristy" passengers. By now it was about 8 p.m. and we were told by her that on finding the Argentinian desk they would take us into town and to a hotel! Of course we were amazed and promptly asked whether it was free, she said yes but we were waiting to believe it when we saw it. The airport had a ring of three and a half months previous experience and familiarity and any fear that we felt, this time was different! We kind of knew what to expect and how to cope! The officials were happy to stamp our passports for overnight and at the Argentinian desk we enquired about the mystery hotel! Did we have a voucher? Of course we didn't and it turned out we were able to get a free ride into the centre but no free hotel! On asking about price it was clear we would have to pay about $100 each, so we told them we wanted to stay in the airport instead. They directed us to the International part of the airport (as the National section was closed) and we headed out into the sea of anxious anticipated faces of families, friends, taxi drivers and tour operators. We were so much more prepared and must have looked confident and known what we were doing as we had no hassles.

The International section was also busy and although there weren't many places to sit, we found some wooden benches near the airline check-in desks and took over one.

The evening was uneventful safe for Simon's search for a British newspaper, making a Tuna sandwich and the coming and goings of Argentinians and foreigners. What was obvious to us was the stronger western feel and more money about. Bolivia and Peru really had been 3rd world! "Lan Chile" were drilling a little too loudly at their check in desks so we moved around to the other section where "Aeroflot" (Russia) and other airlines had all closed up for the evening. By morning the name had changed to "National"- could have been weird to wake up to this, if we hadn't seen them make the change.

We both managed to get a few hours' sleep that night and were both disturbed by cleaners! Same experience as Lima, they all have these expensive floors that demand all night cleaning attention. Anyway, by about 6.30–7 a.m. we were wide awake having slept on the long wooden bench chairs, one each! No need for the sleeping bags as it had been quite warm and by 8.00 a.m. we went back to the "National" section to check-in. We found a British paper (hurray!) and on checking in our bags we were extremely pleasantly surprised to find them accept our story about having already paid their tax to "Bridge the World" (the agency we used in England when we booked our flight tickets)! We couldn't believe they would accept it but they did. What a difference, what a saving!

We hung around the arrivals lounge for a while and tried to get some New Zealand dollars (impossible!) as well as play our game of chess, that had been on going now for about twelve hours! We moved to the departure lounge at about 9.30–10 a.m. and got chatting to an English guy called Simon Taylor who was now living in New Zealand (Dunedin). He had flown in from England that morning having been to his sister's wedding but had also been via Brazil with a friend, so therefore away from New Zealand for about six weeks. Very enthusiastic about New Zealand. He chatted to us about where we should go and what we should see. He even gave us his card and said we could go and stay at his place in Dunedin! Of course he was on our flight but not next to us so we boarded about thirty minutes late with the advice that he had been impressed with American Airlines coming from England. For him the food on his flight had been good and by now we were really desperate for something decent.

What a huge plane and once again they almost got our seats right! We had once again requested Fire Exit seats and were given a couple in front. We were fortunate that they were two seats on their own so no chance of disturbing people and not far from the kitchen area, to spy on what food was coming. The flight was really good for fifteen hours and the attendants were actually very nice. We are convinced that things had been improved somewhat in three and a half months as it didn't seem the same airline. The food was really good, lunch, afternoon tea, dinner and drinks galore! It was strange that it didn't go dark at the normal times as we were heading over the timeline but we slept for a couple of hours before we touched down. The strangest thing was stopping off on the southern tip of Argentina, Rio Gallegos where Santiago came from, to collect some new staff! In the middle of nowhere we all disembarked at what seemed like a service station and took photos of our big plane on the tarmac! Not often you get so close to a jumbo! It was a laugh though as we met up with Simon Taylor again and had a beer!

Getting nearer New Zealand seemed really weird and touching down in Auckland we got off tired but living on adrenalin! What a posh airport, never seen anything like it. It looked and felt like a really up market hotel walking through and seeing such westernisation. What a shock!

A Summary of South America

Simon

I'm sitting here at Buenos Aires airport wondering if this continent has one more page to offer on this our last night. You just never know here. Anything can and does happen.

I've used the phrase "Nothing is as it seems," repeatedly since the start of this trip and I still stand by that. In Argentina, booking a river rafting trip can mean total chaos, numerous telephone calls and a two-hour wait before you are any nearer to establishing if such a transaction is possible. In Chile an agreed price for B&B can suddenly include hospitality and friendship at no extra cost. In Peru, telling a local farmer you are from "Inglaterra" can prompt the reaction "is that place more than an hour from here?" In Bolivia, illegal demands by the police for entry to a town on a bus load of tourists can stop as soon as enough money has been collected for lunch.

You just never know and you never quite get used to not knowing. Here you can predict nothing, save the best laid plans usually end up as just plans.

You also never quite get used to the sheer beauty and diversity of the continent. There is always something wonderful to see, experience, learn and do. Everyday holds something new. The truth is that there is just so much to this continent. There is always something more, or something different to the day before.

The continent has so many different cultures, beliefs, religions, colours, tastes, climates and types of scenery. I would say it is almost impossible to stop learning and I have learnt so much here. This place has forced me to think. Why is robbery almost an accepted part of the culture in Peru?

Is it because the laws there are simply not tough enough on crime? Or is it because a large segment of its people, feel betrayed of a lost heritage, a fall from grace as a great economic power, stolen from beneath their feet?

What is the result of the West's determination to rid the world of cocaine production? Is it a safer, healthier, less threatening and richer society for the lucky few? Or does it mean the elimination of the farming of the coco leaf, an integral part of some of the culture or widespread poverty for the thousands of peasant farmers who have built their lives around it? When we despise the cocaine trade and seek to rid it from our lives, do we really understand the implications of our actions? When the peasant farmers see a gringo, do they see a fellow human being or someone who has so much and cares so little about what he has? Do they see a monster intent on keeping the needy in poverty?

I'm not attempting to pass judgement on these or countless other issues I've thought about over the past few months. However, I'm starting to realise that an overly simplistic picture book is indeed a huge, economic, political, artistic and mathematical library. And now at the end of our time here in South America, I'm itching to read more.